The Mystical

Initiations

of Vision

The Path to Self-Mastery, vol 7

The Mystical Initiations of Vision

KIM MICHAELS

Copyright © 2017 Kim Michaels. All rights reserved. No part of this book may be used, reproduced, translated, electronically stored or transmitted by any means except by written permission from the publisher. A reviewer may quote brief passages in a review.

MORE TO LIFE PUBLISHING

www.morepublish.com

For foreign and translation rights,

contact info@ morepublish.com

ISBN: 978-87-93297-40-1

The information and insights in this book should not be considered as a form of therapy, advice, direction, diagnosis, and/or treatment of any kind. This information is not a substitute for medical, psychological, or other professional advice, counseling and care. All matters pertaining to your individual health should be supervised by a physician or appropriate health-care practitioner. No guarantee is made by the author or the publisher that the practices described in this book will yield successful results for anyone at any time. They are presented for informational purposes only, as the practice and proof rests with the individual.

For more information: *www.ascendedmasterlight.com and www.transcendencetoolbox.com*

CONTENTS

Introduction 7
1 | Introducing the Fifth Ray 9
2 | Introducing Hilarion 11
3 | Guidance at the Temple of Truth 15
4 | Vision Is both Passive and Active 27
5 | Invoking a Higher Vision 51
6 | Getting Results from Your Spiritual Efforts 79
7 | Invoking the Will to Surrender 103
8 | Going from a Lower to a Higher Vision 135
9 | Invoking a Higher Vision of My Motivation 157
10 | How to Stop Projecting out 185
11 | I Invoke Freedom from Projecting Out 211
12 | How to Stop Projecting in 243
13 | I Invoke Freedom from Projecting In 265
14 | Being a True Healer 297
15 | Invoking True Healing 327
16 | Seeing Beyond the Matter Screen 373
17 | Invoking Vision beyond Matter 401

INTRODUCTION

This book is part of the series *The Path to Self-Mastery*. The purpose of the series is to give you a complete course for knowing and passing the mystical initiations of the seven spiritual rays. The books in the series form a progression, and it is recommended that you start by working through the books to the First Ray of God Power, the Second Ray of God Wisdom, the Third Ray of God Love and the Fourth Ray of God Purity before progressing to this book.

The purpose of this book is to teach you about the characteristics of the Fifth Ray, which will show you how to purify and raise your vision. If you are new to ascended master teachings, you will benefit greatly from reading the first book in the series, *The Power of Self,* because it gives a general introduction to the spiritual path as it is taught by the ascended masters. This will give you a good foundation for taking greater advantage of the teachings in this book.

This book is designed as a workbook in order to help you better integrate and apply the teachings. You will get the best results if you give the invocation that corresponds to the chapter you are studying. It is recommended that you give a specific invocation once a day for nine days and then study part of the corresponding dictation before or after giving the invocation. Each evening, make calls to be taken to Hilarion's retreat, the *Temple of Truth,* in the etheric realm over the island of Crete.

You give an invocation by reading it aloud, thereby invoking high-frequency spiritual energy. For more information about invocations and how to give them, please see the website: *www.transcendencetoolbox.com.* In order to learn more about the ascended masters and how they give dictations, see the website *www.ascendedmasterlight.com.* If you are not familiar with the concepts of the fall and of fallen beings, please read *Cosmology of Evil.* That book gives a profound yet easily understood explanation of why there are some beings who have no respect for the free will (or lives) of human beings. It explains why they are willing to do anything in order to control us or destroy those who will not be controlled.

NOTE: Some of the invocations in this book are longer than in the previous books. You might give part of an invocation in the morning and the rest in the evening.

1 | INTRODUCING THE FIFTH RAY

Color of the Fifth Ray: Emerald green
Corresponding chakra: Third eye
Elohim of the Fifth Ray: Cyclopea and Virginia
Archangel and Archeia of the Fifth Ray: Raphael and Mother Mary
Chohan of the Fifth Ray: Hilarion
Decrees for the Fifth Ray: 5.01 Decree to Elohim Cyclopea, 5.02 Decree to Archangel Raphael, 5.03 Decree to Hilarion.

Pure qualities of the Fifth Ray

Traditionally, the Fifth Ray qualities are seen as truth and vision—yet vision of what? The Fifth Ray is the seat of single vision, as illustrated by Jesus in the remark: "If thine eye be single, thy whole body shall be full of light." The single-eyed vision is the Christ vision, which sees beyond duality. This is based on the realization that *any* expression of "truth" in the material world is less than the Spirit of Truth. One must look beyond *any* outer expression in order to experience truth.

When one does, one sees that all divisions are unreal and one sees the need to raise all life. This gives rise to Christ discernment, the ability to instantly identify and see through the lies of duality that always seek to raise up one part of life by putting down another. This is exemplified in the situation in the Garden of Eden where the Serpent said to Eve: "Thou shallt not *surely* die," thus inserting the element of doubt in her consciousness. The Fifth Ray qualities empower you to see through this serpentine logic. You can also see that all appearances in the material world are only temporary, and thus you can hold the immaculate vision for people or conditions to be transformed.

Perversions of the Fifth Ray

The perversions are lack of vision, a lack of ability to discern between the one non-dual Truth and the many dualistic "truths," leading to doubt and a sense of hopelessness or the sense that there is no truth. Another perversion is the belief that there is only one truth, and that it is *our* truth. Also the sense that because we have the only truth, we are locked in a battle against those who promote another thought system, and that it is necessary and justified for us to criticize or even destroy their system. People who are critical of other people or ideas have perverted the Fifth Ray qualities. Another perversion is the tendency to say that if people do or believe certain things, they are bad people. This is a failure to see beyond temporary appearances.

2 | INTRODUCING HILARION

Hilarion was embodied as Saul of Tarsus who later became known as Saint Paul. Consider the psychological aspects of this embodiment. You have Saul who is convinced that Jesus is a fake and who is actively persecuting Christians. What could cause this? It is the human mind's ability to create its own idolatrous image of truth so that you literally weave a filter around your mind. When you view life or a particular issue through the filter, everything you see is colored by the filter. You are convinced that your self-created version of truth is the one and only truth. You have made yourself into a "god" who thinks it knows what is good and evil because it thinks it is surely defined by its own perception filter.

Then, consider the story of how Saul traveled on the road to Damascus and encountered the Living Christ who blinded him by the light but also made the scales fall from his eyes. The word "scales" can be both a physical covering, as fish scales, but it can also be a symbol of the two cups of a scale that weigh everything according to a dualistic standard. When

Saul acknowledged that the light of Christ was from beyond his perception filter, he was blinded for a time. He eventually recovered a vision that was not split by dualistic polarities. He could – after spending considerable time in the desert purifying himself – go out and preach the undivided truth of Christ.

The point being, of course, that because Hilarion has personally gone through this process, he is uniquely trained to help others go through the transformation that is the key element of the Fifth Ray initiations, namely seeing beyond the dualistic world view and grasping – experiencing – the indivisible truth of the Christ mind. Innumerable are the dualistic "truths," yet there is only *one* truth of Christ. Only by experiencing it directly – being willing to be blinded by its light – will you have a frame of reference for extricating yourself from the dualistic filter you have created. This filter looks absolutely real when viewed from the inside, meaning its unreality can only be exposed by looking at the filter from the outside.

When you look at the world today, you see many people who have abandoned religion and have become agnostics or atheists. Many of them are actually going through a phase that is very necessary on the spiritual path. What outer religions offer is a "certainty" that you are right and that you will be saved because religion gives you an absolute truth. You can grow beyond this phase only by being willing to go through a phase of doubting everything until you realize that in this world, there is no absolute truth. Truth can be found beyond this world in a direct experience that is beyond words and intellect.

When you come to this phase of being willing to acknowledge that you don't know, then you can benefit from attending sessions with Hilarion at the *Temple of Truth* over Crete. In the beginning, you will attend assemblies where he appears on a stage with lifestreams who are either students or teachers of

2 | Introducing Hilarion

some capacity. They then discuss and role-play various scenarios and ideas in order to help the audience work through various aspects of the duality consciousness, almost like Greek tragedies or comedies.

As you begin to advance in the initiations offered by Hilarion, you will start attending smaller meetings where you get an opportunity to discourse directly with the master. Hilarion is an expert at confounding the human intellect and the rational mind. If you are willing, he will lead you gradually to see the limitations of these faculties until you realize a profound truth.

Your perception filter was created by using the intellect and the rational mind. Spiritual students go through a phase where they think reaching a higher state of consciousness is a matter of using the rational mind to understand spiritual ideas and solve a certain problem, riddle or enigma. As you approach the graduation level at the Fifth Ray retreat, you need to come to the realization that the problems defined by the intellect simply have no solution—neither with the human mind nor with the Christ mind.

For students who have not completely let go of the dream of certainty, this can be a major disappointment, and they might even deny it for a time. The reality is that the Christ mind does not have answers to dualistic questions or solutions to dualistic problems. There are no answers or solutions to problems that have no reality to them. What the Christ mind does offer is a frame of reference that empowers you to accelerate yourself – your vision – beyond the dualistic filter. Once you see with clear vision, you see that the problems need not be solved, they simply need to be left behind as you continue to transcend yourself on the straight and narrow way – the undivided way – of Christ.

Hilarion finds great joy in seeing a student reach this level of giving up all attempts at solving the problems of unreality, instead turning to Hilarion and asking him to help you see the reality of Christ—as opposed to what the dualistic mind defines as the "reality" of Christ. You will never see a more joyful and sincere look of approval than when Hilarion looks at you with his immaculate vision, and shows you with a fond gesture that he honors your growth and that he gladly sends you on to the Sixth Ray and Lady Master Nada.

3 | GUIDANCE AT THE TEMPLE OF TRUTH

Hilarion I AM, and I am indeed the Chohan, meaning the Head Teacher, of the Fifth Ray. The Fifth Ray has often been called the ray of truth or healing but it can also be seen as the ray of wholeness through enlightened vision, purified vision.

The purity of your vision and God vision

Consider the old statement: "Without vision, the people perish." The background for this statement is, of course, that your co-creative abilities are exercised by formulating a mental image, directing the stream of your self-awareness through that image, and thereby stirring the River of Life to take on the form of the image. Where do you formulate the image? Well, you formulate it in the totality of your being, which involves all of your seven chakras. It is in the third eye chakra that you finalize the image and then project consciousness through it. If there are impurities in your third eye chakra, you will not be able to formulate a pure image, an image that is in alignment with the higher principles used by the Elohim to create the material realm.

If you formulate an impure image, then you will inevitably create circumstances in your life that are not the highest possible. It will cause you resistance, suffering, perhaps even physical disease. What is physical disease? It is in one sense when the cells of your body begin to vibrate with a vibration that is lower than a certain level. You have been brought up to think that the cells of your body are like miniature building blocks, small spheres with a membrane around it and complicated machinery inside. This is not an invalid view, but it is a partial view, for it focuses on that level of vision that sees everything in terms of matter—matter particles. As you know, or *should* know, in 1905 Albert Einstein formulated the theory of relativity. It says that even though your senses detect what you call the matter world, that matter world is made from a finer substance, called energy. Energy is vibration.

The sound of your cells

Another valid way to look at the cells of your body is to see them as something that is akin to a musical instrument. Your cells are truly a kind of instrument, and they do not simply produce protein, they actually emit a vibration. It could be heard as a sound if your ears were sensitive enough. Or rather, they would never be audible to the physical ears, but to the inner ear of the mind it is possible to hear the vibration, the sound, emitted by the cells of your body. Now, you will know that before a musician plays his part in a symphony, he will first tune his

3 | Guidance at the Temple of Truth

instrument. One of the technologies used by musicians to tune their instrument is a tuning fork that is constructed to always emit a certain tone. The question now becomes: What is the tuning fork that you have allowed to set the base vibration of certain cells in your body? You see, if you hold imperfect images and energies in any of your seven chakras, they produce lower energies, meaning energies that vibrate lower than the vibration of love and therefore vibrate in the spectrum of fear and the emotions that spring from fear. If these vibrations are your tuning fork, then your cells will emit a disharmonious sound.

This sound will spread and influence other cells. Of course, the only way a cell can emit a disharmonious sound is by having that sound inside itself. This means that the extremely complex machinery of the cell cannot function at its highest potential. What happens now is that if a cell is emitting a disharmonious sound, it will start spreading that sound to other cells. Then, you can have a situation where each of the cells that make up a certain unit in your body, such as an organ, are now emitting a disharmonious sound.

Over time, this will inevitably interfere with the function of that organ, causing it to either function below its potential or gradually even start to dysfunction, to stop functioning. Eventually, it fails to produce its task in the body, or even fails completely and causes the death of the body, if it is a vital enough organ. If it is not a vital enough part of the body, then you may live for an entire lifetime, or for the rest of that lifetime, with a lower capacity of the body. This will influence your wellbeing but also to some degree your ability to be an open door for spiritual light.

The tightrope initiation at the Temple of Truth

At the *Temple of Truth* you will be given instructions in what it is that is most threatening to the functioning of your particular physical body, what it is in your mind and your chakras that causes parts of your body to be attuned to a lower frequency and therefore to emit a lower frequency. When you come to the *Temple of Truth*, you will first be taken, not to the main halls, but you will be taken to some of the side rooms where you will be given a special opportunity. The first room you will be allowed to enter is what we have jokingly called "The Tightrope Room" or "The High Wire Room." When you enter this room, you will find yourself standing over a platform that extends over an abyss. At first you cannot see what is at the bottom of this abyss, for it is shrouded in mist or fog.

What you *can* see is that from the platform on which you are standing extends a tightrope, it extends into the distance, but you cannot see the other end of the tightrope, for your vision is obscured by a fog. It is now your task to walk this tightrope. The width of the tightrope is carefully adjusted to your state of consciousness so that with your present state of consciousness it is possible for you to walk the tightrope without falling down. It is only possible if you are very concentrated and do not look to either side. On either side of the room in which you find yourself, there are large screens, and as you start walking the tightrope, images will be flashed on both screens.

On the one side will be the images of what you see as evil, bad or impure manifestations with your current sense of vision. On the other side will be images that you see as beautiful, good, right or pure with your current sense of vision. Your challenge now is to walk the tightrope and to avoid looking to either side. If you do, you will soon slip and fall into the mist of the abyss. When you do fall, as most people do at first, you will, of course, be caught in a safety net. You will not know this in the beginning so it requires that you have the courage to walk out not knowing where you will end up, not knowing where you will fall, if you fall. The question of whether you fall or not is determined exclusively by your propensity to look to the images on one or the other side. What do you focus most on, the good, the bad or the ugly? What is it that draws your attention and causes you to fall off the tightrope, to miss your balance and therefore your ability to walk towards your ultimate goal in life, your spiritual goal in life, the fulfillment of your Divine plan?

Once you have started this exercise and fallen for the first time, you will, of course, be given assistance by those of us who serve in the *Temple of Truth*. We will help you see what it is in your consciousness: Do you tend to focus only on the negatives, thinking that you must battle with the negatives, or that the negatives must be removed before you can be truly spiritual? Do you tend to ignore the negatives and only want to look at the positives, do not want to see problems, do not want to see that there are certain manifestations on earth that must be uncreated the same way they were created, namely through the power of vision?

As you are willing to see this, you will transcend the tendency to have your conscious awareness pulled towards either what you see as good or what you see as bad. At least at a certain level, this means that you will now be able to walk further out on the tightrope. When you again enter the room, the tightrope is narrower. What happens now is that the first images that are flashed on the screens will no longer disturb you so you will be able to walk past them. Then, you will come to a part of the screen that will flash deeper images than the first ones you saw.

Now again, your attention will be drawn to one side or the other. You will lose your balance and fall into the safety net that you now know is there. Again, you will, of course, be given guidance. If you are willing to see, then you will be given all the help you need in order to overcome what now pulls your vision into focusing on a matrix that is not the highest potential.

The goal of the Brothers of Truth

Focusing your attention on what is wrong on earth or ignoring what is wrong and focusing on what you define as good, is either way an unbalanced reaction. The goal of the Masters of the Fifth Ray, the Brothers of Truth, is to take you to the point where you can see beyond the dualistic polarities of good and evil, right and wrong, bad and good, pure and impure, true and false. You can see that they are only creations of the mind, the lower mind, the separate mind. They are not created by the mind of Christ, they do not exist in the mind of Christ, in the mind of God or in the mind of ascended beings. In order to walk the tightrope that leads to the ascended state – or at least leads you to pass the initiations of the Fifth Ray and ascend to the Sixth Ray – you must develop that power of vision where you do not ignore the conditions on earth.

You do not ignore the conditions that have the potential to be accelerated, but you *see* them, and you see beyond them, to see the deeper reality that they are simply images projected upon the River of Life and have no real permanence, no real reality or power and thus have no power over you. They have no power to attract your vision, or to limit your vision, or even to limit your physical body and your physical actions.

3 | Guidance at the Temple of Truth

The purification of your third eye chakra

Now, it is entirely possible (and it is indeed the case for most people) that you will have to go through a special process in order to purify your third eye of these impure images that pull you toward one or the other dualistic extreme. As you become ready to take this next step, you will, each time you fall off the tightrope, be offered to go into another room that bears some resemblance to a modern surgery room. However, we do not operate on you with knives. We have an instrument that bears some resemblance to a laser gun or a laser lamp.

This instrument emits a very concentrated ray of the vibrations of the Fifth Ray of truth. In order for this instrument to assist you, two things are required. First of all, we cannot cut out of your third eye any condition that you have not been willing to see and consciously surrender. Second of all, the power that drives this laser surgery is generated by you, through your invocation of the Fifth Ray. It is your own willingness to surrender, to see and surrender, and your own momentum of invoking the energies of the Fifth Ray that will determine the level of assistance we can offer you in this third eye surgery.

Why is this surgery necessary? It is because the false teachers of humankind have developed methods whereby they can insert various implants into your third eye. These implants come in a variety of shapes, and at this point it is not important for you to know them.

What is important is to realize that it is scarcely possible to grow up on planet earth (especially in a modern, Western society where you are exposed to so many images via television, the Internet or books) without having such implants projected into your third eye chakra. Here, they will either block your vision of the higher reality, they will distort your vision or they will lock your vision into focusing on certain conditions on earth. This may be impure conditions that you always notice or it may be seemingly beautiful conditions that you see as right and use as a justification for ignoring anything else. When you have come to see the underlying consciousness, we can use this laser surgery gun to burn away the implant in your third eye.

This is a process that most people at their current level of consciousness could not go through consciously. That is why we offer you that as you travel to the etheric retreat in your finer bodies at night, we can perform the surgery. You will only be consciously aware of the positive effects, but you also will need to be consciously aware of the shift in consciousness, that causes you to suddenly focus your vision in a different way than you have done in the past.

Your potential to help the entire planet

This is a great initiation, a great assistance for those who are willing to go through it. What happens when you are willing to go through this process and walk the increasingly narrow tightrope until you reach the other side? Well, when you have purified your vision to a certain degree, you will be allowed to enter another room. This is a room where you now stand on a platform, but instead of seeing the abyss, you see the entire planet earth beneath you. In front of you, you have what looks like one of these laser guns that you might have seen in certain science fiction movies.

The opportunity you now have is that you can look at the earth with the purified vision you now have. You can see areas where there is an intense concentration of energies that are focused there by an imperfect vision, an imperfect matrix, an imperfect idea or belief. This will be one of the ideas and beliefs that you have accepted at previous times but that you have now been willing to see and that you have transcended. Again, the driving force that drives your laser gun is the momentum you have invoked on the Fifth Ray by giving our decrees and perhaps in other ways in past lifetimes. You will now be able to aim your laser gun at any area on earth that you choose. This is, of course, not in the physical octave but in the emotional, mental and etheric realms, and you will then be able to fire your laser gun with all the momentum built into it. This will transform, first, the energies that cover the underlying matrix. Then, if you have enough momentum to transform these energies, you can transform – raise in vibration – even the matrix itself. Thereby, you can give an invaluable assistance to your brothers and sisters in the physical realm who now will be able to free themselves from this matrix and the momentum that has supported it.

Most people will not be consciously aware of rendering this service, but they might be consciously aware of having a new sense of purpose, a new sense that they are making a difference somehow by being in embodiment on earth. It is, of course, only because you are in embodiment that you have the authority to use this laser gun. We of the ascended masters, who have a far greater momentum on the Fifth Ray, are not allowed to do this for the simple reason that we are not in physical embodiment. You see, again, how *we* cannot change the earth but we can assist *you* in unlocking your ability to raise the earth to a new level. This, of course, is our greatest joy. It is our greatest sense of beauty when we see that you have raised your vision so that you now see what you did not see before. You now see beyond both the ugly and the beautiful manifestations in the material realm. You see the far more sophisticated beauty of the spiritual realm. This is when you will know what beauty is. This is when you will know what truth is. As the Chohan of the Fifth Ray I, of course, feel that there is nothing more beautiful than truth.

The Chohans appreciate all seven rays

Certainly, I would not say this in front of my fellow Chohans on the other rays, for they, of course, each feel that their ray is the most beautiful, and this is the way it should be. You see, the qualities of God are not in competition with each other. It is perfectly possible and perfectly valid that you can have seven Chohans who come together, each feeling that their ray is the most beautiful, and we never get into an argument, we never feel competition. What we will often do is that we will get together, the seven Chohans, and then one of us will be the one who leads that particular session. This Chohan will then begin to speak of, or rather illustrate with the non-verbal language we use, certain qualities of his or her ray.

As one Chohan does this, the other Chohans will tune in to the first Chohan's vibration, and thus each of the seven Chohans will attune their beings to the vibrations of one ray. We will come together in complete union and oneness in one ray, and this, of course, helps each of the seven Chohans to maintain appreciation for all seven rays, and therefore the ability to give a balanced instruction in his or her specific ray. A Chohan is, of course, focused on a particular ray, but a Chohan also knows that this is just one ray. As a Chohan, you are more than the ray upon which you serve, for you are an extension of the Creator's Being. You are, as we have said about you, pure awareness.

Pure awareness can express itself through any of the seven rays, and that means, in a sense, that each of the seven Chohans could serve on each of the rays. This is true mastery, the

3 | Guidance at the Temple of Truth

mastery of the seven rays to which we are seeking to raise those of you who are willing to walk with us on the Path of the Seven Veils.

I thank you with the gratitude of all of the seven Chohans, and of course the Maha Chohan. With this I seal you in the gratitude of our love, the gratitude of the Fifth Ray focused through the love of the Fifth Ray, the special shade of the love ray that *is* the Fifth Ray.

4 | VISION IS BOTH PASSIVE AND ACTIVE

I AM the Ascended Master Hilarion, Chohan of the Fifth Ray. The purpose of this book is to give you the outer stimuli, the outer reminders, that can help you pass and integrate the lessons you receive at the etheric level when you attend my retreat at this level of this course of self-mastery. We will begin, in this first lesson, by looking at an aspect of the Fifth Ray that is normally seen as vision.

It has been said in ancient scriptures that: "Without vision, the people perish." This is somewhat of a dubious statement, for is there anyone who does not have vision? All people have vision whether they are aware of it or not, whether they are classified as visionaries or not. Every human being has vision. The problem is that people are not aware that they have vision and they are not aware of what they do with it. It is not actually correct that without vision the people perish, we need to look at what kind of vision people have.

Vision is not passive

You who are familiar with our teachings know something about duality and non-duality. Therefore, it should be clear that the real statement should be that: "With a dualistic vision, people perish." When they do not have the Christ vision, the vision based on oneness, *then* they will perish. Why is this so? Because it is through the faculty of vision that you project into the cosmic mirror. As we have said, now many, many times: "What can the cosmic mirror do except project back to you what you are projecting out?" This, then, brings us to the central initiation that you face at the first level of my retreat.

The vast majority of people on this planet have grown up with an incorrect vision about vision. They think that vision is passive. If you think back to what you learned in school, you learned that your eyes are receiving instruments. They take in the light that comes to them from your surroundings and then you see what is actually there. *Nothing,* my beloved, could be further from the truth. You do *not* see what is actually there.

We have attempted to explain this many, many times, but at this first level of my retreat you simply cannot move on to the next level until you actually, truly get this point. It is not enough to understand it *theoretically* and *intellectually*. You need to *get it* as this total experience that shifts your consciousness so you realize in all four of your lower bodies that vision is not a *passive* faculty. It is, indeed, an *active* faculty where you are constantly projecting out, and what you project out very much affects what you see.

It is really that what you are projecting out affects what you think is coming to you from without. What you see is not what is coming to you from without; what you see is (as the scientists of quantum physics have started to realize) something that is produced inside your mind. There is no way that you can

4 | Vision Is both Passive and Active

ascend to the 96th level of consciousness without getting and integrating this reality. We might say that for the remainder of this course of self-mastery, one of the primary tasks is for you to clarify, to clear, your vision so that you are aware of what you are projecting out. You have mastery of what you are projecting out and therefore you have mastery of what is coming back from the cosmic mirror, which only reflects back what you are projecting out.

A subtle illusion on the path

This, incidentally, is a great hurdle for many of the students who come to my retreat. It is entirely possible that you can have walked the path up until this point, of having gone through the initiations under the first four Chohans, but you still have not let go of one of the most subtle illusions on the spiritual path. This is the illusion that comes directly from the fallen consciousness; it is the illusion that Jesus talked about when he said: "The kingdom of heaven suffers violence, and the violent take it by force."

The fallen beings have for a very, very long time attempted to take heaven by force. Now, you *cannot* take heaven by force and therefore Jesus' statement is not entirely transcribed correctly, for he knew, of course, the reality. You cannot take heaven by force because you cannot go beyond the four levels of this unascended sphere while you are in embodiment in any of those four levels. You cannot affect the spiritual realm.

What you *can* do, is that you can seek to force the flow of energy to go in such a direction that you take on certain powers, certain abilities, that are beyond what is considered normal on this planet. As we have said before, it is entirely possible to force certain abilities. As Serapis Bey discoursed on, there are certain false teachers who have set themselves up so that they have various abilities that can impress their students. Well, my beloved, if I was to select a spiritual teacher, I would not select one who had certain abilities, but I would select the one who had the purest vision. What do I mean with "pure vision?" Well, that will become clear as we go through the steps in this book.

For now, I want to stay with this idea that there are people who come to my retreat at the first level and they still have not let go of the idea that this course of self-mastery, that the spiritual path in general, is about acquiring certain abilities, certain extraordinary abilities. What is even more devastating is that many people have not understood, have not truly grasped, that the spiritual path is not about acquiring a mechanical ability. This is subtle, I know this very well, but I need you to ponder this very subtle difference.

Now, I have just told you that the universe is the cosmic mirror. It can only reflect back to you what you are projecting out. This does sound like the universe is functioning in a mechanical way. In a way, we could say that the universe *is* as mechanical as a mirror because what you are projecting upon the Mat-er Light, well the Mat-er Light will take on the form of the image you are projecting in a rather mechanical way. It is not like the Mat-er Light is creative in giving you back what you are sending out. It is giving you back *exactly* what you are sending out. The subtlety comes in because there is no way to cheat the system—you understand?

No way to cheat the system

There are many, many gurus and teachers out there in the field of New Age, Positive Mental Attitude, self-empowerment (or whatever they call it) who will attempt to make you believe that by following a few simple steps, by learning a certain formula, by giving certain affirmations, then you can, so to speak, turn your life around very quickly. In very simple ways, you can attract to you the most wonderful love partner, all the money you could ever need or whatever else it is that you desire. This is not so my beloved—right? There is no way to cheat the system.

You may go in with your conscious mind and select some kind of course that is offered out there and you may focus your conscious mind on a positive view of life. You may create treasure maps, you may write down exactly what you want, you may go through all of these exercises and you may focus your vision on something. You may put as much energy as you can muster into projecting that vision into the cosmic mirror, but if you only do this with your conscious mind, it can only have a limited effect. You are still projecting a *different* vision – and possibly a *contrary* vision – with your sub-conscious mind, the three levels of the emotional, mental and identity levels. What you are actually doing (as we have said before) is that instead of resolving the programs or the internal spirits in the three higher layers of the mind, you are creating a new program, a new spirit, and now it is only a matter of which spirit is stronger. Even if there is one spirit that is stronger, the others are still there and the others are still projecting out.

We might go back to the old statement: "Without vision, the people perish." We might say: "Without a *unified* vision, the people perish." What are you projecting out if you do not have a unified vision? You are sending "mixed signals," as they say, and what will the cosmic mirror reflect back to you? Of course, an outer situation that is affected by this. This is why I say that there is no way to cheat the system, there is no *mechanical* way. You cannot create a mechanical formula that will give you the exact conditions you want. You may create some formulas (as I said) where you can temporarily get certain abilities. It is possible for people (and some people have done this) to attract to themselves, for example, great riches in this lifetime.

This does not mean that they have put aside the Law of Karma. Therefore, in a future lifetime they will have to experience the opposite polarity of the unbalanced vision that they projected out. What I am saying here is this: At this first level of my retreat, students need to come to the realization that all of these false promises out there are *false*. You also need to understand *why* they are false. They are false partly because what they make you do is create a program with the conscious mind but they do not resolve the other programs in the other layers of the mind. They are also false in the sense that you have to make a choice between what it is you want in life. Do you want self-mastery or do you want certain physical, material conditions or certain experiences on earth?

Mastery of the world or mastery of self

What have I just said, my beloved? I said that the universe is a mirror; it reflects back to you exactly what you project into it. You may look at some people and you may see that they have a great momentum (and let us just say a great *mastery*) in getting the exact physical conditions they want. You may look at certain people who have managed to produce or attract to themselves great wealth. They live in a beautiful mansion, they have a beautiful spouse, they have the perfect outer conditions where everything is under control exactly as they wanted. You may look at this and say: "Well, I would like to have a life where I don't have to worry about money and where I have a nice place to live and where everything is seemingly under control."

4 | Vision Is both Passive and Active

You may look at this and say: "I want that too. This must be self-mastery when I can manifest these outer conditions."

Well, my beloved, if this is your attitude, if this is your desire, there is absolutely nothing wrong with it. As we have said, the earth is a sort of experience machine where you are allowed to have certain experiences until you have had enough of them and you are ready to move on. As you are probably beginning to realize, the goal of this course in self-mastery is not to empower you to manifest the exact physical conditions you want. It is not a matter of manifesting specific physical conditions; it is a matter of *self*-mastery. What is the difference? Well, the difference is very simple.

The lie promoted by the fallen beings is that when you have certain material conditions, *then* you will be happy, *then* you will be at peace inside yourself. This is the lie they promote because they believe in it. They cannot help but believe in it because they are in the dualistic consciousness. In duality you see yourself as a separate being, and this means that you see a division between what is inside your own mind and being and what is outside. You experience (all the time) that the conditions that are outside your mind are affecting your state of mind.

Therefore, you fall prey to the illusion that the only way to take control over your state of mind is to take control over the external conditions. Once you have the external conditions the way you want them, then the state of mind will automatically follow, will *mechanically* follow. This is what Jesus meant when he said that the violent attempt to take heaven by force. With heaven he, of course, meant the Christ Consciousness where you are in complete inner peace. The violent attempt to take inner peace by forcing the external conditions to live up to the vision they see of what would be the ideal conditions that they think will mechanically produce inner peace

What we, of course, have been telling you over and over again is that you are not a mechanical being. Therefore, regardless of the outer circumstances that you might have, you will not necessarily be at peace. The outer circumstances cannot produce inner peace because inner peace and happiness is an *internal* condition. That is why you are engaged in what we call the course of *self*-mastery. Self-mastery is not to take command over the *external* conditions, the conditions *outside* of self, but to take command over the *internal* conditions, the conditions *inside* your self. Now, you may think that we have said this before—and we have. You may think you have heard this before—and you have. But have you truly *internalized* it? Have you truly locked in to it? Has it clicked in all four levels of your mind? Has the Conscious You been able to step outside of these age-old momentums of seeking to control the outside world? Have you been able to step outside of these age-old desires to have certain conditions in the outside world?

No mechanical formula

That is why I said that the path is not mechanical. You cannot create a formula that produces certain external conditions and then automatically have inner peace. You can (as I said) create a certain formula that will produce certain outside conditions. This is possible. It is not practical for the vast majority of people on this planet, but you will see some people who have used their minds to project a certain vision and thereby gather to themselves great riches, great power or whatever you have.

What you would also see, if you saw with Christ vision, is that almost all of these people are fallen beings who have had a very, very long time to build this momentum of controlling the material realm. They can only do this as a pendulum swinging where they can gradually move towards having greater and greater control as the pendulum swings to one side. When the pendulum is as far out as their momentum is able to carry it, they can seemingly have great power and riches on earth. Then, they inevitably reach the limit of their ability to create an imbalance in the universe and the pendulum starts swinging back. They now go into having less and less control and they might spend many, many lifetimes having virtually no control over their lives. What you see as the great men today will not be the great men of tomorrow and they were not the great men of the past (at least not the distant past).

You see here that if you desire to have a certain experience, and if you desire to have this seeming mastery over matter, then, again, I do not condemn you, I do not criticize you. I acknowledge that the only way for you to overcome this desire is to go out and attempt to manifest it until you have had enough of this experience. Then, I simply say to you: "I am not the teacher you need at this point on your path. Neither are the other Chohans. The course of self-mastery is not what you need at this point. You need to go out and find another teacher who can seemingly deliver what you desire." There are indeed students who come to this point, after having gone through the previous four levels, and when they are confronted with this reality, it finally clicks in them that this path is not what they want at this point in their cosmic evolution—and so they decide to leave.

Then, they will, of course, be welcome back whenever they are ready to come back. They will have to go down and start with Master MORE again, but nevertheless we never condemn anyone, we never send anyone away. You see, it is necessary to confront people at this level, the first level of my retreat, to clarify for them what is their vision of the spiritual path, what is their vision of this course.

Then, they have the choice: Will they transcend a certain vision and align themselves with what the course actually offers, or will they go elsewhere and pursue the vision they see and that it is important for them to live out? When people have passed this hurdle and decided that "Yes," they do want self-mastery, they do want to follow this course, they do want to study under me, then we can move on. That is when we move on to the other hard realization that you need to face at this first level of my retreat, which I already described by saying that you need to realize that vision is not *passive,* vision is very much an *active* faculty.

How your mind distorts your vision

Now, I want you to think back to what you learned in school. You learned that there are certain objects out there. There are tables, chairs, streets, cars, trees, mountains, rivers, oceans, the earth. When you look at them, light rays are bouncing off these objects and the light rays enter your eyes. They hit the retina and then you supposedly see what is actually out there. Now, this is where we need to go beyond what you learned in school.

First of all, we can question whether there *are* actually objects out there, at least objects as you were brought up to see them. Now, I am not saying here that the entire material world does not exist or is produced in your vision. There *are* objects out there.

We could question whether those objects are solid objects or something else. As you know if you have studied our teachings, and if you have looked into Quantum physics just a little bit, then even scientists are beginning to question whether there are actual, solid objects out there. They know, when they think about this, that everything is made of vibrating energy

4 | Vision Is both Passive and Active

waves. You are not necessarily seeing an object, you are seeing an energy field. This is important to keep in mind, and I will return to it in later lessons.

The question I want you to consider now is: "Where do the light rays that hit your eyes actually come from?" Are they just sort of floating around in space, do they come from the sun or from an artificial light source? You know, of course, that when it is dark, you cannot see anything. Does that mean that the objects are not there when it is dark? Nay, they are, of course, there. The energy fields are there and so where do the light rays come from that enter your eye after they have supposedly hit the object? Well, here it is important to recognize that there is a physical aspect of vision and there are non-physical aspects, at least as you define "physical" right now.

If you are a spiritual person, you are no doubt aware that there has always been a concept of "second sight" or "having your third eye opened" so that people can supposedly see the energy fields around other people or things. What you need to recognize is that there is always an emission of light rays from any object that is out there. It is an energy field and it is giving off electromagnetic rays constantly, even at night. What happens, of course, when the sun comes up or when you turn on a light bulb is that now there are the kind of electromagnetic waves that your eyes can physically see and therefore you can see the object.

My beloved, it is entirely possible to have night vision without wearing funny goggles that make everything look green. It is completely possible to be able to see in the dark as clearly as you can see in the daytime with your physical eyes. Why don't you see auras, why can't you see at night? It is because you are not seeing what your eyes are seeing. What I am telling you here is that there are far more light rays entering your physical eyes than you actually see. Why are most people not seeing the auras around other people? It is not because their eyes are not receiving the light rays from people's auras; it is because their minds are filtering out these light rays as irrelevant or unnecessary information.

The four levels of vision

Let us look at what happens when a light ray enters your physical eye. As you have been taught, the light ray hits the retina and the retina sends a signal to the visual cortex in the brain. This is where your school learning probably stopped, but what you need to realize is that this is a very sophisticated and very complicated process. You know that a digital camera has a sensor and when a light ray hits the sensor, the sensor transforms the light ray into the kind of signal that a computer can deal with. You also know that computers are based on a binary system of on and off signals. In other words, there are no nuances, no shades; it is on or off, zero or one, there are only two possibilities. Well, the retina in your eye functions in a similar way but it has more than two possibilities; it is not binary.

There are, in fact, seven levels or seven shades of what the retina can deal with. This means that when the retina sends signals to the visual cortex, they are not sent as on or off signals, they are sent as seven different shades, seven different codings of signals. As the retina converts the light ray (or the impression of the light ray) into one of these signals that your brain can deal with, it is sending them through the wiring in the brain to the visual cortex. What happens in the visual cortex is an even more complex and sophisticated process. It is not that there is a one-on-one correspondence between what the visual cortex receives from the retina and what you see. It is, for that matter, not that there is a one-on-one relationship between the light ray that hits the retina and the signal the retina sends to the brain.

What you need to recognize is the very simple truth that you do not see with your eyes, you see with your brain. Now, you need to go beyond this and realize that the physical aspect of vision (that takes place in the brain) is only the most coarse aspect of vision. This is the foundation for physical vision, but it is only the tip of the iceberg of what vision is really comprised of. There is an aspect of vision that relates to your emotional body, there is an aspect that relates to the mental and one to the identity body. You do not see with the eyes, you do not see with the brain, you see with all four lower bodies.

What is your emotional body? Well, as you can readily imagine, it is an energy field. Now, you need to reach into something you may or may not have learned in school, but otherwise we have written about this and it is very simple. Electromagnetic light or electromagnetic rays are waves. When waves interact, they will, depending on their vibratory characteristics, either interfere with each other or pass through each other. When there is an interference pattern, then it is the characteristics of the two waves that determines the interference pattern and thereby the outcome of the interaction.

How vision happens at the physical level

What I am saying here is this: You have an electromagnetic ray that enters your eye. It hits the retina, which truly is also an electromagnetic field. An interference pattern is created that has seven different shades. As a result of this interference pattern, an impulse is sent to the brain, to the visual cortex. As this impulse hits the visual cortex, which is also an energy field, a new interference pattern is created and what the visual cortex deals with is the outcome of this interference pattern. It is possible (and in fact it happens for the vast majority of people) that the visual cortex itself will affect what you actually see. There is an interpretation imposed upon what you see at the physical level. I will give you a simple example of this. You have no doubt seen these illusions that are out there, very simple optical illusions. The simplest one being two lines, one of them has a normal arrow that points out and the other one has a reversed arrow that points in. When you look at these two lines, it looks like one is longer than the other, even though you can go in and measure that they have the exact same length. It is simply that the direction of the two arrows cheats your eye, as they say, and makes one look longer than the other.

This is what is imposed upon your vision at the level of the visual cortex. There are certain programs in the visual cortex that relate to the physical octave, the material world or how you see things—what they are. This is, of course, much more sophisticated than lines; it relates to shapes, your ability to judge what a shape is. For example, if you go back to primitive men that lived in the forest where they could be attacked by a wild animal, their visual cortex was very, very quick to determine that a certain shape represented danger. The brain could therefore signal to the muscles to take evasive action before the conscious mind actually had time to react to the experience.

You see that there is a certain practical reality here. There are situations in life where you need to react so quickly that you cannot consciously make a decision about this; you need to respond subconsciously. You all do this when you drive your cars, for example, or ride a bicycle. This is at the purely physical level.

There is not necessarily anything wrong with this, even though it must be recognized that because of the very long history of this planet being in the dualistic consciousness, all people have certain, what you might call instincts, programmed into their brains. It is necessary at some point on the spiritual path, although not until you go beyond the 96th level, to start unraveling those.

This is just to give you a feel for the fact that even at the physical level, the level of the brain, there is a distortion of your vision. There is a certain interpretation imposed upon what you see. The simplest one being: "Does this represent danger or does it not?" There are many more, very subtle interpretations.

Vision at the higher levels

When the impulse has passed through the visual cortex, that is when the interference pattern created there is sent to the emotional body. Again, your emotional body is an energy field so there will be another interaction, another interference pattern. What you then see at the emotional level will be affected by what is in your emotional body. The programmings that are there, the kind of energies that are there. If you have a lot of fear in your emotional body, you will tend to interpret many situations as threatening even if they are not particularly threatening. That is why you can see people who are in the same situation but respond differently because one has more fear than the other in their emotional body.

Again, after this interaction in the emotional body, the impulse moves to the mental body. Here, it again creates an interference pattern and then it moves on to the identity body. Now, what is it that you see—the Conscious You? At what point do you see this? Well, that depends on where you, the Conscious You, are focused in your four lower bodies. There are people who are focused at the physical level, the level of the physical body. These are often people who have been in physically dangerous situations. It may be soldiers of war, it may be criminals who are constantly threatened, it may be native people living in the jungle. These people are focused entirely on the physical level so they do not even see (at least not consciously) what happens at the higher levels. We might say that their chain of vision ends at the physical level.

Then, there are people who are focused at the emotional level and they, of course, see the interference pattern that is created after the visual impulse reaches the emotional body. They do not see what happens when it goes on to higher levels, at least not consciously, because they are not thinking consciously. Then, of course, some people are focused at the mental level, some at the identity level. Now, all of the students who come to my retreat are focused either in the higher mental realm or in the identity level. You cannot have walked this far on the path without having risen above the physical and the emotional level. You cannot be totally focused on emotions, for example, and have passed the initiations of Serapis Bey.

What you need to recognize here, and what I am asking you to consider as you are going through this lesson, is that your mental body, your identity body will be distorting your vision. Now, I know that at this point this can seem scary or difficult to see through. After all, if you are wearing yellow glasses and you do not know you are wearing yellow glasses, how do you come to see without the glasses? Of course, it is my job as your teacher on these seven levels of my retreat to gradually make you more aware that you have a filter and that you can take off the filter and attain a more pure, a more clear, vision.

I do not want you to panic, to be discouraged or to feel that this is an impossible task. Of course it is possible and I will make it even more possible as we go along. What I do want you to decide consciously here is whether you actually want to

True and false self-control

Now, you understand that this is a course of *self*-mastery. What the fallen beings are attempting to attain is control over the external world without taking control over the internal world. This may seem like a contradiction because there are false teachers out there who will claim that they have self-control, that they have complete control over their actions or their state of mind. There is some reality here in the sense that you *can* attain a certain level of control over your four lower bodies. This is, indeed, what the people I talked about, who have a certain ability to control their outer situation, have attained.

You cannot cheat the universe; it reflects back to you what you are projecting out. If you want a certain condition to be manifest, well, you have to have some control over what you are projecting out. You can, of course, (as you have seen many times in the past) have one person who has managed to turn an entire population into his slaves so they are all working to give him the physical conditions of a great palace and seemingly a great army and great power. Even this requires a certain mastery of mind where you are able to bend other people's will with *your* will.

Again, this is not self-mastery. It is mastery over the four lower bodies, but it is not the mastery of self because the self is more than the four lower bodies. What, then, is self-mastery? It is purity of intent. Serapis talked about the purity of intention when you come to a point where you are not aggressive. When you are not seeking to bend other people with *your* will by making them relinquish *their* will, *then* you have self-mastery.

This is when you are not seeking to force the universe to give you certain conditions even though you do not have the corresponding conditions inside your self. Do you see, my beloved, what I am saying here? The universe is a mirror. If you want certain conditions (that you need in the outside world), you need to create a vision of those conditions inside your mind and then you need to project that vision upon the Ma-ter Light, the cosmic mirror.

The question is whether you are formulating your vision through the dualistic mind, the separate mind, or through the Christ mind. I must tell you that when you come to this level of my retreat, you will have remnants of this momentum of projecting through the separate mind. This means that you have certain desires, certain needs of the separate mind, that you are thinking (perhaps almost subconsciously) need to be fulfilled. It should be part of the path to self-mastery that you fulfill these desires and become able to manifest these outer conditions.

This may be a certain mastery of mind over matter, but it is not the mastery of mind over mind. There is no mastery of mind over mind, for what we are talking about in the course of self-mastery is that you come to the point where you do not have *two* minds. You have only *one* mind.

Do you not see that duality is based on a fundamental division between self and the world, between *my* self and other selves? The course of self-mastery is the course of overcoming duality, overcoming separation, coming towards that which we have called the Christ Consciousness, which is where you see the Oneness of all life. Do you understand the difference here?

What the fallen beings are doing is they are saying: "I want certain conditions manifest in the external world. I know the universe works like a mirror so I have to create inside my four lower bodies a matrix of the conditions I want manifest in the physical world and then I have to project, with as much force as I can, that matrix upon the Ma-ter Light. Then, after some time, the Ma-ter Light will take on that form." Do you not see what they are doing? As I said earlier, they are creating a new program, a new spirit, and what does it do? It increases the division in their minds.

What they call mastery is when they create one internal spirit that is so powerful that it can temporarily override the other internal spirits. Therefore, as I said, when the pendulum swings to one side, they can manifest these outer conditions. Then, there comes a point where they simply do not have the power to keep going, and now this powerful spirit that they have created runs out of steam. The other spirits begin to take over and suddenly there is division in the mind and the pendulum starts swinging back. Now they experience many embodiments with chaos, turmoil and a low estate in the outer world.

Self-mastery is when you gradually dissolve the internal spirits, dissolve the internal divisions. You transcend the internal divisions and you come closer and closer to a point where your vision is based on oneness.

Compare Jesus to billionaires

Here you may want to take a conscious look at the life and mission of Jesus or the life of the Buddha, if you prefer. Compare Jesus and the Buddha to the people you see today who are rich and powerful, who are billionaires, who have everything they could possibly want, who can control every aspect of their outer lives. Do you think that a rich and powerful person, the richest man in the world, has more self-mastery than Jesus or the Buddha? He has more – perhaps – of this ability to manifest physical conditions. Or does he really have more, for does it not seem likely to you that Jesus and the Buddha had the mastery, for they could have manifested any outer conditions they wanted for themselves.

You need to ask yourself: "Why is it that these two spiritual masters, who had self-mastery, actually lived very simple and, from a materialistic point, very poor lives? They had no possessions, they owned nothing. Jesus had no ashram, no fixed place, but walked around all the time. Why did he not manifest the exact conditions he desired? Well, he did not because he had done this in past lives where he had manifested outer conditions to the point where he had enough of this and he desired a higher experience.

What is the higher experience? It is that you begin to look beyond the self! Your vision is not focused on the separate self, you are not focused on what you want for the separate self. You become more and more focused on the whole, you overcome the division between self and other. You see that either it is all self or the self is part of a whole. The ultimate creative fulfillment for your self is to do something that raises the whole rather than focusing all of your energy, attention and vision on just raising the separate self.

Do you see that there comes a point where you begin to realize that what the fallen beings are doing, is that they are raising their separate selves up above all others? When you consider that there is a certain balance in the universe, a certain action and reaction, a certain Law of Karma, then you realize that if one person raises itself so high above others, it can only be done by creating an imbalance where others are put down. This imbalance cannot go on forever. That is why I said that the person who raises himself up in one lifetime, will in future lifetimes go down. It can be no other way.

What you realize is that in the dualistic consciousness, you are constantly seeking to go towards one extreme. By doing this, you create an imbalance and there will come a point where the pendulum starts swinging back in order to again create some state of balance. When you attain the Christ vision, you come to see that it is possible to act in such a way that you are not raising one separate self by putting other separate selves down, by putting other parts of the universe down. You can actually raise your self in such a way that it raises the whole. This is Christ vision. When you come to the point where your energy, your attention, your time is focused on raising the All, *then* you begin to attain self-mastery.

Change your mind before changing the world

This does not mean that you stop being a human being; it does not mean you cannot live an active life in society. It does not mean you cannot have a house to live in, you cannot have a family, you cannot have any possessions. We are not saying that all people in the modern world should live like Jesus. As we have said, in this day and age, it is more important that you live active lives in society.

You can come to the point where the things you have do not own you because for you they are just means to an end, they are not an end in themselves. You are not focused on producing certain material conditions in order to produce a state of inner peace. Your mind is focused on achieving the inner peace through the powers of the mind itself. When you gain some mastery in producing inner peace regardless of outer conditions, then why do you need these outer conditions? It does not mean you cannot have them, but do you see my point? You are not striving towards material possessions in order to have an inner experience. You are focusing on the inner experience and then the outer conditions are just what they are. They fall into place and you make the best of them, whatever they are.

There are so many people who come to this level of my retreat and they have heard about higher states of consciousness, enlightenment, Christhood, whatever they call it. They still think that until certain outer conditions are fulfilled, they cannot really experience these higher states of consciousness.

You see, my beloved, if you have this attitude, you will never, *ever* reach a point where the outer conditions are so ideal that you will say: "Now, I can manifest a higher state of consciousness." The reason for this is simple; we have said it many times: "Consciousness comes before the physical manifestation." If you think that the physical manifestation must come first – and then, consciousness will follow – you will never have a higher state of consciousness. If you are waiting for ideal conditions before you can manifest a higher state of consciousness, it will never happen.

The point I want to leave you to ponder (and I know I have already given you a lot in this lesson, but I will give you one more thing to ponder) is this: Consider whether you have these very subtle ideas in your mind that in order to truly walk the spiritual path, in order to manifest a higher state of consciousness, in order to truly focus on being spiritual, certain outer conditions, material conditions, must be fulfilled. If you have, then ponder what they are and ponder what I have said: You can keep waiting for the outer ideal conditions indefinitely. You will not manifest Christhood until you decide that regardless of the outer conditions, you will focus your attention within. You will look for the beam in your own eye, you will look at yourself, you will focus on attaining self-mastery rather than mastering outer conditions or waiting for those outer conditions to magically appear.

There are those who think the path of self-mastery is about forcefully manifesting outer conditions. There are those who think it is about passively waiting until some Divine grace manifests those conditions. Neither will happen. In fact, it may be better to seek to force the outer conditions and then realize that the outer conditions will not give you inner peace. Then, you can more quickly move on than those who are waiting forever for some Divine grace to give them the conditions where they can manifest peace.

Consciousness comes before the physical manifestation. Why? Because the physical manifestation is a reflection from the cosmic mirror of what you project into it. Do not focus on the mirror, focus on the images in your mind that you are projecting outside your mind. Focus on the film-strip in the movie projector, not on the screen.

Hilarion I AM, and I look forward to giving you the next lessons in my retreat.

5 | INVOKING A HIGHER VISION

In the name I AM THAT I AM, Jesus Christ, I call to my I AM Presence to flow through the I Will Be Presence that I AM and give this invocation with full power. I call to beloved Elohim Cyclopea and Virginia and Hercules and Amazonia, Archangel Raphael and Mother Mary and Michael and Faith, Hilarion and Master MORE to help me know how my vision works. Help me see and surrender all patterns that block my oneness with Hilarion and with my I AM Presence, including …

[Make personal calls]

Part 1

1. It is through the faculty of vision that I project into the cosmic mirror. What can the cosmic mirror do except reflect back to me what I am projecting out?

Cyclopea so dear, the truth you reveal,
the truth that duality's ailments will heal,
your Emerald Light is like a great balm,
our emotional bodies are perfectly calm.

**Cyclopea so dear, in Emerald Sphere,
in raising perception we shall persevere,
as deep in our hearts your truth we revere,
to immaculate vision the earth does adhere.**

2. If I want to get a different return from the cosmic mirror, I must start by acknowledging that vision is not passive. I project with my vision.

Cyclopea so dear, with you we unwind,
all negative spirals clouding the mind,
we know pure awareness is truly our core,
the key to becoming the wide-open door.

**Cyclopea so dear, in Emerald Sphere,
in raising perception we shall persevere,
as deep in our hearts your truth we revere,
to immaculate vision the earth does adhere.**

3. I do not simply understand this theoretically and intellectually. I am having a total experience that shifts my consciousness so I realize in all four of my lower bodies that vision is not a passive faculty. I am constantly projecting out, and what I project out affects what I see.

5 | Invoking a Higher Vision

Cyclopea so dear, clear our inner sight,
empowered, we pierce the soul's fearful night,
we now see our life through your single eye,
beyond all disease we're ready to fly.

**Cyclopea so dear, in Emerald Sphere,
in raising perception we shall persevere,
as deep in our hearts your truth we revere,
to immaculate vision the earth does adhere.**

4. What I am projecting out affects what I think is coming to me from without. What I see is not what is coming to me from without; what I see is something that is produced inside my mind.

Cyclopea so dear, life can only reflect,
the images that the mind does project,
the key to our healing is clearing the mind,
from the images the ego is hiding behind.

**Cyclopea so dear, in Emerald Sphere,
in raising perception we shall persevere,
as deep in our hearts your truth we revere,
to immaculate vision the earth does adhere.**

5. I am clarifying my vision so that I am aware of what I am projecting out. I have mastery of what I am projecting out and therefore I have mastery of what is coming back from the cosmic mirror, which only reflects back what I am projecting out.

Cyclopea so dear, we want to aim high,
to your healing flame we ever draw nigh,
through veils of duality we now take flight,
bathed in your penetrating Emerald Light.

**Cyclopea so dear, in Emerald Sphere,
in raising perception we shall persevere,
as deep in our hearts your truth we revere,
to immaculate vision the earth does adhere.**

6. One of the most subtle illusions on the spiritual path comes directly from the fallen consciousness. It is the illusion that Jesus described when he said: "The kingdom of heaven suffers violence, and the violent take it by force."

Cyclopea so dear, your Emerald Flame,
exposes every subtle, dualistic power game,
including the game of wanting to say,
that truth is defined in only one way.

**Cyclopea so dear, in Emerald Sphere,
in raising perception we shall persevere,
as deep in our hearts your truth we revere,
to immaculate vision the earth does adhere.**

7. I cannot take heaven by force because I cannot go beyond the four levels of this unascended sphere while I am in embodiment in any of those four levels. I cannot affect the spiritual realm.

5 | Invoking a Higher Vision

Cyclopea so dear, we're feeling the flow,
as your Living Truth upon us you bestow,
from all dual vision we are now set free,
planet earth in immaculate matrix will be.

**Cyclopea so dear, in Emerald Sphere,
in raising perception we shall persevere,
as deep in our hearts your truth we revere,
to immaculate vision the earth does adhere.**

8. I surrender the idea that this course of self-mastery, that the spiritual path in general, is about acquiring certain extraordinary abilities. The spiritual path is *not* about acquiring a mechanical ability.

Cyclopea so dear, the truth is now clear,
we see higher purpose for which we are here
we know truth transcends all systems below,
immersed in your light, we continue to grow.

**Cyclopea so dear, in Emerald Sphere,
in raising perception we shall persevere,
as deep in our hearts your truth we revere,
to immaculate vision the earth does adhere.**

9. I surrender the idea that by following a few simple steps, by learning a certain formula, by giving certain affirmations, then I can turn my life around very quickly and force the universe to give me what I desire.

Cyclopea so dear, we're feeling your joy,
as creative vision we now do employ,
in lifting earth out of serpentine cage,
to manifest Saint Germain's Golden Age.

**Cyclopea so dear, in Emerald Sphere,
in raising perception we shall persevere,
as deep in our hearts your truth we revere,
to immaculate vision the earth does adhere.**

Part 2

1. Without a unified vision, the people perish. I am willing to look at my subconscious mind and work towards a unified vision based on my Divine plan.

O Hercules Blue, we're one with your will,
all space in our beings with Blue Flame you fill,
a beacon that radiates light to the earth,
bringing about our planet's rebirth.

**O Hercules Blue, all life you defend,
giving us power to always transcend,
in you the expansion of self has no end,
as we in God's infinite spirals ascend.**

2. There is no way to cheat the system. I cannot create a mechanical formula that will give me the exact conditions I want. All of the false promises out there are false.

O Hercules Blue, your wisdom so great,
within us a sense of knowing create,
a new frame of reference we suddenly gain,
for going beyond duality's pain.

**O Hercules Blue, all life you defend,
giving us power to always transcend,
in you the expansion of self has no end,
as we in God's infinite spirals ascend.**

3. I surrender all desire to create a program with the conscious mind. I want to resolve the programs in the other layers of the mind.

O Hercules Blue, we lovingly raise,
our voices in giving God infinite praise,
in feeling your flame, so clearly we see,
transcending the self is the true alchemy.

**O Hercules Blue, all life you defend,
giving us power to always transcend,
in you the expansion of self has no end,
as we in God's infinite spirals ascend.**

4. I make the conscious choice that I want self-mastery rather than certain physical, material conditions or certain experiences on earth.

O Hercules Blue, all life now you heal,
enveloping all in your Blue-flame Seal,
we're grateful for playing a personal part,
In God's infinitely intricate work of art.

> O Hercules Blue, all life you defend,
> giving us power to always transcend,
> in you the expansion of self has no end,
> as we in God's infinite spirals ascend.

5. The goal of this course of self-mastery is not to empower me to manifest the exact physical conditions I want. It is not a matter of manifesting specific physical conditions; it is a matter of *self*-mastery.

> O Hercules Blue, your Temple of Light,
> revealed to us all through our inner sight,
> your power allows us to forge on until,
> we pierce every veil and climb every hill.

> O Hercules Blue, all life you defend,
> giving us power to always transcend,
> in you the expansion of self has no end,
> as we in God's infinite spirals ascend.

6. The lie promoted by the fallen beings is that when I have certain material conditions, then I will be happy, then I will be at peace inside myself.

> O Hercules Blue, I pledge now my life,
> in helping this planet transcend human strife,
> duality's lies are pierced by your light,
> restoring the fullness of our inner sight.

> O Hercules Blue, all life you defend,
> giving us power to always transcend,
> in you the expansion of self has no end,
> as we in God's infinite spirals ascend.

7. In duality, I see myself as a separate being. I see a division between what is inside my own mind and what is outside. I experience that the conditions that are outside my mind are affecting my state of mind.

> O Hercules Blue, we set all life free,
> from the subtlest lies of duality,
> the prince of this world no more has a bond,
> for with you we go completely beyond.

> **O Hercules Blue, all life you defend,**
> **giving us power to always transcend,**
> **in you the expansion of self has no end,**
> **as we in God's infinite spirals ascend.**

8. In duality, I fall prey to the illusion that the only way to take control over my state of mind is to take control over the external conditions. Once I have the external conditions the way I want them, then the state of mind will automatically follow.

> O Hercules Blue, in oneness with thee,
> we open our hearts to your reality,
> your electric-blue fire within us reveal,
> our innermost longing for all that is real.

> **O Hercules Blue, all life you defend,**
> **giving us power to always transcend,**
> **in you the expansion of self has no end,**
> **as we in God's infinite spirals ascend.**

9. The violent attempt to take inner peace by forcing the external conditions to live up to their vision of what would be the ideal conditions that they think will mechanically produce inner peace.

> O Hercules Blue, you fill every space,
> with infinite Power and infinite Grace,
> you embody the key to creativity,
> the will to transcend into Infinity.
>
> **O Hercules Blue, all life you defend,**
> **giving us power to always transcend,**
> **in you the expansion of self has no end,**
> **as we in God's infinite spirals ascend.**

Part 3

1. I am not a mechanical being and therefore, regardless of the outer circumstances, I will not necessarily be at peace. The outer circumstances cannot produce inner peace because inner peace and happiness is an internal condition.

> Raphael Archangel, your light so intense,
> raise us beyond all human pretense.
> Mother Mary and you have a vision so bold,
> to see that our highest potential unfold.
>
> **Raphael Archangel, for vision we pray,**
> **Raphael Archangel, show us the way,**
> **Raphael Archangel, your emerald ray,**
> **Raphael Archangel, our lives a new day.**

5 | Invoking a Higher Vision

2. Self-mastery is *not* to take command over the external conditions, the conditions outside of self, but to take command over the internal conditions, the conditions inside of self.

> Raphael Archangel, in emerald sphere,
> to immaculate vision we always adhere.
> Mother Mary enfolds us in her Sacred Heart,
> from Mother's true love, we're never apart.

> **Raphael Archangel, for vision we pray,**
> **Raphael Archangel, show us the way,**
> **Raphael Archangel, your emerald ray,**
> **Raphael Archangel, our lives a new day.**

3. I have heard this before, but now I am truly internalizing it. I am locking in to it. It is clicking in all four levels of my mind. My Conscious You is stepping outside of these age-old momentums of seeking to control the outside world.

> Raphael Archangel, all ailments you heal,
> each cell in our bodies in light now you seal.
> Mother Mary's immaculate concept we see,
> perfection of health our new reality.

> **Raphael Archangel, for vision we pray,**
> **Raphael Archangel, show us the way,**
> **Raphael Archangel, your emerald ray,**
> **Raphael Archangel, our lives a new day.**

4. The path is not mechanical. I cannot create a formula that produces certain external conditions and then automatically have inner peace.

Raphael Archangel, your light is so real,
the vision of Christ in us you reveal.
Mother Mary now helps us to truly transcend,
in emerald light with you we ascend.

**Raphael Archangel, for vision we pray,
Raphael Archangel, show us the way,
Raphael Archangel, your emerald ray,
Raphael Archangel, our lives a new day.**

5. I am willing to clarify what is my vision of the spiritual path and this course. I will transcend any lower vision and align myself with what the course actually offers.

Raphael Archangel, diseases are done,
as you help us see that all life is One,
we no longer do your true love reject,
immaculate vision on all we project.

**Raphael Archangel, for vision we pray,
Raphael Archangel, show us the way,
Raphael Archangel, your emerald ray,
Raphael Archangel, our lives a new day.**

6. I live in a world where there are no solid objects because everything is made of vibrating energy waves. I am not seeing an object, I am seeing an energy field.

Raphael Archangel, we're healing the earth,
in immaculate vision we give her rebirth,
a new era has on this day begun,
your emerald light now shines like a sun.

> Raphael Archangel, for vision we pray,
> Raphael Archangel, show us the way,
> Raphael Archangel, your emerald ray,
> Raphael Archangel, our lives a new day.

7. There is a physical aspect of vision and there are non-physical aspects.

> Raphael Archangel, the fall is behind,
> as all of earth's people the Christ path do find,
> we call now to you all people to heal,
> as four lower bodies in love you do seal.

> Raphael Archangel, for vision we pray,
> Raphael Archangel, show us the way,
> Raphael Archangel, your emerald ray,
> Raphael Archangel, our lives a new day.

8. There are far more light rays entering my physical eyes than I actually see. My mind is filtering out many light rays as irrelevant or unnecessary information.

> Raphael Archangel, as you bring the light,
> the forces of darkness swiftly take flight,
> their day is now done as we claim the earth,
> spreading to all an innocent mirth.

> Raphael Archangel, for vision we pray,
> Raphael Archangel, show us the way,
> Raphael Archangel, your emerald ray,
> Raphael Archangel, our lives a new day.

9. I do not see with my eyes, I see with my brain. Yet the physical aspect of vision, that takes place in the brain, is only the most coarse aspect of vision.

> Raphael Archangel, our vision set free,
> as we can now see God's reality,
> as Saint Germain's vision is manifest here,
> the earth is now sealed in immaculate sphere.

> **Raphael Archangel, for vision we pray,**
> **Raphael Archangel, show us the way,**
> **Raphael Archangel, your emerald ray,**
> **Raphael Archangel, our lives a new day.**

Part 4

1. There is an aspect of vision that relates to my emotional body, there is an aspect that relates to the mental and one to the identity body. I do not see with the eyes, I do not see with the brain, I see with all four lower bodies.

> Michael Archangel, in your flame so blue,
> there is no more night, there is only you.
> In oneness with you, we're filled with your light,
> what glorious wonder, revealed to our sight.

> **Michael Archangel, your Knowing so strong,**
> **Michael Archangel, oh sweep us along.**
> **Michael Archangel, we're singing your song,**
> **Michael Archangel, with you we belong.**

2. At each level, there is a distortion because of the interaction of energy waves. What I consciously see is a result of an external stimuli creating interference patterns with my four lower bodies.

> Michael Archangel, protection you give,
> within your blue shield, we ever shall live.
> Sealed from all creatures, roaming the night,
> we remain in your sphere, of electric blue light.
>
> **Michael Archangel, your Knowing so strong,**
> **Michael Archangel, oh sweep us along.**
> **Michael Archangel, we're singing your song,**
> **Michael Archangel, with you we belong.**

3. My emotional body, mental body and identity body will be distorting my vision. I want to become more aware that I have a filter and that I can take off the filter and attain a more pure vision.

> Michael Archangel, what power you bring,
> as millions of angels, praises will sing.
> Consuming the demons, of doubt and of fear,
> we know that your Presence, will always be near.
>
> **Michael Archangel, your Knowing so strong,**
> **Michael Archangel, oh sweep us along.**
> **Michael Archangel, we're singing your song,**
> **Michael Archangel, with you we belong.**

4. The fallen beings are attempting to attain control over the external world without taking control over the internal world. They can attain a certain level of control over their four lower bodies and have some control over what they are projecting out.

> Michael Archangel, God's will is your love,
> you bring to us all, God's light from Above.
> God's will is to see, all life taking flight,
> transcendence of self, our most sacred right.

> **Michael Archangel, your Knowing so strong,**
> **Michael Archangel, oh sweep us along.**
> **Michael Archangel, we're singing your song,**
> **Michael Archangel, with you we belong.**

5. This is not self-mastery; it is mastery over the four lower bodies, but it is not the mastery of self because the self is more than the four lower bodies.

> Michael Archangel, you are the best friend,
> from all worldly dangers you do us defend,
> the devil no match for your power of light,
> and therefore our souls can freely take flight.

> **Michael Archangel, your Knowing so strong,**
> **Michael Archangel, oh sweep us along.**
> **Michael Archangel, we're singing your song,**
> **Michael Archangel, with you we belong.**

6. Self-mastery is purity of intent. I surrender any desire to bend other people with *my* will by making them relinquish *their* will.

5 | Invoking a Higher Vision

Michael Archangel, as children we play,
we're bringing the earth into a new day,
we raise it from all of the patterns so old,
our planet's life story is by us retold.

**Michael Archangel, your Knowing so strong,
Michael Archangel, oh sweep us along.
Michael Archangel, we're singing your song,
Michael Archangel, with you we belong.**

7. I surrender any desire to force the universe to give me certain conditions even though I do not have the corresponding conditions inside my self.

Michael Archangel, God's power you show,
that you are invincible, this we do know,
you are undivided and thus can withstand,
anything coming from serpentine band.

**Michael Archangel, your Knowing so strong,
Michael Archangel, oh sweep us along.
Michael Archangel, we're singing your song,
Michael Archangel, with you we belong.**

8. The universe is a mirror. If I want certain conditions, I need to create a vision of those conditions inside my mind and then I need to project that vision upon the Ma-ter Light.

Michael Archangel, come raise now the earth,
giving her thus a complete rebirth,
collective the mind that we do now raise,
for this we do give our infinite praise.

**Michael Archangel, your Knowing so strong,
Michael Archangel, oh sweep us along.
Michael Archangel, we're singing your song,
Michael Archangel, with you we belong.**

9. The question is whether I am formulating my vision through the dualistic mind, the separate mind, or through the Christ mind, the undivided mind.

Michael Archangel, the earth is now new,
covered in Blue-flame as the morning dew,
our planet now sparkles throughout all of space,
as we are receiving your infinite Grace.

**Michael Archangel, your Knowing so strong,
Michael Archangel, oh sweep us along.
Michael Archangel, we're singing your song,
Michael Archangel, with you we belong.**

Part 5

1. I surrender all remnants of this momentum of projecting through the separate mind. I surrender all desires, all needs of the separate mind. I surrender the idea that it should be part of the path to self-mastery that I fulfill these desires and become able to manifest these outer conditions.

Hilarion, on emerald shore,
we're free from all that's gone before.
Hilarion, we let all go,
that keeps us out of sacred flow.

5 | Invoking a Higher Vision

**Hilarion, with light so green,
we see behind the matter screen,
immaculate our inner sight,
we see the earth is taking flight.**

2. I surrender the desire to have mastery of mind over matter, for I truly want the mastery of mind over mind. Yet there is no mastery of mind over mind, for I want to come to the point where I do not have *two* minds. I have only *one* mind.

Hilarion, the secret key,
is wisdom's own reality.
Hilarion, all life is healed,
the ego's face no more concealed.

**Hilarion, with light so green,
we see behind the matter screen,
immaculate our inner sight,
we see the earth is taking flight.**

3. Duality is based on a fundamental division between self and the world. The course of self-mastery is the course of overcoming duality, overcoming separation, coming towards the Christ Consciousness, which is where I see the Oneness of all life.

Hilarion, your love for life,
helps us surrender inner strife.
Hilarion, your loving words,
thrill our hearts like song of birds.

> Hilarion, with light so green,
> we see behind the matter screen,
> immaculate our inner sight,
> we see the earth is taking flight.

4. What the fallen beings call mastery is when they create one internal spirit that is so powerful that it can temporarily override the other internal spirits. Self-mastery is when I gradually dissolve the internal spirits, dissolve the internal divisions.

> Hilarion, invoke the light,
> your sacred formulas recite.
> Hilarion, your secret tone,
> philosopher's most sacred stone.
>
> **Hilarion, with light so green,
> we see behind the matter screen,
> immaculate our inner sight,
> we see the earth is taking flight.**

5. I desire to transcend the internal divisions and come closer and closer to a point where my vision is based on oneness.

> Hilarion, with love you greet,
> us in your temple over Crete.
> Hilarion, your emerald light,
> the third eye sees with Christic sight.
>
> **Hilarion, with light so green,
> we see behind the matter screen,
> immaculate our inner sight,
> we see the earth is taking flight.**

5 | Invoking a Higher Vision

6. Jesus and the Buddha had the mastery, but they were not focused on manifesting material conditions. They were focused on manifesting their Divine plans.

> Hilarion, you give us fruit,
> of truth that is so absolute.
> Hilarion, all stress decrease,
> as our ambitions we release.

> **Hilarion, with light so green,**
> **we see behind the matter screen,**
> **immaculate our inner sight,**
> **we see the earth is taking flight.**

7. I want the higher experience of looking beyond the self! My vision is not focused on the separate self, I am not focused on what I want for the separate self. I am focused on the whole, I overcome the division between self and other.

> Hilarion, our chakras clear,
> as we let go of subtlest fear.
> Hilarion, we are sincere,
> as freedom's truth we do revere.

> **Hilarion, with light so green,**
> **we see behind the matter screen,**
> **immaculate our inner sight,**
> **we see the earth is taking flight.**

8. The ultimate creative fulfillment for my self is to do something that raises the whole, rather than focusing all of my energy, attention and vision on just raising the separate self.

Hilarion, you balance all,
the seven rays upon our call.
Hilarion, you keep us true,
as we remain all one with you.

**Hilarion, with light so green,
we see behind the matter screen,
immaculate our inner sight,
we see the earth is taking flight.**

9. The fallen beings are raising their separate selves up above all others. Through the Christ vision I see that it is possible to act in such a way that I am not raising one separate self by putting other separate selves down. I am raising my self in such a way that it raises the whole.

Hilarion, your Presence here,
filling up the inner sphere.
Life is now a sacred flow,
God Vision we on all bestow.

**Hilarion, with light so green,
we see behind the matter screen,
immaculate our inner sight,
we see the earth is taking flight.**

Part 6

1. When I come to the point where my energy, my attention, my time is focused on raising the All, then I begin to attain self-mastery.

5 | Invoking a Higher Vision

Master MORE, come to the fore,
we will absorb your flame of MORE.
Master MORE, our will so strong,
our power centers cleared by song.

**Master MORE, your Sacred Heart,
from this we will no more depart,
we are forever in your flow,
of Diamond Will that you bestow.**

2. I am moving towards the point where the things I have do not own me. For me, they are just means to an end, they are not an end in themselves.

Master MORE, your wisdom flows,
as our attunement ever grows.
Master MORE, we have a tie,
that helps us see through Serpent's lie.

**Master MORE, your Sacred Heart,
from this we will no more depart,
we are forever in your flow,
of Diamond Will that you bestow.**

3. I am not focused on producing certain material conditions in order to produce a state of inner peace. My mind is focused on achieving inner peace through the powers of the mind itself.

Master MORE, your love so pink,
there is no purer love, we think.
Master MORE, you set us free,
from all conditionality.

> **Master MORE, your Sacred Heart,**
> **from this we will no more depart,**
> **we are forever in your flow,**

4. When I gain some mastery in producing inner peace regardless of outer conditions, then why do I need these outer conditions?

> Master MORE, we will endure,
> your discipline that makes us pure.
> Master MORE, intentions true,
> as we are always one with you.

> **Master MORE, your Sacred Heart,**
> **from this we will no more depart,**
> **we are forever in your flow,**
> **of Diamond Will that you bestow.**

5. I am not striving towards material possessions in order to have an inner experience. I am focusing on the inner experience and then the outer conditions are just what they are. They fall into place and I make the best of them, whatever they are.

> Master MORE, our vision raised,
> the will of God is always praised.
> Master MORE, creative will,
> raising all life higher still.

> **Master MORE, your Sacred Heart,**
> **from this we will no more depart,**
> **we are forever in your flow,**
> **of Diamond Will that you bestow.**

6. I will never, *ever* reach a point where the outer conditions are ideal for manifesting a higher state of consciousness. Consciousness comes before the physical manifestation.

> Master MORE, your peace is power,
> the demons of war it will devour.
> Master MORE, we serve all life,
> our flames consuming war and strife.
>
> **Master MORE, your Sacred Heart,**
> **from this we will no more depart,**
> **we are forever in your flow,**
> **of Diamond Will that you bestow.**

7. I surrender all of the subtle ideas saying that in order to truly walk the spiritual path and manifest a higher state of consciousness, certain material conditions must be fulfilled.

> Master MORE, we are so free,
> eternal bond from you we see.
> Master MORE, we find rebirth,
> in flow of your eternal mirth.
>
> **Master MORE, your Sacred Heart,**
> **from this we will no more depart,**
> **we are forever in your flow,**
> **of Diamond Will that you bestow.**

8. I can keep waiting for the ideal conditions indefinitely. I will not manifest Christhood until I decide that regardless of the outer conditions, I will focus my attention within. I will look for the beam in my own eye, I will look at myself, I will focus on attaining self-mastery rather than mastering outer conditions or waiting for those outer conditions to magically appear.

> Master MORE, you balance all,
> the seven rays upon our call.
> Master MORE, forever MORE,
> we are the Spirit's open door.

> **Master MORE, your Sacred Heart,**
> **from this we will no more depart,**
> **we are forever in your flow,**
> **of Diamond Will that you bestow.**

9. Consciousness comes before the physical manifestation because the physical manifestation is a reflection from the cosmic mirror of what I project into it. I do not focus on the mirror, I focus on the images in my mind that I am projecting outside my mind.

> Master MORE, your Presence here,
> filling up the inner sphere.
> Life is now a sacred flow,
> God Power we on all bestow.

> **Master MORE, your Sacred Heart,**
> **from this we will no more depart,**
> **we are forever in your flow,**
> **of Diamond Will that you bestow.**

Sealing:

In the name of the Divine Mother, I fully accept that the power of these calls is used to set free the River of Life, so it can outpicture the perfect vision of Christ for my own life, for all people and for the planet. In the name I AM THAT I AM, it is done! Amen.

6 | GETTING RESULTS FROM YOUR SPIRITUAL EFFORTS

I AM the Ascended Master Hilarion. On the second level of the initiations at my retreat, you are facing the combination of the Fifth Ray with the Second Ray of Wisdom. "Wisdom is the principal thing, and with all thy getting, get understanding," as it says in the Scriptures. Let us focus on getting some understanding about vision.

I would like to begin by asking you to consider your reactions as you were reading or hearing my first discourse. Particularly, I want you to think back to your reaction when I said that the universe is the cosmic mirror and it will reflect back to you exactly what you are projecting out. Did you have a reaction to that statement, such as: "But I have attempted to project out a certain vision and I have not gotten back exactly what I projected out."

Why you are not getting results

You see, at the second level of my retreat it is very important that you come to an understanding of exactly how the universe works and exactly how vision works. This is particularly important for those who have been on the spiritual path for a long time. I have many people who come to my retreat at this level and they say to me, when we have our informal discussions: "Hilarion, I have been on the path for thirty or forty years. I have given countless decrees. I have invoked the Violet Flame. I have studied the teachings of the ascended masters. I have gone to psychologists. I have worked on my psychology. I have done treasure maps. I have done vision. I have done positive affirmations. But still I do not have the outer situation that I desire to have."

There are many people who have not been on the spiritual path for so long but they come to me and they have gone into the more superficial things that are available out there (as I said, Positive Mental Attitude, positive affirmations, treasure maps and so on), but they think that they can very quickly project out a positive vision and manifest that vision. Again, they have been disappointed and they come and they ask me: "Does this actually work? And then, if it does, why haven't we gotten the results that we desire to have?"

This is the point where we go into taking a deeper look at exactly how life works. I have already hinted at some of the conditions here in my first discourse because I said that if you are projecting out one vision with the conscious mind but you have not looked at the subconscious mind, you could be projecting out an unclear vision, a divided vision, or even opposite visions with the conscious and subconscious minds.

This, of course, is one possible explanation why you have not received back from the universe what you desire to have.

There is no other way to deal with this than to systematically go through the layers of the subconscious mind and root out these visions that are not conducive to what you want to manifest. This is, of course, what you do as you go through the seven levels of this course in self-mastery and as you use our other teachings and tools, especially the tools for healing your cosmic birth trauma and some of the deeper traumas that you have received in past lives.

Nevertheless, even if you come to a point where you have cleared your four lower bodies sufficiently so that you are not putting out contrary visions, then you will still see that it is not always that you get back exactly what you project out. Now, you may say to me, as some people do: "But Hilarion, you said that the universe is almost mechanical because the cosmic mirror will reflect back to us exactly what we project out." Well, as with everything, there is always a deeper understanding.

The universe *will* reflect back to you exactly what you are projecting out but not necessarily what you *think* you are projecting with your conscious mind. Let us begin by taking a look at the vast majority of people who are currently in embodiment on earth. Most of these people are not very conscious of the power of vision and they are not very conscious of the vision they hold in their minds of how life works. They are often not very willing to take responsibility for themselves. They are not very willing to admit that their outer situation could have something to do with their state of consciousness.

What are they projecting out? They still have some vision (even though they are not conscious of it) and they are projecting that vision into the cosmic mirror. It is a very fuzzy, a very unclear vision where they are actually projecting that they do not want to take responsibility for themselves and they do not want to be so conscious of everything they do. What have they received back from the cosmic mirror? They have received back exactly what they projected out: A situation where they feel that their lives are limited by so many outer circumstances that they have limited possibility to take command over their lives. This frees them from the sense of responsibility. This frees them from the sense where they have to be consciously evaluating their state of consciousness all the time. From that perspective, these people are getting back exactly what they are projecting out.

Many of these people, of course, have conscious desires for a certain situation, such as a comfortable lifestyle, and they are not getting back exactly that vision, that conscious vision. You see, they *are* getting back (from a certain viewpoint) exactly what they are projecting out. The same, of course, can be applied to you as a spiritual person.

Vision and your Divine plan

With a spiritual person, there are other considerations that come into play. The most important thing here is that as a spiritual person (who is open to the ascended masters in this lifetime), it is guaranteed that you created a Divine plan before you came into embodiment. Do I hereby say that not all people on earth have a Divine plan? Yes, I am indeed saying this. The majority of the people who are living largely unconscious lives and have done so for many lifetimes, are simply not at a level of awareness where they are willing or able to work directly with us between embodiments so that they can consciously make a Divine plan before they come into their next embodiment. Those who are spiritual people (of course, in this I count many people who are not in ascended master teachings), it is guaranteed that you did make a Divine plan before you came into embodiment. This Divine plan is first of all focused on your spiritual goals. If you have been following this course of self-mastery through the first four levels, then your Divine plan definitely involves the possibility of you manifesting Christhood. The purpose of the course of self-mastery is, of course, to get you to a point at the 96th level of consciousness where you can choose to move on and truly work on manifesting and expressing your Christhood, and this will be in your Divine plan.

This is where you need to come to this recognition that it is entirely possible that you have so far had conscious desires for a certain outer situation (often created by the culture that you grew up in), but those desires are contrary to your Divine plan. At least, they are not constructive to the fulfillment of your Divine plan. If that is the case, then you will actually have in your identity body a certain awareness of your Divine plan (even though it may not have been conscious yet) that will sabotage your conscious goals. You will actually stop yourself, at the identity body, from directing the necessary force into your conscious goals so that they will be projected out with enough force to come back as manifest circumstances.

Why this is so, I would like to leave aside for now, because I want to focus on this issue that you have a conscious vision, a conscious goal, a conscious desire. You formulate a vision in your mind, whether you use a treasure map or some other way. You hold an image of a particular material situation that you want to manifest and then you are putting your conscious attention on this and you are putting your conscious psychic, (emotional, mental and identity) energy into projecting this vision out into the universe, out into the cosmic mirror.

Why a vision cannot be manifest

I have already addressed the issue of whether this vision is whole. Is it consistent? Do you have something contrary in your emotional body or your mental body? This is one issue that can prevent manifestation. How scattered is the vision?

Let us just say that you have a relatively focused vision that you are projecting out. The next consideration then becomes: How much force are you putting into this projection? This will depend on several issues. I said in my previous discourse that there are fallen beings who have worked up a great momentum on manifesting certain material circumstances. They have therefore worked up a great momentum on taking a force-based approach to manifesting what they desire. They have tremendous psychic power that they have gathered over many, many lifetimes and so they are able to direct tremendous power into their vision in this lifetime.

Now, if you are a spiritual person who is open to this course, it is extremely unlikely that you are a fallen being. I do not rule out that it is possible for a fallen being to have followed the course to this point, but it is very unlikely. This means that you will not have this momentum of directing psychic energy. Right here, there is a limit to how much force you can put into projecting your vision into the cosmic mirror.

Beyond this, it is possible that you are directly limiting the force that you are projecting with. You are doing this at the level of your mental body or your identity body because, as I said, there is an awareness that the conscious vision you desire is not conducive to the fulfillment of your Divine plan. Therefore, at the identity level, for example, you are refusing to release enough power from that level and therefore you only have the power that is available to you at the conscious, physical level. The power with which you are projecting this vision out, is limited. Now, we have established that when you are attempting to manifest something, the question is: How unified is your vision and how much force are you putting into projecting it into the cosmic mirror?

The next consideration is what happens when the vision, the projection, has left your mind. It has now gone out from your mind and it is now moving into what we have called the cosmic mirror. Of course, there is always a difficulty in giving a teaching in that, on the one hand, we desire to simplify it so people can easily understand and grasp the teaching but on the other hand, in simplifying it, we make it seem easier than it is.

You might get the idea that the cosmic mirror is like an ordinary mirror where you are standing in front of it and the light rays that are coming from your body are hitting the mirror and are reflected back to your eyes. In the cosmic mirror, of course, we are dealing with a much more complex situation because what is the cosmic mirror? Well, it is the four levels of the material universe in the energy system of earth. The earth is the center of that system but it is not the only planet or the only unit in that system.

You also, of course, have the four levels, the identity, mental, emotional and material. What you need to realize, as I said in my last discourse, is that everything is an electromagnetic wave. When you are projecting out a vision, what are you projecting out? An electromagnetic wave or at least a complex of waves! In order for this vision or this projection to come back to you as a physical circumstance, it has to pass through these four levels of the identity, mental, emotional levels of the energy system of earth. Naturally, the question now becomes: What is contained in these four levels? The four levels are energy fields and in those energy fields are many energy waves. As your projection comes out, it is inevitable that the energy waves that make up your projection are going to start creating interference patterns with the energy waves that are in the entire energy unit in which you are living. This is, again, simple wave mechanics.

When you consider how much turmoil, how much impure energy, is found in the four lower bodies of earth – how dense the material matter is – then you can see that, right here, there can be a reason why you have projected out a certain vision but you have not (yet, at least) received the desired result. This may make you doubt whether the path that we describe actually works. Do you get the results of your efforts?

A more sophisticated understanding of vision

What you realize here is that you need to be more sophisticated in your understanding. When I say "understanding," I do not mean an understanding of the mechanics so much as the purpose of the energy system of earth. Here we run into a particular issue that is difficult for many spiritual people. Why are you a spiritual person following ascended master teachings? Well, it is because, even if you have no conscious memory of your Divine plan, you do have an inner intuitive knowing, an inner intuitive sense, that there is more to life than this material existence that you see many people around you pursuing.

You are not only and exclusively focused on material conditions. You may desire certain material conditions but they are not defining your life completely or you would not be following the spiritual path. This inner intuitive knowing for many, many people involves a certain knowing of what life is like when you are on a planet that has a higher collective consciousness than earth. There are quite few of the people who follow ascended master teachings who started out their sojourn in the material universe on earth. Most of you have come from other planets where you incarnated and reached a certain level of consciousness before you then volunteered to incarnate on earth. This means that you can have a, not conscious memory, but a subconscious memory of how it was to live on some of these planets where life was indeed much easier. You see, on a planet with less dense matter and with a less dense collective consciousness, it is far easier for you to manifest your visions. There is not the resistance from the collective consciousness. There is not so much interference that your projection has to pass through before it is returned to you as a physical circumstance.

This is what can sometimes make people discouraged because you have a certain feeling that you have actually put out enough effort that you should have reaped the physical rewards of those efforts. Yet you see that the effort is not manifest and so you begin to become discouraged and start doubting whether the path works. That, of course, is when you become vulnerable to the projections of the fallen beings who are always seeking to get you back off the path once you have gotten on it. They are also trying to prevent you from getting on the path in the first place, but once you are on it, they are always looking to trip you up so that you get off the path again.

This is where you need to recognize that the earth is a very different kind of planet than the other planets upon which you have embodied. The earth is a very dark planet; it is a very dense planet. One of the purposes of the earth is to serve as a sort of halfway house for lifestreams who are not yet ready to take full responsibility for themselves.

You may look at the planet and you may see how few people are open to ascended master teachings. This gives you the awareness that many people are not yet ready to take responsibility for themselves. What is the essence of ascended master teachings? It is that you take responsibility for your self, for your own state of consciousness. Many people are not ready for this and that is why it is so difficult to project a vision and have it become manifest, exactly as you project it out.

Then, you might go on and ask yourself: "Well, why did I volunteer to embody on this planet?" The answer is very simple. You came here to demonstrate to the people that it is possible to live in a different way than what they are doing. You came here to demonstrate that there is a higher way, there is a higher approach to life, a more spiritual approach. This is why you are here.

Once you begin to truly realize this at the inner levels, I see a shift in many of the students who have had doubts about the path. It is as if a light bulb switches on in their minds. I am hoping that I can help you have the experience at the conscious level that you are having at the identity level. It is as if people suddenly realize: "Oh, I am not here to manifest a particular outer situation, a comfortable lifestyle, a nice house, the perfect partner, lots of money, this and that. This is not actually why I am here. I am here to walk and demonstrate the path of Christhood."

Making peace with your life

Once again, you can look at the life of Jesus. He did not manifest the perfect love partner, the perfect family, the perfect house, lots of money, a position in society, all of these things that people desire. If you look at Jesus and his life with a measurement of what most people have today, you must say that Jesus was a complete failure compared to the goals and the vision of these people. All he did was wander around and utter words that most people did not understand and then in the end he got himself killed, without having achieved anything at the time. Maybe later some people took some of his teachings and made something out of it, but in Jesus' own lifetime, he could be said to be a complete failure. He manifested none of the goals that normal people at the time thought were desirable and that normal people today think are desirable.

You can look at your own life and say: "Well, have I manifested anything desirable compared to the goals of normal people?" If the answer is "No," then you might say: "But is that really so bad? Is that maybe not what is in accordance with my Divine plan. If part of my Divine plan is to manifest Christhood, then my Divine plan probably does not involve the same materialistic goals that normal people have in my culture. So is it possible that I can come to a point where I look at my life as it has formed itself so far, and I make peace with the fact that it has been the way it has been?"

You see, my beloved, when you truly acquire understanding, then you see that with "all thy getting" you may not have gotten what you consciously wanted. When you get understanding, you realize that what you consciously wanted was not what you really want in this life. What you really want is the fulfillment of your Divine plan, not the superficial goals defined by your culture. When you see this, you can look at your life and say: "But I have followed the path that I could follow, given who I was, what my level of consciousness was when I embodied and given what my culture was."

You do not need to look at yourself and see whether you made a mistake here, or whether you did this wrong or that wrong. When you begin to realize that you have a Divine plan and that your Divine plan involves demonstrating the path to Christhood (and that the path to Christhood is very different from the life lived by normal people), then you can begin to make peace with your life. You see, as ascended masters, we are not the kind of teachers who want you to look at every aspect of your life and analyze everything you did and find out what you did wrong and what you should have done better.

My goal, at this level of my retreat, is to help you make complete peace with your life as it has been so far. I want to help you come to that point where you can look at your life and say: "It was what it was. I did what I did for a reason. Maybe that reason was that I had to have this experience in order to realize that I don't actually want what I desired. I don't actually want those material goals, those material conditions. I want something more. I want something higher."

Turning the spiritual path into a race

You see, my beloved, there can be a period of your life where you always feel like you are behind. You are always chasing a pot of gold at the end of the rainbow. You are always chasing a goal out there and you are always feeling like you are never manifesting it. Many, many students have actually used the spiritual path (and even the teachings of the ascended masters) to magnify this process.

When you find the spiritual path, you realize that you have spiritual goals. You want a higher state of consciousness and you are putting your energy into striving for it. You still feel like you are not there and whatever you do is not enough, it is not good enough because you have not manifested this higher state of consciousness, however you see it.

What I desire to help you achieve is to come to a point where you realize that your life (up until this point) has been exactly the way it should be, given your state of consciousness and your outer situation. You have done exactly what you *should* do. All that remains is that you consciously learn the lesson you were meant to learn from doing what you did.

It is not a matter of blaming yourself. It is not a matter of finding out what you did wrong. It is a matter of coming to the point where you realize: "I actually had to grow up in a certain situation among people in a certain culture, a certain family, a certain nationality. I had to grow up there and I had to go through a period of adjusting to that situation. I had to immerse myself in it, I had to pursue certain goals but I did not do this in order to pursue those goals for the rest of my life. I did this in order to demonstrate that I am a person that, from an outer perspective, is just like the other people in that culture. Now, what I have the opportunity to do is to go beyond this and demonstrate that I can be more than that kind of person, that I can live my life in a different way."

You see, my beloved, what I am guiding you towards here is the realization that you have lived your life up until this point based on a certain vision that you had. You are now at a point where you are attending my retreat in the etheric and you are reading and studying this lesson at the conscious level. You have the opportunity to change your life and embrace a higher vision, namely the vision that you built into your Divine plan.

You see what I am saying, I hope. So far, you have lived your life based on a certain vision. There was nothing wrong with that vision but it was limited, partly by your own state of consciousness, your own psychology, partly by the culture in which you lived. This was all in order. It was all part of your Divine plan that you immersed yourself in a certain culture, in a certain situation. As we have said before, life, growth, is a process where you first immerse yourself and then you awaken. The point you are at right now is the point of awakening where you realize that there is a higher vision than the one you have lived by so far. It is the vision in your Divine plan, and that vision may be very different from the vision you have had up until this point.

The reason it is so important for you to understand this is very simple, but also very profound, very decisive, very fundamental. You see, my beloved, you cannot project into the cosmic mirror anything higher than your current vision. This means that in order to embrace a higher vision than you have right now, you have to be willing to give up the vision you have had so far. You have to be willing to come to the realization: "I have had a limited vision. I want to embrace a higher vision and that means I am willing to let go of the old vision."

When people get this at the identity level, when they get this in my retreat, their entire demeanor shifts. I am hoping that by following this course, you can have a similar shift at the conscious level where you realize that your life can take an entirely different direction.

Now, I know that many of you have been on the spiritual path for a very long time. I know that many of you have studied ascended master teachings for a long time and you may look back at that time and you may say: "But I have already gone through many shifts in the twenty or thirty years I have been on the path. I have changed so much compared to where I was." This is true, and you have, but then it should not be such a big step for you to realize that there is an even higher vision than what you have seen so far. After all, did you expect that you were attending a course on the Fifth Ray of Vision, under the Chohan of the Fifth Ray, and it would not expand your vision? Of course, even though you have gone through dramatic shifts and a dramatic raising of your vision, there is more that can be achieved. There is a higher vision that you have not yet grasped.

The Alpha and Omega of higher vision

It is, of course, my joy and my privilege to help you grasp that vision and the vision has two aspects, an Alpha and an Omega. What is it you need to see in yourself in order to manifest your Christhood? What does manifesting and expressing your Christhood mean in terms of what you do in the outer world?

We are now back to the point where we can look at your Divine plan and vision. I said earlier that in many cases you have subconsciously blocked the manifestation of a vision you were sending out with your conscious mind. You can now begin to look at the visions you have had, the goals, the desires you have had and what you have been projecting out with your conscious mind. You can begin to ask yourself: "I have had certain goals throughout my lifetime, but now I am willing to compare those goals to my Divine plan and I am willing to consider whether I simply need to let go of some of these goals."

You see, my beloved, here is where we come to a very subtle point. I have contrasted the lives of certain fallen beings who have great material control over their situation with the life of Jesus. When you look at the life of Jesus, you could say that he had very little material control over his situation. After all, he was arrested by the authorities, condemned to death and killed in a very unpleasant manner. Did this show great material control of his situation? Would the fallen beings have allowed themselves to do this?

When you begin to open your mind to this higher vision of what it means for you personally to walk the path of

Christhood and to express your Christhood, you can see that in some cases this means that you will not have total control over your physical circumstances. I am not hereby saying that you need to be arrested, persecuted, tortured and killed like Jesus was. This is not what we are looking at today because the situation has, at least in most countries, changed.

I am not hereby saying that there are not people in certain countries who have it as part of their Divine plan to allow themselves to be persecuted, tortured or killed in order to bring the judgment of certain fallen beings. In the countries where this book is likely to become known, you hopefully do not have that situation. Nevertheless, even in the more peaceful countries in the world, it may very well be that part of you demonstrating the path to Christhood means going through certain situations where you do not have full control over your physical, material circumstances.

The cosmic evolution of earth

Why is this so, my beloved? Well, in order to understand this, you need to understand where the earth is at in its cosmic evolution. The earth is naturally on a path where we are moving it towards Saint Germain's Golden Age, but the earth has not yet fully entered that golden age consciousness. There will come a point where the earth is so far into the Golden Age that a natural aspect of manifesting Christhood will be to manifest some higher material situation.

At this stage, there are still so many people who are trapped in a lower state of consciousness that the primary goal of the path to Christhood is actually not to demonstrate an *outer* mastery where you can manifest the exact physical situation you want. It is to demonstrate an *inner* mastery where you demonstrate that, regardless of outer situations, you can be who you are. You are not allowing your peace to be taken away by unfavorable outer circumstances. You are pursuing your vision of your Divine plan regardless of not having the ideal outer circumstances.

Thereby, you demonstrate to people that instead of waiting for the ideal material conditions before you manifest peace of mind, a joyful life or pursuit of higher goals, you can do so right now, you can start right now. You need to demonstrate to people the opposite of the lies of the fallen beings that people have come to believe. As I said in my first discourse, one of these lies is that you need to wait for ideal conditions before you can be spiritual and before you can manifest your Christhood. Naturally, part of demonstrating the path to Christhood at this stage is to demonstrate that even though you do not have ideal conditions, you can manifest your Christhood.

When you come to this realization, you can suddenly see that: "Oh, but it is pointless for me to put my energy and my attention into manifesting certain material conditions. I need to start right now, focusing on attaining my Christhood and then demonstrating it." Now, I am not saying here that you should jump ahead. You are naturally at a certain level of this course of self-mastery and we are aiming to take you quite higher than the level you are at right now. What I am saying is that when you have the vision of where you are going, then you can make peace with your outer situation as it is.

The biggest hindrance to Christhood

You understand that there is a principle here, a very important principle. We have said before, that you will not actually manifest a different situation until you have made peace with the situation you have. This is something that applies especially to spiritual people who are at the point where part of their Divine plan is Christhood. The most common way that people delay their Christhood is because in their conscious minds they have become attached to manifesting a certain outer situation and they are so focused on this outer situation that they are subconsciously saying: "I can't manifest my Christhood until I have these outer conditions."

The only way to break free of that Catch-22 is to come to the point where you realize that no outer condition can bring about your Christhood and no outer condition can prevent it. Christhood is an internal condition, and it will start being manifest when you decide that it is *now*. You need to come to that point where you look at your situation and say: "Regardless of how difficult it is, regardless of the conditions I have or the conditions I don't have, I am going to focus on manifesting Christhood now." *That* is when you have made peace with your situation.

Many of you have already experienced that when you come to that point, suddenly the outer situation changes. Many of you have the potential to go through this experience when you come to the point where you look at a certain outer situation that has focused your attention and then you suddenly make peace with it and say: "But this cannot stop my Christhood, so why am I worried about it?" That is when you will experience that the outer situation suddenly changes. What seemed to be locked and beyond your power to change, suddenly becomes fluid and now things start to shift.

The principle here is this: Your outer situation is not what matters when you are on the path to Christhood. Your outer situation is not a *hindrance,* it is an *opportunity* to demonstrate that you cannot and will not be defined by material circumstances. What is Christhood? Well, what is anti-Christ?

Think of the situation where Jesus says to Peter: "Get thee behind me, Satan. You are not favoring the things of God but the things of men." The satanic consciousness is the consciousness that demands that Spirit should conform to current conditions in matter. This is what Peter was projecting upon Jesus, namely that Jesus (as the representative of the Christ consciousness) should conform to Peter's expectations of what should or should not happen to him.

There were many people who, when Jesus started becoming known in Israel, wanted him to be the warrior king who could free Israel from the Romans. When he did not want to fulfill that role, they rejected him or became angry with him. They also were projecting upon the Christ that he should conform to current conditions in matter, but what is the goal of the Christ? It is to set people free from the current conditions in matter. How can you set them free from current conditions by conforming to those conditions? You can set them free only by demonstrating that regardless of current conditions, this cannot define you as a spiritual being; you are more than these conditions. *This* is how you demonstrate Christhood.

The importance of letting go of the old vision

As long as you feel that you are being limited in the expression of your Christhood by current material conditions, then you cannot manifest your Christhood, you cannot fulfill your Divine plan. Therefore, you need to come to the realization where you see that current conditions in matter are the product of a limited vision. The limited vision of most people on this earth has been projected into the cosmic mirror for a very long time and it has produced the current conditions in matter, including the density of matter, including all of the chaos, warfare, struggle and conflict you see on the planet. How are you, as a representative of the Living Christ, going to help set people free unless you live by a higher vision? How are you going to consciously open yourself to that higher vision unless you consciously recognize that you need to let go of the old vision, you need to see that it is limited. You need to let the self based on this vision die and then say: "What is that to me? I will follow thee," and then you follow the Living Christ until you see that higher vision.

This is the only way that you are going to demonstrate your Christhood and that is why you need to come to that point where you do not hold on to your old vision. You may have had this vision for a long time, but you need to take another look at it. You need to realize that you are the Conscious You. You are pure awareness and therefore you can step outside of the perception filter of your current vision. You can take off those colored glasses, you can look at your life without that vision, without that perception filter, without that coloring and now you can see what you have not been able to see so far.

This is where I sometimes have the greatest difficulty in helping students who have been following ascended master teachings for a very long time. You may think, my beloved, that the only people who come to my retreat are the people who are reading this book but this is not so. You who are reading this book, you are riding a wave where there are many people (some who have not even heard of ascended master teachings) who are still tuned in and who are still following this progressive, collective movement where millions of people are ready to take these steps.

There are people who are not reading this book (who are not even recognizing this messenger as a genuine messenger) but they have followed ascended master teachings for decades. They have used those teachings to create a specific vision of their own path, their own life but also of the planet and what we of the ascended masters want. In many cases, that vision is limiting their Divine plan and the expression of their Christhood, and it can be very, very difficult for me as an ascended master to help these people let go of their limiting vision. They think this is the only true vision because it is based on the teachings of the ascended masters. They are very reluctant to admit that they have used the teachings of the ascended masters to validate a limited vision. *We* have not validated it, but *they* themselves have done so.

It can be very painful for people to come to this recognition; it can especially be painful for them to come to it at the conscious level. I must tell you that there is a significant number of people who have followed ascended master teachings for decades but who have actually aborted their Christhood through a misuse, a misinterpretation, of those teachings. This has caused them to fixate their minds on a vision that is not what is in their Divine plan and that is not conducive to their personal Christhood.

What can I do for such students? In some cases, I can do nothing other than wait and hope that they will tire of this old vision and they will become open to something higher in their conscious minds. Why is it so important to let go of the old vision? Well, my beloved, how are you ever going to take a step up to a higher level of consciousness unless you let go of the vision that you have created at your current level? This is the very principle of Christhood.

Letting go of the old self

We have talked about internal spirits, we have talked about a certain self. Right now, you are at a specific level of consciousness.

You have created a certain self, which gives you continuity at this level. There is nothing wrong with this. You can do nothing else, but in order to rise to the next level of consciousness, you cannot take that self with you. You cannot transfer it, you cannot perfect it, you cannot develop it. You need to let it die and then, of course, you form another self at the next level of consciousness.

Most people are not aware that when they shift from one level of consciousness to the next, the old self dies and the new is born. This happens in a way that is hidden to the conscious awareness, it happens so smoothly, so gradually, that they do not realize that there is a self that dies. You can come to the point where you become conscious of this, or at least you become conscious that in order to rise to a higher level on the path, there is something (there is an old vision, an old self) that you need to let go of. The more you can do this consciously, the quicker you will grow because the less you are likely to get stuck at a certain level.

For each level you go up on the spiritual path, it is a decisive victory, it is a quantum leap. It is not just a gradual evolution; it is a distinct, decisive leap in consciousness. It is a victory, but the fallen beings are always trying to make sure that your last victory will be your *last* victory and that you will become attached to something at that level and not go higher. It is not that the ascended master students I am talking about have not made progress and have not reached a level that was higher than when they found the ascended master teachings. If they stop at that level, then they have not made full use of the ascended master teachings because our goal is to lead you to the ascension. This requires you to continue to rise through the 144 levels of consciousness until you reach that highest level and now you can make the ultimate quantum leap into the ascended state.

It is always, always necessary to let go of the old before you can be reborn into the new self, the new vision, that will take you higher. Is it not, my beloved, a beautiful process? Why look upon it as a threat? Why look upon it as if you have to give up something? If you find that you have a certain sense of being attached to something, being reluctant to let go of something, then this is ego, this is remnants of the ego, because only the ego holds on. I can assure you, my beloved, that when you reach this level on this course of self-mastery, you have come to the point where you have embraced growth, you *want* to grow, you *desire* to grow.

Why not consciously embrace this and realize that growth means letting go of the old? There will always be a certain sense of wanting to hold on to something, but when you can become conscious of the fact that this is just ego (it has no major significance, it is just there), you just look at it without going into it and you say: "Oh well, I know what this is, but I'm still going to let it go. I'm still going to let that old self, that old vision, go."

That is when you make the path so much easier for yourself because now every step up becomes a greater joy, instead of a constant battle with the ego (with that dweller on the threshold, as we have called it) that is always seeking to keep you at the old level and will not let you go. It is true that the ego or the dweller will never let you go, but that does not mean that *you* cannot let *it* go. When you let it go, it is gone, and *you move on*.

7 | INVOKING THE WILL TO SURRENDER

In the name I AM THAT I AM, Jesus Christ, I call to my I AM Presence to flow through the I Will Be Presence that I AM and give this invocation with full power. I call to beloved Elohim Cyclopea and Virginia and Apollo and Lumina, Archangel Raphael and Mother Mary and Jophiel and Christine, Hilarion and Lord Lanto to help me truly see my old vision and surrender it. Help me see and surrender all patterns that block my oneness with Hilarion and with my I AM Presence, including ...

[Make personal calls]

Part 1

1. If I am projecting out one vision with the conscious mind but have not looked at the subconscious mind, I could be projecting out an unclear vision, a divided vision, or even opposite visions with the conscious and subconscious minds.

> Cyclopea so dear, the truth you reveal,
> the truth that duality's ailments will heal,
> your Emerald Light is like a great balm,
> our emotional bodies are perfectly calm.
>
> **Cyclopea so dear, in Emerald Sphere,
> in raising perception we shall persevere,
> as deep in our hearts your truth we revere,
> to immaculate vision the earth does adhere.**

2. I am willing to systematically go through the layers of the subconscious mind and root out the visions that are not conducive to what I want to manifest.

> Cyclopea so dear, with you we unwind,
> all negative spirals clouding the mind,
> we know pure awareness is truly our core,
> the key to becoming the wide-open door.
>
> **Cyclopea so dear, in Emerald Sphere,
> in raising perception we shall persevere,
> as deep in our hearts your truth we revere,
> to immaculate vision the earth does adhere.**

7 | Invoking the Will to Surrender

3. Even if I have cleared my four lower bodies and I am not putting out contrary visions, then it is not always that I get back exactly what I project out.

> Cyclopea so dear, clear our inner sight,
> empowered, we pierce the soul's fearful night,
> we now see our life through your single eye,
> beyond all disease we're ready to fly.

> **Cyclopea so dear, in Emerald Sphere,**
> **in raising perception we shall persevere,**
> **as deep in our hearts your truth we revere,**
> **to immaculate vision the earth does adhere.**

4. The universe will reflect back to me exactly what I am projecting out but not necessarily what I think I am projecting with my conscious mind.

> Cyclopea so dear, life can only reflect,
> the images that the mind does project,
> the key to our healing is clearing the mind,
> from the images the ego is hiding behind.

> **Cyclopea so dear, in Emerald Sphere,**
> **in raising perception we shall persevere,**
> **as deep in our hearts your truth we revere,**
> **to immaculate vision the earth does adhere.**

5. Most people are projecting that they do not want to take responsibility for themselves and they do not want to be so conscious of everything they do. They have received back a situation where they feel that their lives are limited by so many outer circumstances that they have limited possibility to take command over their lives.

> Cyclopea so dear, we want to aim high,
> to your healing flame we ever draw nigh,
> through veils of duality we now take flight,
> bathed in your penetrating Emerald Light.
>
> **Cyclopea so dear, in Emerald Sphere,**
> **in raising perception we shall persevere,**
> **as deep in our hearts your truth we revere,**
> **to immaculate vision the earth does adhere.**

6. As a spiritual person, I have created a Divine plan before I came into embodiment. This Divine plan is first of all focused on my spiritual goals. My Divine plan involves the possibility of me manifesting Christhood.

> Cyclopea so dear, your Emerald Flame,
> exposes every subtle, dualistic power game,
> including the game of wanting to say,
> that truth is defined in only one way.
>
> **Cyclopea so dear, in Emerald Sphere,**
> **in raising perception we shall persevere,**
> **as deep in our hearts your truth we revere,**
> **to immaculate vision the earth does adhere.**

7 | Invoking the Will to Surrender

7. It is possible that I have conscious desires for a certain outer situation, but those desires are contrary to or not constructive to the fulfillment of my Divine plan.

> Cyclopea so dear, we're feeling the flow,
> as your Living Truth upon us you bestow,
> from all dual vision we are now set free,
> planet earth in immaculate matrix will be.

> **Cyclopea so dear, in Emerald Sphere,**
> **in raising perception we shall persevere,**
> **as deep in our hearts your truth we revere,**
> **to immaculate vision the earth does adhere.**

8. I have in my identity body a certain awareness of my Divine plan, and it will block my conscious goals. I will stop myself at the identity body from directing the necessary force into my conscious goals so that they will be projected out with enough force to come back as manifest circumstances.

> Cyclopea so dear, the truth is now clear,
> we see higher purpose for which we are here
> we know truth transcends all systems below,
> immersed in your light, we continue to grow.

> **Cyclopea so dear, in Emerald Sphere,**
> **in raising perception we shall persevere,**
> **as deep in our hearts your truth we revere,**
> **to immaculate vision the earth does adhere.**

9. Because I am not a fallen being, I do not have a momentum of directing psychic energy. There is a limit to how much force I can put into projecting my vision into the cosmic mirror.

> Cyclopea so dear, we're feeling your joy,
> as creative vision we now do employ,
> in lifting earth out of serpentine cage,
> to manifest Saint Germain's Golden Age.
>
> **Cyclopea so dear, in Emerald Sphere,**
> **in raising perception we shall persevere,**
> **as deep in our hearts your truth we revere,**
> **to immaculate vision the earth does adhere.**

Part 2

1. It is possible that I am directly limiting the force that I am projecting with. I am doing this at the level of my mental body or identity body because there is an awareness that the conscious vision I desire is not conducive to the fulfillment of my Divine plan.

> Beloved Apollo, with your second ray,
> you open our eyes to see a new day,
> We see through duality's lies and deceit,
> transcending the mindset producing defeat.
>
> **Beloved Apollo, thou Elohim Gold,**
> **your radiant light our eyes now behold,**
> **as pages of wisdom you gently unfold,**
> **our planet is free from all that is old.**

2. When I am attempting to manifest something, the question is: How unified is my vision and how much force am I putting into projecting it into the cosmic mirror?

7 | Invoking the Will to Surrender

> Beloved Apollo, in your flame we know,
> that your living wisdom is always a flow,
> in your light we see our own highest will,
> immersed in the stream that never stands still.
>
> **Beloved Apollo, thou Elohim Gold,**
> **your radiant light our eyes now behold,**
> **as pages of wisdom you gently unfold,**
> **our planet is free from all that is old.**

3. The cosmic mirror is the four levels of the material universe in the energy system of earth, which is a complex field of electromagnetic waves.

> Beloved Apollo, your light makes it clear,
> why we have taken embodiment here,
> exposing all lies causing the fall,
> you help us reclaim the oneness of all.
>
> **Beloved Apollo, thou Elohim Gold,**
> **your radiant light our eyes now behold,**
> **as pages of wisdom you gently unfold,**
> **our planet is free from all that is old.**

4. As my projection comes out, the energy waves that make up my projection are going to start creating interference patterns with the energy waves that are in the entire energy unit in which I am living. This is simple wave mechanics.

> Beloved Apollo, exposing all lies,
> we hereby surrender all ego-based ties,
> we know our perception is truly the key,
> to transcending the serpentine duality.

> **Beloved Apollo, thou Elohim Gold,**
> **your radiant light our eyes now behold,**
> **as pages of wisdom you gently unfold,**
> **our planet is free from all that is old.**

5. The amount of impure energy found in the four lower bodies of earth can be one reason I have projected out a certain vision but I have not received the desired result.

> Beloved Apollo, we heed now your call,
> drawing us into Wisdom's Great Hall,
> working to raise our own cosmic sphere,
> together we form the tip of the spear.

> **Beloved Apollo, thou Elohim Gold,**
> **your radiant light our eyes now behold,**
> **as pages of wisdom you gently unfold,**
> **our planet is free from all that is old.**

6. I am a spiritual person, following ascended master teachings, because I have an intuitive knowing that there is more to life and that I have a Divine plan.

> Beloved Apollo, your wisdom so clear,
> in oneness with you, no serpent we fear,
> the beam in our eye we willingly see,
> we're free from the serpent's own duality.

> **Beloved Apollo, thou Elohim Gold,**
> **your radiant light our eyes now behold,**
> **as pages of wisdom you gently unfold,**
> **our planet is free from all that is old.**

7 | Invoking the Will to Surrender

7. I am not only and exclusively focused on material conditions. I may desire certain material conditions but they are not defining my life completely.

> Beloved Apollo, you help us to see
> through your knowing eyes we truly are free,
> we willingly stand in your piercing gaze,
> empowered, we exit duality's maze.

> **Beloved Apollo, thou Elohim Gold,**
> **your radiant light our eyes now behold,**
> **as pages of wisdom you gently unfold,**
> **our planet is free from all that is old.**

8. My intuitive knowing involves an awareness of what life is like when I am on a planet that has a higher collective consciousness than earth. On a less dense planet it is far easier to manifest my visions.

> Beloved Apollo, our vision we raise,
> we see that the earth is in a new phase,
> for nothing can stop the knowledge you bring,
> exposing that there's no separate thing.

> **Beloved Apollo, thou Elohim Gold,**
> **your radiant light our eyes now behold,**
> **as pages of wisdom you gently unfold,**
> **our planet is free from all that is old.**

9. I choose not to be discouraged even though I have a feeling that I have put out enough effort that I should have reaped the physical rewards of those efforts. I accept that the path does work, but it takes more time on a dense planet like earth.

> Beloved Apollo, in wisdom's great mirth,
> we all are together uplifting the earth,
> as you now the true Flame of Wisdom reveal,
> all of earth's people can see what is real.
>
> **Beloved Apollo, thou Elohim Gold,**
> **your radiant light our eyes now behold,**
> **as pages of wisdom you gently unfold,**
> **our planet is free from all that is old.**

Part 3

1. One of the purposes of the earth is to serve as a sort of halfway house for lifestreams who are not yet ready to take full responsibility for themselves.

> Raphael Archangel, your light so intense,
> raise us beyond all human pretense.
> Mother Mary and you have a vision so bold,
> to see that our highest potential unfold.
>
> **Raphael Archangel, for vision we pray,**
> **Raphael Archangel, show us the way,**
> **Raphael Archangel, your emerald ray,**
> **Raphael Archangel, our lives a new day.**

2. The essence of ascended master teachings is that I take responsibility for my *self,* for my own state of consciousness. Many people are not ready for this and that is why it is so difficult to project a vision and have it become manifest.

7 | Invoking the Will to Surrender

> Raphael Archangel, in emerald sphere,
> to immaculate vision we always adhere.
> Mother Mary enfolds us in her Sacred Heart,
> from Mother's true love, we're never apart.
>
> **Raphael Archangel, for vision we pray,**
> **Raphael Archangel, show us the way,**
> **Raphael Archangel, your emerald ray,**
> **Raphael Archangel, our lives a new day.**

3. I volunteered to come here in order to demonstrate to the people that it is possible to live in a different way than what they are doing. I came here to demonstrate that there is a higher way, there is a higher approach to life, a more spiritual approach. This is why I am here.

> Raphael Archangel, all ailments you heal,
> each cell in our bodies in light now you seal.
> Mother Mary's immaculate concept we see,
> perfection of health our new reality.
>
> **Raphael Archangel, for vision we pray,**
> **Raphael Archangel, show us the way,**
> **Raphael Archangel, your emerald ray,**
> **Raphael Archangel, our lives a new day.**

4. I am not here to manifest a particular outer situation, a comfortable lifestyle, a nice house, the perfect partner, lots of money, this and that. This is not actually why I am here. I am here to walk and demonstrate the path of Christhood.

Raphael Archangel, your light is so real,
the vision of Christ in us you reveal.
Mother Mary now helps us to truly transcend,
in emerald light with you we ascend.

Raphael Archangel, for vision we pray,
Raphael Archangel, show us the way,
Raphael Archangel, your emerald ray,
Raphael Archangel, our lives a new day.

5. Maybe I have not manifested anything desirable compared to the goals of normal people. Yet is that really so bad if it is in accordance with my Divine plan?

Raphael Archangel, diseases are done,
as you help us see that all life is One,
we no longer do your true love reject,
immaculate vision on all we project.

Raphael Archangel, for vision we pray,
Raphael Archangel, show us the way,
Raphael Archangel, your emerald ray,
Raphael Archangel, our lives a new day.

6. If part of my Divine plan is to manifest Christhood, then my Divine plan does not involve the same materialistic goals that normal people have in my culture. I am looking at my life as it has formed itself so far, and I am making peace with the fact that it has been the way it has been.

7 | Invoking the Will to Surrender

> Raphael Archangel, we're healing the earth,
> in immaculate vision we give her rebirth,
> a new era has on this day begun,
> your emerald light now shines like a sun.
>
> **Raphael Archangel, for vision we pray,**
> **Raphael Archangel, show us the way,**
> **Raphael Archangel, your emerald ray,**
> **Raphael Archangel, our lives a new day.**

7. When I get understanding, I realize that what I consciously wanted was not what I really want in this life. What I really want is the fulfillment of my Divine plan, not the superficial goals defined by my culture.

> Raphael Archangel, the fall is behind,
> as all of earth's people the Christ path do find,
> we call now to you all people to heal,
> as four lower bodies in love you do seal.
>
> **Raphael Archangel, for vision we pray,**
> **Raphael Archangel, show us the way,**
> **Raphael Archangel, your emerald ray,**
> **Raphael Archangel, our lives a new day.**

8. I have followed the path that I could follow, given who I was, what my level of consciousness was when I embodied and given what my culture was.

> Raphael Archangel, as you bring the light,
> the forces of darkness swiftly take flight,
> their day is now done as we claim the earth,
> spreading to all an innocent mirth.

**Raphael Archangel, for vision we pray,
Raphael Archangel, show us the way,
Raphael Archangel, your emerald ray,
Raphael Archangel, our lives a new day.**

9. I have a Divine plan and it involves demonstrating the path to Christhood. The path to Christhood is very different from the life lived by normal people. Therefore, I make peace with my life.

Raphael Archangel, our vision set free,
as we can now see God's reality,
as Saint Germain's vision is manifest here,
the earth is now sealed in immaculate sphere.

**Raphael Archangel, for vision we pray,
Raphael Archangel, show us the way,
Raphael Archangel, your emerald ray,
Raphael Archangel, our lives a new day.**

Part 4

1. My life was what it was. I did what I did for a reason. Maybe the reason was that I had to have this experience in order to realize that I don't actually want what I desired. I don't actually want those material goals, those material conditions. I want something more. I want something higher.

7 | Invoking the Will to Surrender

Jophiel Archangel, in wisdom's great light,
all serpentine lies exposed to our sight.
So subtle the lies that creep through the mind,
yet you are the greatest teacher we find.

Jophiel Archangel, exposing all lies,
Jophiel Archangel, cutting all ties.
Jophiel Archangel, clearing the skies,
Jophiel Archangel, the mind truly flies.

2. I surrender the sense that I am behind, that I am chasing a pot of gold at the end of the rainbow. I surrender chasing a goal out there and always feeling like I am never manifesting it.

Jophiel Archangel, your wisdom we hail,
your sword cutting through duality's veil.
As you show the way, we know what is real,
from serpentine doubt, we instantly heal.

Jophiel Archangel, exposing all lies,
Jophiel Archangel, cutting all ties.
Jophiel Archangel, clearing the skies,
Jophiel Archangel, the mind truly flies.

3. I surrender the tendency to use the spiritual path to magnify this process. I surrender the sense that whatever I do is not enough, it is not good enough because I have not manifested this higher state of consciousness.

Jophiel Archangel, your reality,
the best antidote to duality.
No lie can remain in your Presence so clear,
with you on our side, no serpent we fear.

> **Jophiel Archangel, exposing all lies,**
> **Jophiel Archangel, cutting all ties.**
> **Jophiel Archangel, clearing the skies,**
> **Jophiel Archangel, the mind truly flies.**

4. My life up until this point has been exactly the way it should be, given my state of consciousness and my outer situation. I have done exactly what I should do. All that remains is that I consciously learn the lesson I was meant to learn from doing what I did.

> Jophiel Archangel, God's mind is in me,
> and through your clear light, its wisdom we see.
> Divisions all vanish, as we see the One,
> and truly, the wholeness of mind we have won.

> **Jophiel Archangel, exposing all lies,**
> **Jophiel Archangel, cutting all ties.**
> **Jophiel Archangel, clearing the skies,**
> **Jophiel Archangel, the mind truly flies.**

5. I actually had to grow up in a certain situation among people in a certain culture, a certain family, a certain nationality. I had to grow up there and I had to go through a period of adjusting to that situation. I had to immerse myself in it.

> Jophiel Archangel, now show us the way,
> that leads us beyond duality's fray,
> we long to discern the truth and the lie,
> so we the serpentine knots can untie.

7 | Invoking the Will to Surrender

Jophiel Archangel, exposing all lies,
Jophiel Archangel, cutting all ties.
Jophiel Archangel, clearing the skies,
Jophiel Archangel, the mind truly flies.

6. I had to pursue certain goals, but I did not do this in order to pursue those goals for the rest of my life. I did this in order to demonstrate that I am a person just like the other people in that culture. Yet I can go beyond this and demonstrate that I can be more than that kind of person, that I can live my life in a different way.

Jophiel Archangel, your Presence is here,
and therefore our minds are perfectly clear,
in wisdom's great fount we do take a bath,
and now we withstand the devil's own wrath.

Jophiel Archangel, exposing all lies,
Jophiel Archangel, cutting all ties.
Jophiel Archangel, clearing the skies,
Jophiel Archangel, the mind truly flies.

7. I have lived my life up until this point based on a certain vision. I now have the opportunity to change my life and embrace a higher vision, namely the vision that I built into my Divine plan.

Jophiel Archangel, it is your great task,
to raise all mankind, if only we ask,
so now on behalf of those who are blind,
we ask for your help in wisdom to find.

**Jophiel Archangel, exposing all lies,
Jophiel Archangel, cutting all ties.
Jophiel Archangel, clearing the skies,
Jophiel Archangel, the mind truly flies.**

8. It was part of my Divine plan that I immersed myself in a certain situation. Growth is a process where I first immerse myself and then I awaken. I am now at the point of awakening.

> Jophiel Archangel, your Presence we hail,
> your Light cutting through the serpentine veil,
> the serpents can no longer people deceive,
> for all now your Flame of Wisdom receive.

**Jophiel Archangel, exposing all lies,
Jophiel Archangel, cutting all ties.
Jophiel Archangel, clearing the skies,
Jophiel Archangel, the mind truly flies.**

9. There is a higher vision than the one I have lived by so far. It is the vision in my Divine plan, and that vision is very different from the vision I have had up until this point.

> Jophiel Archangel, where else can we go,
> when we long the highest wisdom to know?
> You share with us gladly all that you are,
> and now our vision goes ever so far.

**Jophiel Archangel, exposing all lies,
Jophiel Archangel, cutting all ties.
Jophiel Archangel, clearing the skies,
Jophiel Archangel, the mind truly flies.**

7 | Invoking the Will to Surrender

Part 5

1. I cannot project into the cosmic mirror anything higher than my current vision. In order to embrace a higher vision than I have right now, I have to be willing to give up the vision I have had so far.

> Hilarion, on emerald shore,
> we're free from all that's gone before.
> Hilarion, we let all go,
> that keeps us out of sacred flow.
>
> **Hilarion, with light so green,**
> **we see behind the matter screen,**
> **immaculate our inner sight,**
> **we see the earth is taking flight.**

2. I realize that I have had a limited vision. I want to embrace a higher vision and that means I am willing to let go of the old vision and have my life take an entirely different direction.

> Hilarion, the secret key,
> is wisdom's own reality.
> Hilarion, all life is healed,
> the ego's face no more concealed.
>
> **Hilarion, with light so green,**
> **we see behind the matter screen,**
> **immaculate our inner sight,**
> **we see the earth is taking flight.**

3. I want to see what I need to see in myself in order to manifest my Christhood.

> Hilarion, your love for life,
> helps us surrender inner strife.
> Hilarion, your loving words,
> thrill our hearts like song of birds.

> **Hilarion, with light so green,**
> **we see behind the matter screen,**
> **immaculate our inner sight,**
> **we see the earth is taking flight.**

4. I want to see what manifesting and expressing my Christhood means in terms of what I do in the outer world.

> Hilarion, invoke the light,
> your sacred formulas recite.
> Hilarion, your secret tone,
> philosopher's most sacred stone.

> **Hilarion, with light so green,**
> **we see behind the matter screen,**
> **immaculate our inner sight,**
> **we see the earth is taking flight.**

5. I am willing to look at my visions, goals and desires and what I have been projecting out with my conscious mind. I have had certain goals throughout my lifetime, but now I am willing to compare those goals to my Divine plan. I am willing to consider whether I simply need to let go of some of these goals.

7 | *Invoking the Will to Surrender*

Hilarion, with love you greet,
us in your temple over Crete.
Hilarion, your emerald light,
the third eye sees with Christic sight.

**Hilarion, with light so green,
we see behind the matter screen,
immaculate our inner sight,
we see the earth is taking flight.**

6. In some cases, expressing my Christhood means that I will not have total control over my physical circumstances. Demonstrating the path to Christhood may mean going through certain situations where I do not have full control over my physical, material circumstances.

Hilarion, you give us fruit,
of truth that is so absolute.
Hilarion, all stress decrease,
as our ambitions we release.

**Hilarion, with light so green,
we see behind the matter screen,
immaculate our inner sight,
we see the earth is taking flight.**

7. At this stage of the cosmic evolution of earth, so many people are trapped in a lower state of consciousness that the primary goal of the path to Christhood is *not* to demonstrate an outer mastery. It is to demonstrate that regardless of outer situations, I can be who I am.

Hilarion, our chakras clear,
as we let go of subtlest fear.
Hilarion, we are sincere,
as freedom's truth we do revere.

**Hilarion, with light so green,
we see behind the matter screen,
immaculate our inner sight,
we see the earth is taking flight.**

8. I am not allowing my peace to be taken away by unfavorable outer circumstances. I am pursuing my vision of my Divine plan regardless of not having the ideal outer circumstances.

Hilarion, you balance all,
the seven rays upon our call.
Hilarion, you keep us true,
as we remain all one with you.

**Hilarion, with light so green,
we see behind the matter screen,
immaculate our inner sight,
we see the earth is taking flight.**

9. I demonstrate to people that instead of waiting for the ideal material conditions before I manifest peace of mind, I can do so right now, I can start right now.

Hilarion, your Presence here,
filling up the inner sphere.
Life is now a sacred flow,
God Vision we on all bestow.

> **Hilarion, with light so green,**
> **we see behind the matter screen,**
> **immaculate our inner sight,**
> **we see the earth is taking flight.**

Part 6

1. It is pointless for me to put my energy and my attention into manifesting certain material conditions. I am focusing on attaining my Christhood and then demonstrating it. Because I have the vision of where I am going, I am at peace with my outer situation as it is.

> Master Lanto, golden wise,
> expose in us the ego's lies.
> Master Lanto, will to be,
> we will to win our mastery.

> **Master Lanto, Wisdom's Fount,**
> **with blessings we can hardly count,**
> **you are for earth a shining light,**
> **your Golden Wisdom oh so bright.**

2. I will not manifest a different situation until I have made peace with the situation I have. The most common way to delay Christhood is to be attached to manifesting a certain outer situation, saying: "I can't manifest my Christhood until I have these outer conditions."

Master Lanto, balance all,
for wisdom's balance we do call.
Master Lanto, help us see,
that balance is the Golden Key.

Master Lanto, Wisdom's Fount,
with blessings we can hardly count,
you are for earth a shining light,
your Golden Wisdom oh so bright.

3. No outer condition can bring about my Christhood and no outer condition can prevent it. Christhood is an internal condition, and it will start being manifest when I decide that it is *now*.

Master Lanto, from Above,
we call forth discerning love.
Master Lanto, love's not blind,
through love, God vision we do find.

Master Lanto, Wisdom's Fount,
with blessings we can hardly count,
you are for earth a shining light,
your Golden Wisdom oh so bright.

4. Regardless of how difficult my situation is, regardless of the conditions I have or the conditions I don't have, I am going to focus on manifesting Christhood *now*.

Master Lanto, we are sure
as Christic lamb intentions pure.
Master Lanto, we'll transcend,
acceleration is our truest friend.

> **Master Lanto, Wisdom's Fount,**
> **with blessings we can hardly count,**
> **you are for earth a shining light,**
> **your Golden Wisdom oh so bright.**

5. I look at outer situations that have focused my attention and I say: "But this cannot stop my Christhood, so why am I worried about it?"

> Master Lanto, we are whole,
> no more division in the soul.
> Master Lanto, healing flame,
> all balance in your sacred name.

> **Master Lanto, Wisdom's Fount,**
> **with blessings we can hardly count,**
> **you are for earth a shining light,**
> **your Golden Wisdom oh so bright.**

6. My outer situation is not what matters when I am on the path to Christhood. My outer situation is not a hindrance, it is an opportunity to demonstrate that I cannot and will not be defined by material circumstances.

> Master Lanto, serve all life,
> as we transcend all inner strife.
> Master Lanto, peace you give,
> to all who want to truly live.

> **Master Lanto, Wisdom's Fount,**
> **with blessings we can hardly count,**
> **you are for earth a shining light,**
> **your Golden Wisdom oh so bright.**

7. The satanic consciousness is the consciousness that demands that Spirit should conform to current conditions in matter. The goal of the Christ is to set people free from the current conditions in matter. How can I set them free from current conditions by conforming to those conditions?

> Master Lanto, free to be,
> in balanced creativity.
> Master Lanto, we employ,
> your balance as the key to joy.

> **Master Lanto, Wisdom's Fount,**
> **with blessings we can hardly count,**
> **you are for earth a shining light,**
> **your Golden Wisdom oh so bright.**

8. I can set them free only by demonstrating that regardless of current conditions, this cannot define me as a spiritual being. I am more than these conditions.

> Master Lanto, balance all,
> the seven rays upon our call.
> Master Lanto, we take flight,
> the threefold flame a blazing light.

> **Master Lanto, Wisdom's Fount,**
> **with blessings we can hardly count,**
> **you are for earth a shining light,**
> **your Golden Wisdom oh so bright.**

7 | *Invoking the Will to Surrender*

9. Current conditions in matter are the product of a limited vision. The limited vision of most people on this earth has been projected into the cosmic mirror for a very long time and it has produced the current conditions in matter.

> Lanto dear, your Presence here,
> filling up the inner sphere.
> Life is now a sacred flow,
> God Wisdom we on all bestow.

> **Master Lanto, Wisdom's Fount,**
> **with blessings we can hardly count,**
> **you are for earth a shining light,**
> **your Golden Wisdom oh so bright.**

Part 7

1. How am I, as a representative of the Living Christ, going to help set people free unless I live by a higher vision? How am I going to consciously open myself to that vision unless I recognize that I need to let go of the old vision, I need to see that it is limited.

> O blessed Mary, Mother mine,
> there is no greater love than thine,
> as we are one in heart and mind,
> my place in hierarchy I find.

**O Mother Mary, generate,
the song that does accelerate,
the earth into a higher state,
all matter does now scintillate.**

2. I need to let the self based on this vision die and then say: "What is that to me? I will follow thee," and then I follow the Living Christ until I see that higher vision.

I came to earth from heaven sent,
as I am in embodiment,
I use Divine authority,
commanding you to set earth free.

**O Mother Mary, generate,
the song that does accelerate,
the earth into a higher state,
all matter does now scintillate.**

3. I do not hold on to my old vision. I am willing to take another look at it. I am the Conscious You. I am pure awareness and therefore I am steeping outside of the perception filter of my current vision.

I call now in God's sacred name,
for you to use your Mother Flame,
to burn all fear-based energy,
restoring sacred harmony.

**O Mother Mary, generate,
the song that does accelerate,
the earth into a higher state,
all matter does now scintillate.**

7 | Invoking the Will to Surrender

4. I am taking off those colored glasses. I am looking at my life without that vision, without that perception filter, without that coloring and now I see what I have not been able to see so far.

> Your sacred name I hereby praise,
> collective consciousness you raise,
> no more of fear and doubt and shame,
> consume it with your Mother Flame.
>
> **O Mother Mary, generate,**
> **the song that does accelerate,**
> **the earth into a higher state,**
> **all matter does now scintillate.**

5. I am willing to consciously see if I have used the teachings of the ascended masters to validate a limited vision. I am willing to surrender any limited vision based on a misinterpretation of the teachings.

> All darkness from the earth you purge,
> your light moves as a mighty surge,
> no force of darkness can now stop,
> the spiral that goes only up.
>
> **O Mother Mary, generate,**
> **the song that does accelerate,**
> **the earth into a higher state,**
> **all matter does now scintillate.**

6. How am I ever going to step up to a higher level of consciousness unless I let go of the vision I have created at my current level? This is the very principle of Christhood.

All elemental life you bless,
removing from them man-made stress,
the nature spirits are now free,
outpicturing Divine decree.

**O Mother Mary, generate,
the song that does accelerate,
the earth into a higher state,
all matter does now scintillate.**

7. In order to rise to the next level of consciousness, I cannot take my current self with me. I cannot transfer it, I cannot perfect it, I cannot develop it. I am willing to consciously let it die and then form another self at the next level of consciousness.

I raise my voice and take my stand,
a stop to war I do command,
no more shall warring scar the earth,
a golden age is given birth.

**O Mother Mary, generate,
the song that does accelerate,
the earth into a higher state,
all matter does now scintillate.**

8. It is always necessary to let go of the old before I can be reborn into the new self, the new vision, that will take me higher. If I am attached to something, being reluctant to let go of something, then this is remnants of the ego because only the ego holds on.

> As Mother Earth is free at last,
> disasters belong to the past,
> your Mother Light is so intense,
> that matter is now far less dense.
>
> **O Mother Mary, generate,**
> **the song that does accelerate,**
> **the earth into a higher state,**
> **all matter does now scintillate.**

9. I consciously embrace growth and realize that growth means letting go of the old. There will always be a sense of wanting to hold on to something, but this is just ego, it has no major significance. I just look at it without going into it and say: "Oh well, I know what this is, but I'm still going to let it go. I'm still going to let that old self, that old vision, go."

> In Mother Light the earth is pure,
> the upward spiral will endure,
> prosperity is now the norm,
> God's vision manifest as form.
>
> **O Mother Mary, generate,**
> **the song that does accelerate,**
> **the earth into a higher state,**
> **all matter does now scintillate.**

Sealing:

In the name of the Divine Mother, I fully accept that the power of these calls is used to set free the River of Life, so it can outpicture the perfect vision of Christ for my own life, for all people and for the planet. In the name I AM THAT I AM, it is done! Amen.

8 | GOING FROM A LOWER TO A HIGHER VISION

I AM the ascended master Hilarion. At the third level of my retreat, you are facing the initiation of the Fifth Ray combined with the Third Ray of Love. When you come to my retreat and participate in the classes at this level, I am attempting to help you reconnect to the original love that caused you to come into embodiment. The other chohans have, of course, helped you do the same thing. I try to do it specifically to help you see that there is a vision that is part of your Divine plan and you love this vision more than any vision you have had so far on your spiritual path.

The hard way or the love way

You see, my beloved, there are two ways to give up something on earth: the hard way or the love way. The hard way is when you come to a point where you realize that you have been suffering from an illusion, you have been holding an illusion in your mind, and it simply is not in accordance with what many people call reality. Reality, of course, is a dubious concept because what many people call reality is only the temporary manifestation brought about by the fact that the earth has sunk so far below its original level.

Nevertheless, there are many people who have had one of these awakening or hitting-the-concrete experiences or they have suddenly realized that what they have believed to be true is not true at all. This is the hard way to give up something. It is not that, as the ascended masters, we are against students giving up something the hard way because it is better that you give up something and move on than you keep holding on to an illusion. We are not seeking to have you give up something the hard way; we are seeking to have you give up something by reconnecting to the love in your being so that you can let it go from a position of love because you know there is something more. When you give up something the hard way, it is often as if you feel like something has been taken from you. You feel empty, you feel like your world has fallen apart. You feel like there is a vacuum inside of you and you do not know what is going to fill it.

What I hope to help you achieve at this level of my retreat is to reconnect to the love you have for the higher vision so that you can see that this higher vision is so much more than what you have seen so far. Therefore, you want to see that vision and it is no difficulty to let go of the old vision because you know you would get so much more instead. This is fairly easy to achieve at the etheric level in the identity body at my retreat. The difficulty is, of course, to bring it down into your conscious mind and that is the purpose of giving this outer dictation that you can read and study. We, of course, have no desire to take you through a process at our retreats where you attain a higher consciousness in your identity body but it is not carried through the mental, emotional and into the physical, conscious level. What can you do at the conscious level to connect to what you are going through at my retreat? Well, you can build on what I gave you in my last discourse where I said that you have a higher vision in your Divine plan. You can realize what I also said, namely that in order to grasp a higher vision, you must first be willing to let go of your current vision. Here, we run into a peculiar problem.

The desire to feel important

There are people who have started the spiritual path and even people who have started this course of self-mastery with a particular vision, a particular goal, a particular desire. They have, for instance, a desire to be important people who are doing something important for saving the earth or raising the consciousness, for bringing in the Golden Age of Saint Germain. This is a positive vision. There is nothing inherently wrong with it, but mixed into this is a certain ego desire to feel that you are special compared to other people because you are following the ascended master teachings, a particular guru or a particular outer teaching.

You are doing so many things, giving invocations and decrees, you are working on your psychology, you are doing this, you are doing that. There is an element of ego desire in this of wanting to feel that you have done something special, you have done something decisive. Therefore, you are more spiritual, you are in a special category of people. Here comes the real subtlety: You now think that God or the ascended masters should pay special attention to you or should reward you in some way.

It is very possible to build a desire where you think that your spiritual path is moving you towards a goal where you can manifest a particular outer situation. I have said that some people have the goal of manifesting a nice house, a perfect spouse and plenty of money. Many spiritual people also have the goal of either manifesting recognition from the world, recognition from the ascended masters or at least the sense that they have done something decisive to bring about a new age on earth.

Now, you may say: "Is there anything wrong with having this desire?" This is where things get subtle, my beloved. You understand that the entire purpose of the ascended masters is that we want to meet people at whatever consciousness they are at. If a person at the absolute lowest level of consciousness currently allowed on earth could attune to us, we would be willing to work with that person. We would meet that person at the person's level of consciousness and seek to help that person come to the next level up. This is our general approach to helping people on earth. In practice, there is, of course, a barrier where many people below the 48th level of consciousness cannot connect to us and therefore we cannot work with them directly. As soon as a person is able to tune in to us in some way, even if only in glimpses, we are willing to work with that person and therefore we must, of course, meet them at the level of consciousness they are at.

Giving up your lower vision

When you start this course of self-mastery, you start (in many cases) at the 48th level. Some can even start it a bit lower than the 48th level and so it is natural, unavoidable and fully acceptable to us that you need a motivation to start the spiritual path, to start this course. Your motivation is, of course, based on your desires, based on the vision that you have at that level of consciousness. Again, there is nothing wrong with this. You

8 | Going from a Lower to a Higher Vision

are at a certain level of consciousness and you cannot at that level see beyond a certain threshold. You cannot grasp a higher vision than what corresponds to your level of consciousness. Naturally, your outlook on life and your desires, ambitions and goals are influenced or based upon the vision that you have at that level.

What we are also seeking to help you see is that you need to continually move up. There are people who come to this level at my retreat and they have followed the course of self-mastery so far, but they have not given up the desire they had when they started. They still have in their minds that as they go through this course, they should build a certain self-mastery that should give them control of mind over matter and help them manifest the same outer situation that they desired when they started the course.

Now, my beloved, I do not think it is possible to go through this entire course and maintain the same vision and the same desire you had when you started. I can assure you that if it *was* possible, you would have failed the course. What you would do when you reached the 96th level of this course was (and mind you, I am saying the 96th level of this course and not the 96th level of consciousness) is that you would use whatever momentum you had gathered on the path to manifest this specific outer situation you desire. Instead of taking you higher towards the 144th level and Christhood, it would actually start taking you lower again. You would start going into using force to manifest that vision and therefore you would start descending the levels of consciousness.

You see, my beloved, it is an absolute requirement to pass the initiations of the course that you are willing to let go of the old vision in order to grasp a higher vision, a higher desire, a higher goal. This is where, at this particular level at my retreat, you need to really take a look at how you are using vision.

How you use or misuse vision actively

I have said before that vision is not a passive faculty; it also has an active aspect. Now, it is true that for most people on earth, vision is primarily passive in the sense that they are taking in. They are not projecting out very much because they are not willing to take responsibility for themselves. They are not willing to even admit that they have the power in their minds to change their outer situation. They are accepting that there is not much they can do about their outer situation and therefore they are not using their vision in its most active way of projecting out.

They are, of course, using their vision in an active way where their vision is affecting the impressions that come to them from the outside. I talked about this earlier of how the filters in your three higher bodies (and even at the level of the physical brain) will distort your perception, will distort what you see. What happens is, of course, that these filters will filter out anything that challenges the basic vision you have of life. If the vision is that there is not much you can do about your outer situation, then your perception filters will filter out what goes beyond this belief. You will therefore see the world as being limiting to your own ability to change.

When you are a spiritual person, and you become more active in accepting that there may be something you can do about your situation by changing your consciousness, then you will begin to use your power of vision in a more active manner. At my retreat I have what we might call a technological device where I am able to show you what you cannot see with your conscious mind. I am able to show you the projections, the impulses, that you are sending out from your four lower bodies. This is something we do very gradually because for most people it would be shocking to see how much you are actually projecting out constantly, so we take this in a very gradual way. What we do is that we seek to help you see that what you are projecting out always has a consequence because, as I said, it will go into the cosmic mirror. It may, in the cosmic mirror, be almost neutralized or decreased by opposition from the collective consciousness but it still has an effect on you.

You see, my beloved, when you are projecting something out, you know, even at the subconscious level, that the world is based on the principle of action and reaction. If you are holding on to a certain vision (for example, the desire to be recognized or acknowledged by the world), then you are subconsciously projecting out an impulse where you are expecting to get some kind of return. Whether you feel a return or whether you do not, this has an impact on your subconscious mind. If you are not feeling a return, then you subconsciously think you are not putting enough force into your projection, and therefore you put more into it. This ties up more and more of your energy in projecting this out. It may also cause you, at the conscious level, to feel an almost compulsive desire to do more of whatever you are doing.

We see many spiritual people, for example, who find some spiritual teaching that prescribes a certain practice and they now become almost obsessed with performing that practice. It can be meditation, it can be yoga, it can be decrees, it can be invocations. They do more and more because they are subconsciously expecting that when they do this, there is going to be a return current in the form of the outer situation they desire. When it does not happen, they think: "Oh, I have to do more."

On the other hand, if you do feel a return current, then many students also go into thinking: "But then I also have to do more because it isn't enough I'm getting back." Students can go through a phase of doing more and more. Probably, most of you will, if you look at your lives, admit that you have gone through this phase or you are in this phase of becoming almost obsessed with performing the outer practice. Again, this is not said to in any way criticize or condemn you. When I was in embodiment myself, I went through this phase even over many lifetimes where I was very, very driven to perform a certain practice.

Again, there is nothing wrong with it, but it is a phase on your path and it is now time that you step back and reconsider this. It is time you realize that if you have a compulsive need to perform a certain spiritual practice, then this is going to block your vision. It is going to block your ability to lock in to the vision in your Divine plan because you are (in the four lower bodies) thinking that performing this practice is more important than opening your mind to the vision.

The two basic functions of the mind

Do you see the underlying principle I am seeking to bring to your attention here? Your mind is a very sophisticated, very delicate, instrument but if you boil it down to its basic functions, then it has two basic functions. This is illustrated in what Mother Mary has called the expansive force of the Father and the contracting force of the Mother.

This can be subtle to understand, and I see many students who have trouble grasping this. I have just said that one aspect of the mind is that you are projecting out, and since the Father is expansive, you might think that when you are projecting out, you are using the Father aspect of the mind to project out. This is not actually the case. You see, my beloved, the Father is the expansive force and this means that in your case, the

8 | Going from a Lower to a Higher Vision

Father aspect of your being is your I AM Presence. Your I AM Presence is like a sun radiating. It is also the open door for the ascended masters to radiate energy, light and vision to you. The Mother aspect of your mind is the four lower bodies and, of course, the Conscious You. Now, what have we said about the Conscious You? It is pure awareness. We have also said that the Conscious You is able to focus its attention in or through the four lower bodies and it is able to step outside the four lower bodies and thereby open itself to the I AM Presence. You cannot do both at the same time.

This is something that many students have not quite grasped. They have not quite had that "Aha" experience of the conscious mind where they see this. You know that you cannot give out and take in at the same time, you cannot direct your attention effectively in two different places at the same time. What happens is that, as the Conscious You is identifying itself with the four lower bodies and is focused on expressing itself in the material world, you are actually using the contracting force of the Mother to create a concentration of energy and attention in your four lower bodies.

It is true that when you have a certain goal that you envision, you are directing light out of this. It is, in a way, the Father element you are using to direct the light out. What I am pointing out to you here is that in order to direct light out, you must have something to direct it through, you must have some thought matrix, some matrix of vision, that you are directing the light through. In order to create this matrix, and in order to actually focus your energies on going through this matrix (and not just generally going out), you are creating a contraction, a concentration in your four lower bodies.

How much energy you can project out

Most of this might be subconscious to you. What I am saying is that when you have this kind of concentration in your four lower bodies, this will draw the attention of the Conscious You. Therefore, you cannot step outside your four lower bodies and receive a higher vision, the vision from your Divine plan, from your I AM Presence. You cannot do both at the same time, my beloved; it just cannot be done. You are either focused on a particular goal or you are open to receiving a new vision from above. What I help students see with the device I have at my retreat is how they have these subconscious matrices that are drawing their attention.

In many cases, students are surprised about this because they are not consciously aware that they have this. They do not realize how much of their energy is fed into this subconscious matrix. They are surprised to see this because I can illustrate for them, I can show on a screen visually, how much energy is coming in from their I AM Presence, how much energy is coming into your identity body, and then I can show how (at the bottom level) the output that is coming out of your aura at the conscious level. What I can show is that there is a certain amount going in and there is a certain amount going out (that you are able to direct consciously). For most students they are very shocked to see the difference between what is actually coming in and what they are able to use consciously.

If you see, for example, that there is a certain amount of energy coming in from your I AM Presence, then you realize, of course, that ideally this is the creative energy that you should be able to use at the conscious level to manifest a certain goal. If you see that you only have 10 percent of that energy available at the conscious level, then naturally you are wondering what is happening to the other 90 percent, or whatever the

8 | Going from a Lower to a Higher Vision

percentage may be in your individual case. This is when I can show you where you have a concentration, a matrix, in one of your three higher bodies that is eating up your energy. The energy is flowing through this matrix, but it is not something you are consciously aware of and therefore you are not consciously directing it. The reason I am telling you this is that, if you are to make the fastest possible progress at this level of my retreat, you need to be willing to consciously look at your goals, your approach, your basic approach, to the spiritual path.

Look at your motivation

What has motivated you on the spiritual path up until this point? If I ask you this question, what is the first thing that comes to your mind? What is your basic motivation for walking the path? What do you hope to get out of it for yourself? What do you hope to get out of it for the world, and what does this show about what you hope to get out of it for yourself?

I have many students who immediately will say: "Well, I want to raise the consciousness, I want to set people free, I want to help Saint Germain's Golden Age, I want to help the ascended masters." When you are more honest and take a closer look, you realize that, yes, these are outer goals but if those goals were manifest, you would get a certain feeling out of knowing that you had been part of manifesting that goal. This, then, is your personal motivation, meaning what you hope to get out of it for yourself.

What is the experience that you are seeking to have by following the spiritual path? Now, for many students this can be a difficult exercise. I know also that at the conscious level this can be very difficult to go through because you have perhaps spent many years walking the spiritual path, studying certain teachings, performing certain practices. As I said, most of the people who come to this level, which is a fairly high level on the spiritual path, they have spent quite a lot of time and put quite a lot of effort into performing certain practices. What unfortunately has happened is that, as a result of all of this effort, the subconscious matrix (which is the matrix of what you hope you get out of following the spiritual path) has become more and more reinforced. You have fed more energy into it; you have sometimes solidified the vision of it.

The stain-glass window of the subconscious mind

Let me give you a crude illustration of how this works in the subconscious mind. It is crude because no illustration that refers to physical things can fully cover what happens in the energy field, but still it is helpful to many students. Imagine that your energy field is an enclosed space and in order to manifest anything, in order to manifest a particular situation in the material world, you have to send light and energy, you have to direct and project light and energy out from your energy field. You, of course, do not want to just direct light randomly; you want the light to have a certain form so that what you are projecting is not just light but a certain matrix.

Let us imagine that your energy field is like one of the old cathedrals that have stained glass windows that are colored. They have an intricate pattern where the glass pieces are set in a certain pattern, and then the glass pieces are colored. You have created in your energy field these round rose windows, and they have a matrix and a coloring, a shape and a coloring, that is forming the light you are projecting out. You are now using these matrices to project into the world. When I make visible to you that there is a subconscious matrix that is tying up a lot of your energy, when you take a closer look at this, it looks like one of these rose windows in the cathedrals, a round window with an intricate pattern and the glass pieces are colored. Many times, you will realize, when you take a closer look, that as you have been walking the path up until this point, your spiritual studies, your spiritual practice, they have actually reinforced this matrix. You have solidified the window, the glass has become thicker, the lead strings that are holding the glass pieces have become more solid, the colors have become more intense, more dense. The result of this is that it now becomes more difficult for you to let go of this matrix.

It is a natural tendency, my beloved (which we all have), that when we have put a lot of effort into something, we feel there should also be a certain return current from the universe. The more we project out, the more we desire to receive back that which corresponds to what we are projecting out. Strangely, I must say, even people who do something considered "wrong" actually want to be punished for what they are doing.

Whether people do what they think is good or whether they do what they think is evil, they subconsciously want to receive a return current from the universe. Why is this so? Because the entire purpose of the material world is actually that you are experimenting with your creative powers. You are sending something out, and if nothing comes back, how do you know what you sent out and what the effect of it is?

Uncovering self-centered motives

What I am pointing out here is that when you come to this point at my retreat, you need to take a critical look at your spiritual practice, at how you have approached the spiritual path and what is your motivation for walking the path. What is your motivation for putting forth an effort? There are many students who at the level of my retreat become almost shocked when they take a look at this. They become shocked to see that what they actually (in their conscious minds) are convinced is a completely altruistic motive is really, truly a very self-centered motive. They are simply using the spiritual path to get a certain recognition from the world. At least they are hoping to get a certain recognition from the world.

I know that it will be shocking for you at the conscious level to come to realize this. I also know that if you do not realize this, you cannot move on in consciousness. You cannot actually overcome what is the greatest hurdle on the spiritual path. Again, this is subtle and it may at first seem contradictory.

I have just said that the purpose of life, the purpose of taking embodiment, is to experiment with your creative abilities. You are formulating a matrix in your mind, you are directing creative energy and light through that matrix and then you wait to see what is coming back from the cosmic mirror. Based on what is coming back, you then adjust the matrix in your mind and then you direct energy through it again. Then, you keep doing this and you keep refining the matrix until you get back from the universe exactly what you want—or at least so you think.

You see, my beloved, everything is a phase, everything is a stage. There is a point where it is perfectly correct, perfectly right and perfectly constructive for you to do what I just described. During this phase it is natural and unavoidable that you form this very subtle idea that you are supposed to get better and better at formulating matrices. You are supposed to get more and more momentum of directing light through them so that you come to the point where you have mastery and can therefore manifest any material condition you desire. It is natural that you form this idea but it is also, as I have said earlier, only the fallen beings who actually build up enough momentum where they can force the material universe (on a temporary basis, mind you) to comply with their vision.

You are a spiritual person; you are not walking the left-handed path of the fallen beings and the false hierarchy. You are walking the path of Christhood, the path of the ascended masters. The purpose of this path is that you come to a point where you realize that the desire to control the material universe is not your real goal.

As we have said before, the purpose of taking embodiment is that you have two phases. First, you go into the immersion phase where you are completely immersed in the life that is available on whatever planet you are embodying upon. You are immersing yourself in it; you are seeking to know it, to understand how life works. You are seeking to expand your awareness and you are also seeking to expand your ability to manifest certain outer situations. Then, you start the awakening phase, and those who are participating in this course have long ago started the awakening phase.

The purpose of the awakening phase is not that you attain complete control over what you can manifest materially so that you can manifest any material condition you desire. The purpose of the awakening phase is that you come to the realization that you are a spiritual being not a material being. Therefore, as I said in my last discourse, your goals are not material. It is not the real goal in your Divine plan to manifest certain material conditions in this lifetime. Your real goal is to demonstrate the path to Christhood where you become independent of material conditions.

A great challenge on the spiritual path

Do you see that it is entirely possible to walk the spiritual path, even for many years, but still you have in your subconscious mind this matrix where you think that if you attain the highest state of spiritual consciousness (however you see it), then you will be able to completely control matter and manifest any material condition you desire? Now, my beloved, there are many students who have become fascinated, obsessed one might say, with the concept of alchemy or manifestation. They have put considerable effort into coming to the point where they can materialize, for example, gold or an amethyst jewel or any other thing they desire. Some have tried to bend spoons or perform other such feats. All this does for you is to reinforce the subconscious matrix. The stronger this matrix becomes, the more it pulls on the attention of the Conscious You. The more this pull prevents the Conscious You from stepping outside of your four lower bodies and opening itself completely to the vision of your Divine plan.

Do you begin to see what I am taking you towards, my beloved? I am taking you towards the realization here that the key to vision is not concentration but openness. Of course, even this statement needs to be qualified. You live in a world where there is a very chaotic state of the collective consciousness, meaning that the four lower bodies of planet earth (in which your four lower bodies exist) is very chaotic. It is perfectly true that if you open yourself to the many different ideas and visions that are out there, then your attention will be so scattered that you will not be able to accomplish anything. That is why you can say, and rightly so, that in order to accomplish any particular thing, you need to focus, you need to concentrate. You need to block out all of these things coming from the material realm. I have students who say to me: "But

8 | Going from a Lower to a Higher Vision

Hilarion, how could I have walked as far as I have walked on the spiritual path without focusing on it?" This is, again, perfectly true. You needed to focus on it, but everything on earth must be balanced.

Whenever you take something towards one extreme, you create an imbalance and at some point this imbalance will hinder your progress on the path. This is what I am telling you. You have reached the point now where I am *not* telling you to open yourself to any other visions that are out there in the four levels of the material universe around earth. I am asking you to open yourself to your own I AM Presence and the vision in your Divine plan.

In order to do this, you do need to take a look at the subconscious matrix you have created, the matrix that has motivated you, that has driven you, on your spiritual path up to this point. You need to start seeing its limitations. You need to start consciously acknowledging these limitations, and then you need to come to that point of surrender, as Mother Mary describes. You realize that what you have done so far has taken you to this point, but it cannot take you beyond it. Therefore, you need to get to that point of openness where you say: "But then what is my next step? What is it that I have not done before that I need to do? What is it that I have not seen before that I need to see?" The more open you can be, the more clear of a vision you will receive.

Evaluating your spiritual practice

Now, my beloved, there are students who can have a very hard time getting this point. Sometimes I must tell them that they need to stop whatever practice they have been doing so far. I am not saying that this necessarily applies to you. I know there are students who have been practicing invoking spiritual light for decades. What I am asking you is to take a look at the spiritual practice you have been doing and then ask yourself: "If I was to stop this right now, how would I react?"

What are the thoughts, what are the feelings that come to you when you contemplate stopping your practice, taking a break? Do you feel fear, do you feel panic? Is there all kinds of thoughts that start revolving, arguing why you should not do this, why you need to keep doing what you are doing? Then, the more intense this is and the more of an intense reaction you have, the more of an attachment you have to that practice. The stronger the attachment, the more it will prevent you from seeing a new vision. It can be no other way, my beloved.

You see, there comes a point on the path to Christhood where you need to recognize a very simple fact. I say it is simple but it is, of course, very difficult to grasp it and you will have to grasp it in stages. It is exemplified in Jesus' statement: "I can of my own self do nothing." He also made the remark that: "The Father within me, he doeth the work." There comes a point on the spiritual path where you cannot go further with the outer mind.

When you start the spiritual path, your first stage of the path is to pull yourself above the magnetic force of the collective consciousness, the mass consciousness. This requires focus, determination. It requires what you have been doing so far, namely a concentrated focus on practice where you do not look right or left. You do not contemplate whether you should do this or not because you have decided you are going to do it. You need to keep doing it in order to build the momentum. There also comes a point where now you have pulled yourself above the magnetic force of the mass consciousness and now you do not need to keep going the same way. You need something different on a higher level. If your outer mind is not open to this, then this will be hindering your progress. There are many students of the ascended masters who have been giving decrees for so long that it is actually hindering their progress. It is not that they necessarily need to stop completely, but they do need to change the way they go about it. They cannot receive that vision until they are willing to consider giving up the practice. You see, my beloved, in the phase where you are seeking to pull yourself above the mass consciousness, there are all kinds of dark forces (and even the forces of other people and the mass consciousness itself) that are pulling on you to give up your practice so you stop doing it, you give up the thought that you could pull yourself above the mass consciousness. They say you should be like everybody else.

Then, there comes that point, that you are at now, where you need to give up the practice, meaning UP to the I AM Presence. You need to be willing to say to your I AM Presence: "OK, I am giving UP this focus in my outer mind of what I think I should be doing and I am willing to be completely open and listen to you. Show me what I need to be doing in order to go higher on the path." This is giving UP, and my beloved, the path to Christhood requires you to do this over and over again. Give UP the vision you have right now in order to receive a higher vision.

The principle of giving UP

At each step you have taken so far, you have given up something. What I need you to do at this point is to fix in your conscious mind this principle of giving UP what you see with the outer mind, with the conscious mind, what you are focused on. You need to give UP the matrices in the subconscious mind. In a sense, asking for higher vision has two aspects. You need to ask your I AM Presence or an ascended master (that you feel you are working with) to show you the matrices or the matrix in your subconscious mind that you are dealing with right now and that is preventing you from taking the next step on your path. What is that internal spirit, what is that self, what is that matrix that you are focusing your energies through?

You need to be willing to see it and to see the limitations of it. Then, you need to ask what is the higher matrix, what is the higher vision. You now have the Alpha and the Omega action. What will it take to do this? It will take love. I said that there is the hard way and the love way. I do not wish you to continue your spiritual path by going through it the hard way of having one of these shocking awakening experiences over and over and over again.

It is possible to walk from the 48th to the 96th level of consciousness and for each level you go up, you have one of these shocking experiences. It is possible and some people have done it, but would it not be preferable to you to do it the soft way? Well, then you need to cultivate this willingness to always (not every moment but at certain intervals when you feel it appropriate) step back and ask for the vision: "What is the limitation, what is the higher vision?"

In order to do this, you need to become conscious of your real motivation for walking the path. I have said that you have had a motivation that has driven you up until this point. When you formulated your Divine plan for this lifetime, you had a higher motivation and that is the one you need to lock in to if you are willing to do what I have explained: be open to receiving it. I will, of course, help you, your I AM Presence will help you, any other master that is close to you will help you—if you will but ask.

As you give the invocation associated with this chapter, when you are done, then take some moments to be as centered

8 | Going from a Lower to a Higher Vision

in your heart as you can be and then ask. Ask to see, first of all, your real motivation for walking the path, what it is you truly desire to accomplish in this lifetime. Then, ask to see the limitation you are dealing with right now, the matrix in the subconscious mind that you are dealing with right now. Then, ask to see the higher vision that will take you beyond that limitation so that you can simply let the limitation go without feeling you have to force yourself, or you have to destroy it or you have to blame yourself.

You will have a limited vision

You see, my beloved, Serapis Bey made a magnificent effort in helping you come to the point where you are open to seeing what you need to see and just moving on. I know this is a process that has stages, and that is why I am also helping you come to the point where you realize that there is no shame associated with acknowledging that you have had a limited vision.

I am the master of vision. My goal is to give you a higher vision than you have right now. Well, if you already had the highest vision, what would my job be? I know you have a limited vision when you come to my retreat, otherwise you would not be coming. It is my love to help you attain a higher vision. I am not focused on the fact that you have a limited vision. I am not seeking to point out that vision and analyze it and dissect it with a knife. I am seeking to help you grasp the higher vision and then effortlessly and lovingly let go of the limited vision and embrace the higher.

I am focused on the higher vision, not the lower. It is just that in some cases you need to come to see some aspect of that lower vision, and see how it is limiting you, before you can let it go. There is no shame here. There is no criticism from my side. I am focused constantly on the higher vision. When you are focused on the higher vision, why would you be concerned about seeing a lower vision, seeing that you have a lower vision? It is seeing that you have a lower vision that is the very foundation for embracing the higher. Seeing that you have a limited vision is the tool that helps you move on. Why resist it? Why use it to criticize yourself? Why feel bad about it at all?

Love, my beloved, is not the rosy-pink thing that people make it out to be. You could say that one aspect of love is to see a limitation and love yourself free of it. This is what you ideally realize consciously at the third level of my retreat. Then, you lock in to that love-based vision in your Divine plan. You may not see it clearly at this point, but you will see that in order for you to walk your personal path to Christhood (that you have the potential to do in this lifetime), you need to go far beyond the vision of the spiritual path that you have had so far.

You need to go far higher than you have done so far and you are willing to do so. You are looking with anticipation to going through those higher steps. I am looking with anticipation to taking you through those higher steps, and thus I seal you for now in the love, the loving vision, that I Am. Hilarion I AM.

9 | INVOKING A HIGHER VISION OF MY MOTIVATION

In the name I AM THAT I AM, Jesus Christ, I call to my I AM Presence to flow through the I Will Be Presence that I AM and give this invocation with full power. I call to beloved Elohim Cyclopea and Virginia and Heros and Amora, Archangel Raphael and Mother Mary and Chamuel and Charity, Hilarion and Paul the Venetian to help me reconnect to the love-based motivation in my Divine plan. Help me see and surrender all patterns that block my oneness with Hilarion and with my I AM Presence, including …

[Make personal calls]

Part 1

1. There are two ways to give up something on earth: the hard way or the love way.

> Cyclopea so dear, the truth you reveal,
> the truth that duality's ailments will heal,
> your Emerald Light is like a great balm,
> our emotional bodies are perfectly calm.
>
> **Cyclopea so dear, in Emerald Sphere,**
> **in raising perception we shall persevere,**
> **as deep in our hearts your truth we revere,**
> **to immaculate vision the earth does adhere.**

2. I am reconnecting to my love for the higher vision and I see that this higher vision is so much more than what I have seen so far.

> Cyclopea so dear, with you we unwind,
> all negative spirals clouding the mind,
> we know pure awareness is truly our core,
> the key to becoming the wide-open door.
>
> **Cyclopea so dear, in Emerald Sphere,**
> **in raising perception we shall persevere,**
> **as deep in our hearts your truth we revere,**
> **to immaculate vision the earth does adhere.**

3. I want to see that vision and it is no difficulty to let go of the old vision because I know I get so much more instead.

> Cyclopea so dear, clear our inner sight,
> empowered, we pierce the soul's fearful night,
> we now see our life through your single eye,
> beyond all disease we're ready to fly.

> Cyclopea so dear, in Emerald Sphere,
> in raising perception we shall persevere,
> as deep in our hearts your truth we revere,
> to immaculate vision the earth does adhere.

4. I surrender all desires for being an important person who is doing something for saving the earth or raising the consciousness or bringing in the Golden Age of Saint Germain.

> Cyclopea so dear, life can only reflect,
> the images that the mind does project,
> the key to our healing is clearing the mind,
> from the images the ego is hiding behind.

> Cyclopea so dear, in Emerald Sphere,
> in raising perception we shall persevere,
> as deep in our hearts your truth we revere,
> to immaculate vision the earth does adhere.

5. I surrender all ego desire to feel that I am special compared to other people because I am following the ascended master teachings, a particular guru or a particular outer teaching.

> Cyclopea so dear, we want to aim high,
> to your healing flame we ever draw nigh,
> through veils of duality we now take flight,
> bathed in your penetrating Emerald Light.

> Cyclopea so dear, in Emerald Sphere,
> in raising perception we shall persevere,
> as deep in our hearts your truth we revere,
> to immaculate vision the earth does adhere.

6. I surrender the ego desire of wanting to feel that I have done something special, I have done something decisive. Therefore, I am more spiritual, I am in a special category of people and God or the ascended masters should pay special attention to me or should reward me in some way.

> Cyclopea so dear, your Emerald Flame,
> exposes every subtle, dualistic power game,
> including the game of wanting to say,
> that truth is defined in only one way.

> **Cyclopea so dear, in Emerald Sphere,**
> **in raising perception we shall persevere,**
> **as deep in our hearts your truth we revere,**
> **to immaculate vision the earth does adhere.**

7. I surrender the desire for having my spiritual path move me towards a goal where I can manifest a particular outer situation, such as having recognition from the world, recognition from the ascended masters or the sense that I have done something decisive to bring about a new age on earth.

> Cyclopea so dear, we're feeling the flow,
> as your Living Truth upon us you bestow,
> from all dual vision we are now set free,
> planet earth in immaculate matrix will be.

> **Cyclopea so dear, in Emerald Sphere,**
> **in raising perception we shall persevere,**
> **as deep in our hearts your truth we revere,**
> **to immaculate vision the earth does adhere.**

9 | Invoking a Higher Vision of My Motivation

8. My motivation for starting this course has been based on my desires, the vision I had at that level of consciousness. I need to continually move up. I surrender the desire I had when I started.

> Cyclopea so dear, the truth is now clear,
> we see higher purpose for which we are here
> we know truth transcends all systems below,
> immersed in your light, we continue to grow.
>
> **Cyclopea so dear, in Emerald Sphere,**
> **in raising perception we shall persevere,**
> **as deep in our hearts your truth we revere,**
> **to immaculate vision the earth does adhere.**

9. I surrender the idea that as I go through this course, I should build the self-mastery that should give me control of mind over matter and help me manifest the same outer situation that I desired when I started the course.

> Cyclopea so dear, we're feeling your joy,
> as creative vision we now do employ,
> in lifting earth out of serpentine cage,
> to manifest Saint Germain's Golden Age.
>
> **Cyclopea so dear, in Emerald Sphere,**
> **in raising perception we shall persevere,**
> **as deep in our hearts your truth we revere,**
> **to immaculate vision the earth does adhere.**

Part 2

1. Vision is not a passive faculty; it also has an active aspect. I am willing to see the projections, the impulses, that I am sending out from my four lower bodies.

> O Heros-Amora, in your love so pink,
> we care not what others about us may think,
> in oneness with you, we claim a new day,
> as innocent children, we frolic and play.
>
> **O Heros-Amora, we reap what we sow,**
> **yet this is Plan B for helping us grow,**
> **for truly, Plan A is that we join the flow,**
> **immersed in the Infinite Love you bestow.**

2. What I am projecting out always has a consequence because it will go into the cosmic mirror. It may be neutralized or decreased by opposition from the collective consciousness but it still has an effect on me.

> O Heros-Amora, a new life begun,
> we laugh at the devil, the serious one,
> the serpent is stuck in his duality,
> but we are set free by Love's reality.
>
> **O Heros-Amora, we reap what we sow,**
> **yet this is Plan B for helping us grow,**
> **for truly, Plan A is that we join the flow,**
> **immersed in the Infinite Love you bestow.**

9 | Invoking a Higher Vision of My Motivation

3. The world is based on the principle of action and reaction. If I am holding on to a certain vision, then I am subconsciously projecting out an impulse where I am expecting to get some kind of return.

> O Heros-Amora, awakened we see,
> in true love is no conditionality,
> we bathe in your glorious Ruby-Pink Sun,
> knowing our God allows life to be fun.
>
> **O Heros-Amora, we reap what we sow,**
> **yet this is Plan B for helping us grow,**
> **for truly, Plan A is that we join the flow,**
> **immersed in the Infinite Love you bestow.**

4. Whether I feel a return or not, this has an impact on my subconscious mind. If I am not feeling a return, then I subconsciously think I am not putting enough force into my projection, and therefore I put more into it.

> O Heros-Amora, life is such a joy,
> we see that the world is like a great toy,
> whatever the mind into it projects,
> the mirror of life exactly reflects.
>
> **O Heros-Amora, we reap what we sow,**
> **yet this is Plan B for helping us grow,**
> **for truly, Plan A is that we join the flow,**
> **immersed in the Infinite Love you bestow.**

5. This ties up more and more of my energy in projecting this out. It may also cause me, at the conscious level, to feel an almost compulsive desire to do more of whatever I am doing.

O Heros-Amora, conditions you burn,
we know we are free to take a new turn,
Immersed in the stream of infinite Love,
we know that the Spirit came from Above.

**O Heros-Amora, we reap what we sow,
yet this is Plan B for helping us grow,
for truly, Plan A is that we join the flow,
immersed in the Infinite Love you bestow.**

6. I am willing to see if I have become obsessed with performing a spiritual practice, subconsciously expecting that there is going to be a return current in the form of the outer situation I desire.

O Heros-Amora, we feel that at last,
we've risen above the trap of the past,
in true love we claim our freedom to grow,
forever we're one with Love's Infinite Flow.

**O Heros-Amora, we reap what we sow,
yet this is Plan B for helping us grow,
for truly, Plan A is that we join the flow,
immersed in the Infinite Love you bestow.**

7. I realize that if I have a compulsive need to perform a certain spiritual practice, this will block my vision. It is going to block my ability to lock in to the vision in my Divine plan because I am thinking that performing this practice is more important than opening my mind to the vision.

9 | Invoking a Higher Vision of My Motivation

O Heros-Amora, conditions are ties,
forming a net of serpentine lies,
but you have the antidote setting us free,
you take us beyond conditionality.

**O Heros-Amora, we reap what we sow,
yet this is Plan B for helping us grow,
for truly, Plan A is that we join the flow,
immersed in the Infinite Love you bestow.**

8. The Conscious You is able to focus its attention in or through the four lower bodies. It is also able to step outside the four lower bodies and thereby open itself to the I AM Presence. I cannot do both at the same time.

O Heros-Amora, your love is no bond,
for love only wants to take us beyond,
your love has no bounds, forever it flies,
raising all life into Ruby-Pink skies.

**O Heros-Amora, we reap what we sow,
yet this is Plan B for helping us grow,
for truly, Plan A is that we join the flow,
immersed in the Infinite Love you bestow.**

9. When the Conscious You is identifying itself with the four lower bodies and is focused on expressing itself in the material world, I am using the contracting force of the Mother to create a concentration of energy and attention in my four lower bodies.

O Heros-Amora, love bathing the earth,
filling all people with infinite mirth,
for fear and despair there is no more room,
as all are awakened by love's sonic boom.

**O Heros-Amora, we reap what we sow,
yet this is Plan B for helping us grow,
for truly, Plan A is that we join the flow,
immersed in the Infinite Love you bestow.**

Part 3

1. In order to direct light out, I must have something to direct it through, I must have some thought matrix, some matrix of vision that I am directing the light through.

Raphael Archangel, your light so intense,
raise us beyond all human pretense.
Mother Mary and you have a vision so bold,
to see that our highest potential unfold.

**Raphael Archangel, for vision we pray,
Raphael Archangel, show us the way,
Raphael Archangel, your emerald ray,
Raphael Archangel, our lives a new day.**

2. In order to create this matrix, and in order to focus my energies on going through this matrix and not just generally going out, I am creating a contraction, a concentration in my four lower bodies.

9 | Invoking a Higher Vision of My Motivation

> Raphael Archangel, in emerald sphere,
> to immaculate vision we always adhere.
> Mother Mary enfolds us in her Sacred Heart,
> from Mother's true love, we're never apart.
>
> **Raphael Archangel, for vision we pray,**
> **Raphael Archangel, show us the way,**
> **Raphael Archangel, your emerald ray,**
> **Raphael Archangel, our lives a new day.**

3. When I have this kind of concentration in my four lower bodies, this will draw the attention of the Conscious You. I cannot step outside my four lower bodies and receive a higher vision, the vision from my Divine plan.

> Raphael Archangel, all ailments you heal,
> each cell in our bodies in light now you seal.
> Mother Mary's immaculate concept we see,
> perfection of health our new reality.
>
> **Raphael Archangel, for vision we pray,**
> **Raphael Archangel, show us the way,**
> **Raphael Archangel, your emerald ray,**
> **Raphael Archangel, our lives a new day.**

4. I want to see my subconscious matrices that are drawing my attention and how much of my energy is fed into this subconscious matrix.

> Raphael Archangel, your light is so real,
> the vision of Christ in us you reveal.
> Mother Mary now helps us to truly transcend,
> in emerald light with you we ascend.

> **Raphael Archangel, for vision we pray,**
> **Raphael Archangel, show us the way,**
> **Raphael Archangel, your emerald ray,**
> **Raphael Archangel, our lives a new day.**

5. I want to know how much of the creative energy from my I AM Presence I am able to use at the conscious level and how much is consumed by my subconscious matrices.

> Raphael Archangel, diseases are done,
> as you help us see that all life is One,
> we no longer do your true love reject,
> immaculate vision on all we project.

> **Raphael Archangel, for vision we pray,**
> **Raphael Archangel, show us the way,**
> **Raphael Archangel, your emerald ray,**
> **Raphael Archangel, our lives a new day.**

6. I am willing to consciously look at my goals and my basic approach to the spiritual path. I am willing to look at what has motivated me on the spiritual path up until this point, what I hope to get out of it for myself.

> Raphael Archangel, we're healing the earth,
> in immaculate vision we give her rebirth,
> a new era has on this day begun,
> your emerald light now shines like a sun.

> **Raphael Archangel, for vision we pray,**
> **Raphael Archangel, show us the way,**
> **Raphael Archangel, your emerald ray,**
> **Raphael Archangel, our lives a new day.**

9 | Invoking a Higher Vision of My Motivation

7. I am willing to look at what I hope to get out of it for the world, and what this shows about what I hope to get out of it for myself.

> Raphael Archangel, the fall is behind,
> as all of earth's people the Christ path do find,
> we call now to you all people to heal,
> as four lower bodies in love you do seal.

> **Raphael Archangel, for vision we pray,**
> **Raphael Archangel, show us the way,**
> **Raphael Archangel, your emerald ray,**
> **Raphael Archangel, our lives a new day.**

8. I am willing to look at my outer goals and consider the feeling I would get if those goals were manifest. This is my personal motivation, meaning what I hope to get out of it for myself.

> Raphael Archangel, as you bring the light,
> the forces of darkness swiftly take flight,
> their day is now done as we claim the earth,
> spreading to all an innocent mirth.

> **Raphael Archangel, for vision we pray,**
> **Raphael Archangel, show us the way,**
> **Raphael Archangel, your emerald ray,**
> **Raphael Archangel, our lives a new day.**

9. I am willing to see how I have used spiritual teachings to reinforce the subconscious matrix, which is the matrix of what I hope to get out of following the spiritual path.

Raphael Archangel, our vision set free,
as we can now see God's reality,
as Saint Germain's vision is manifest here,
the earth is now sealed in immaculate sphere.

Raphael Archangel, for vision we pray,
Raphael Archangel, show us the way,
Raphael Archangel, your emerald ray,
Raphael Archangel, our lives a new day.

Part 4

1. Whether people do what they think is good or whether they do what they think is evil, they subconsciously want to receive a return current from the universe.

Chamuel Archangel, in ruby ray power,
we know we are taking a life-giving shower.
Love burning away all perversions of will,
we suddenly feel our desires falling still.

Chamuel Archangel, descend from Above,
Chamuel Archangel, with ruby-pink love,
Chamuel Archangel, so often thought-of,
Chamuel Archangel, o come Holy Dove.

2. The purpose of the material world is that I am experimenting with my creative powers. I am sending something out, and if nothing comes back, how do I know what I sent out and what the effect of it is?

9 | Invoking a Higher Vision of My Motivation

Chamuel Archangel, a spiral of light,
as ruby ray fire now pierces the night.
All forces of darkness consumed by your fire,
consuming all those who will not rise higher.

**Chamuel Archangel, descend from Above,
Chamuel Archangel, with ruby-pink love,
Chamuel Archangel, so often thought-of,
Chamuel Archangel, o come Holy Dove.**

3. I am willing to take a critical look at my spiritual practice, at how I have approached the spiritual path and what is my motivation for walking the path. What is my motivation for putting forth an effort?

Chamuel Archangel, your love so immense,
with clarified vision, our lives now make sense.
The purpose of life you so clearly reveal,
immersed in your love, God's oneness we feel.

**Chamuel Archangel, descend from Above,
Chamuel Archangel, with ruby-pink love,
Chamuel Archangel, so often thought-of,
Chamuel Archangel, o come Holy Dove.**

4. I am willing to see if what I, in my conscious mind, am convinced is a completely altruistic motive is really a self-centered motive. I want to see if I am using the spiritual path to get recognition from the world or other such goals.

> Chamuel Archangel, what calmness you bring,
> we see now that even death has no sting.
> For truly, in love there can be no decay,
> as love is transcendence into a new day.

> **Chamuel Archangel, descend from Above,**
> **Chamuel Archangel, with ruby-pink love,**
> **Chamuel Archangel, so often thought-of,**
> **Chamuel Archangel, o come Holy Dove.**

5. There is a phase where I need to experiment with my creative abilities. I formulate a matrix in my mind, I am directing creative energy through it and then I wait to see what is coming back from the cosmic mirror. I keep refining the matrix until I get back from the universe exactly what I want.

> Chamuel Archangel, God's Love Flame bestow,
> on all those longing God's true love to know,
> conditions we know can never be real,
> and this is the love you always reveal.

> **Chamuel Archangel, descend from Above,**
> **Chamuel Archangel, with ruby-pink love,**
> **Chamuel Archangel, so often thought-of,**
> **Chamuel Archangel, o come Holy Dove.**

6. I surrender the very subtle idea that I am supposed to get better and better at formulating matrices, that I am supposed to get more and more momentum of directing light through them so that I have mastery and can manifest any material condition I desire.

9 | Invoking a Higher Vision of My Motivation

Chamuel Archangel, love's seed you have sown,
in hearts of all those who don't seek to own,
for love that possesses is nothing but fear,
that pierces the heart with duality's spear.

**Chamuel Archangel, descend from Above,
Chamuel Archangel, with ruby-pink love,
Chamuel Archangel, so often thought-of,
Chamuel Archangel, o come Holy Dove.**

7. Only the fallen beings have actually built up enough momentum where they can force the material universe to comply with their vision.

Chamuel Archangel, we don't want control,
for this is the devil's hold on the soul,
your love will now break the serpentine chain,
so we are set free God's love to reclaim.

**Chamuel Archangel, descend from Above,
Chamuel Archangel, with ruby-pink love,
Chamuel Archangel, so often thought-of,
Chamuel Archangel, o come Holy Dove.**

8. I am a spiritual person; I am not walking the left-handed path of the fallen beings. I am walking the path of Christhood, and the purpose of this path is not simply to control the material universe.

Chamuel Archangel, you are so adept,
at helping us God's true love to accept,
we know that the love for which we so yearn,
is not something we on earth have to earn.

**Chamuel Archangel, descend from Above,
Chamuel Archangel, with ruby-pink love,
Chamuel Archangel, so often thought-of,
Chamuel Archangel, o come Holy Dove.**

9. Being in embodiment is a process with two phases. First, I am in the immersion phase and then I go into the awakening phase.

Chamuel Archangel, for love to accept,
we do not need to be so perfect,
for love is not static but always a flow,
demanding only we're willing to grow.

**Chamuel Archangel, descend from Above,
Chamuel Archangel, with ruby-pink love,
Chamuel Archangel, so often thought-of,
Chamuel Archangel, o come Holy Dove.**

Part 5

1. The purpose of the awakening phase is not that I attain complete control over what I can manifest materially. The purpose is that I come to the realization that I am a spiritual being, not a material being, and therefore my goals are not material.

Hilarion, on emerald shore,
we're free from all that's gone before.
Hilarion, we let all go,
that keeps us out of sacred flow.

**Hilarion, with light so green,
we see behind the matter screen,
immaculate our inner sight,
we see the earth is taking flight.**

2. It is not the real goal in my Divine plan to manifest certain material conditions in this lifetime. My real goal is to demonstrate the path to Christhood where I become independent of material conditions.

Hilarion, the secret key,
is wisdom's own reality.
Hilarion, all life is healed,
the ego's face no more concealed.

**Hilarion, with light so green,
we see behind the matter screen,
immaculate our inner sight,
we see the earth is taking flight.**

3. I surrender the belief that if I attain the highest state of spiritual consciousness, then I will be able to completely control matter and manifest any material condition I desire.

Hilarion, your love for life,
helps us surrender inner strife.
Hilarion, your loving words,
thrill our hearts like song of birds.

**Hilarion, with light so green,
we see behind the matter screen,
immaculate our inner sight,
we see the earth is taking flight.**

4. I see that focusing on manifesting material conditions reinforces a subconscious matrix that closes my mind to the vision in my Divine plan. The key to vision is not concentration but openness.

> Hilarion, invoke the light,
> your sacred formulas recite.
> Hilarion, your secret tone,
> philosopher's most sacred stone.
>
> **Hilarion, with light so green,**
> **we see behind the matter screen,**
> **immaculate our inner sight,**
> **we see the earth is taking flight.**

5. I want to open myself to my own I AM Presence and the vision in my Divine plan. In order to do this, I am willing to see the limitations of my approach to the spiritual path.

> Hilarion, with love you greet,
> us in your temple over Crete.
> Hilarion, your emerald light,
> the third eye sees with Christic sight.
>
> **Hilarion, with light so green,**
> **we see behind the matter screen,**
> **immaculate our inner sight,**
> **we see the earth is taking flight.**

6. I am willing to surrender everything that has brought me to this point on my path because I realize that it cannot take me beyond it.

Hilarion, you give us fruit,
of truth that is so absolute.
Hilarion, all stress decrease,
as our ambitions we release.

**Hilarion, with light so green,
we see behind the matter screen,
immaculate our inner sight,
we see the earth is taking flight.**

7. I am at the point of openness where I say: "What is my next step? What is it that I have not done before that I need to do? What is it that I have not seen before that I need to see?"

Hilarion, our chakras clear,
as we let go of subtlest fear.
Hilarion, we are sincere,
as freedom's truth we do revere.

**Hilarion, with light so green,
we see behind the matter screen,
immaculate our inner sight,
we see the earth is taking flight.**

8. I am willing to take a look at the spiritual practice I have been doing and then ask: "If I was to stop this right now, how would I react?" The more intense my reaction to this question, the more severe my attachment to my practice.

Hilarion, you balance all,
the seven rays upon our call.
Hilarion, you keep us true,
as we remain all one with you.

> **Hilarion, with light so green,
> we see behind the matter screen,
> immaculate our inner sight,
> we see the earth is taking flight.**

9. The stronger the attachment, the more it will prevent me from seeing a new vision. Yet I want that higher vision more than I want to hold on to the old vision.

> Hilarion, your Presence here,
> filling up the inner sphere.
> Life is now a sacred flow,
> God Vision we on all bestow.

> **Hilarion, with light so green,
> we see behind the matter screen,
> immaculate our inner sight,
> we see the earth is taking flight.**

Part 6

1. I realize I am at the point where I need to give up my practice, meaning UP to my I AM Presence. I say to my I AM Presence: "OK, I am giving UP this focus in my outer mind of what I think I should be doing and I am willing to be completely open and listen to you. Show me what I need to be doing in order to go higher on the path."

9 | Invoking a Higher Vision of My Motivation

> Master Paul, venetian dream,
> your love for beauty's flowing stream.
> Master Paul, in love's own womb,
> your power shatters ego's tomb.
>
> **Master Paul, your love so true,**
> **and therefore we apply to you,**
> **to set all free in the great love,**
> **that you are shining from Above.**

2. The path to Christhood requires me to do this over and over again. Give UP the vision I have right now in order to receive a higher vision.

> Master Paul, your counsel wise,
> our minds are raised to lofty skies.
> Master Paul, in wisdom's love,
> such beauty flowing from Above.
>
> **Master Paul, your love so true,**
> **and therefore we apply to you,**
> **to set all free in the great love,**
> **that you are shining from Above.**

3. I fix in my conscious mind this principle of giving UP what I see with the outer mind, with the conscious mind, what I am focused on. I give UP the matrices in the subconscious mind.

> Master Paul, love is an art,
> it opens up the secret heart.
> Master Paul, love's rushing flow,
> our hearts awash in sacred glow.

> **Master Paul, your love so true,**
> **and therefore we apply to you,**
> **to set all free in the great love,**
> **that you are shining from Above.**

4. I do not wish to continue my spiritual path by going through it the hard way of having shocking awakening experiences over and over. Instead, I cultivate the willingness to step back and ask for the vision: "What is the limitation, what is the higher vision?"

> Master Paul, accelerate,
> upon pure love we meditate.
> Master Paul, intentions pure,
> our self-transcendence will ensure.

> **Master Paul, your love so true,**
> **and therefore we apply to you,**
> **to set all free in the great love,**
> **that you are shining from Above.**

5. I want to become conscious of my real motivation for walking the path, the motivation that is in my Divine plan for this lifetime.

> Master Paul, your love will heal,
> our inner light you do reveal.
> Master Paul, all life console,
> with you we're being truly whole.

9 | Invoking a Higher Vision of My Motivation

**Master Paul, your love so true,
and therefore we apply to you,
to set all free in the great love,
that you are shining from Above.**

6. I ask you, Hilarion, and I ask you, my I AM Presence, to show me my real motivation for walking the path, what it is I truly desire to accomplish in this lifetime.

Master Paul, you serve the All,
by helping us transcend the fall.
Master Paul, in peace we rise,
as ego meets its sure demise.

**Master Paul, your love so true,
and therefore we apply to you,
to set all free in the great love,
that you are shining from Above.**

7. I ask to see the limitation I am dealing with right now, the matrix in the subconscious mind that I am dealing with right now. I ask to see the higher vision that will take me beyond that limitation so that I can let the limitation go without feeling I have to force myself, I have to destroy it or I have to blame myself.

Master Paul, love all life free,
your love is for eternity.
Master Paul, you are the One,
to help us make the journey fun.

> **Master Paul, your love so true,**
> **and therefore we apply to you,**
> **to set all free in the great love,**
> **that you are shining from Above.**

8. I realize that because I am at Hilarion's retreat, it is a given that I have a lower vision. There is no shame in seeing this and I am willing to see it because, as Hilarion, I am focused on getting a higher vision.

> Master Paul, you balance all,
> the seven rays upon our call.
> Master Paul, you paint the sky,
> with colors that delight the I.

> **Master Paul, your love so true,**
> **and therefore we apply to you,**
> **to set all free in the great love,**
> **that you are shining from Above.**

9. Seeing that I have a limited vision is the tool that helps me move on. I do not resist it. I have enough love to see a limitation and love myself free of it. I am locked in to the love-based vision in my Divine plan.

> Master Paul, your Presence here,
> filling up the inner sphere.
> Life is now a sacred flow,
> God Love we do on all bestow.

**Master Paul, your love so true,
and therefore we apply to you,
to set all free in the great love,
that you are shining from Above.**

Sealing:

In the name of the Divine Mother, I fully accept that the power of these calls is used to set free the River of Life, so it can outpicture the perfect vision of Christ for my own life, for all people and for the planet. In the name I AM THAT I AM, it is done! Amen.

10 | HOW TO STOP PROJECTING OUT

I AM the Ascended Master Hilarion. What do you encounter when you get to the fourth level at my retreat? You encounter the need to deal with another subtle illusion, another very difficult illusion, another very difficult initiation. I have previously talked about the fact that it is possible to have been on the spiritual path for many years, even to have studied ascended master teachings for many years, and still have certain illusions about what the path is all about.

Now, my beloved, you can look at this in two ways. You know the old story, of course, of whether the glass is half full or half empty. Likewise, you have spiritual students who have a certain attitude that if they encounter a situation where they feel that they have harbored an illusion or done something that was not the highest possible, then they tend to look at this from the negative and see that they have done something wrong. There may be certain feelings associated with this, such as fear, shame or guilt.

There may be other students who look at it more positively and see that it is good that they now see that they have so far held on to an illusion. Because this sets them free to move to a higher level of the path. This last attitude is, of course, what I wish all of you to achieve when you reach this level of my retreat.

An illusion for each of the 144 steps

If you step back and look at the spiritual path, you can see that we have told you that there are 144 levels before you are ready to ascend. We have also told you that at each of these levels, there is a certain state of consciousness that is associated with that level. Built into the state of consciousness at any given level is a certain illusion. It is not that this is necessarily a negative illusion.

When you are below the 48th level of consciousness, you hold certain illusions that affirm the idea that you are a separate being and that you can either get away with doing things to others or that you have a right to do things to other people. When you go above the 48th level, you go into a different kind of illusions that are more geared towards holding yourself at a certain level. These are not necessarily aggressive or destructive illusions, and therefore there is no particular reason to feel negative about having them.

You could say that it is completely inevitable that at your current level of consciousness you cannot see through the illusion associated with that level. If you had seen through the illusion, you would have ascended to the next level up. You could look at the spiritual path as simply a process where you step-by-step come to see, and therefore let go of and overcome, certain illusions.

10 | How to Stop Projecting out

This could be said to be what the path is all about, and therefore you can come to a point where you are not looking at this as a negative. You are not having any reluctance to see the illusion. You are open; you are willing to see the illusion. You are, in fact, looking for what is the next illusion: "What is the illusion at this step that I need to overcome?" Then, when you begin to see it, you rejoice in the fact that you are now seeing it and therefore it is almost like a sporting game.

You have these computer games where you are walking through underground worlds and various monsters jump out at you and you shoot them. You could look at the path the same way: You are walking and at any level there is a certain illusion and when that illusion jumps out at you, it is a chance to see it, to really look at it, to see through it and then to let it go and overcome it.

Making the path easier for yourself

If you can adopt this attitude, then the rest of this course and the rest of the path until you are ready to ascend will become much easier for you. You do not have to go into the inevitable reaction of the ego (or the dweller on the threshold), which will seek to make you attached to the illusion you have at any level.

Just imagine, my beloved, having to go through all of the illusions between your present level and the 144th level of consciousness and fighting the ego and the dweller on each step. Why would you want to do that if you can make it easier for yourself by stepping back and adopting the attitude that the path really is about seeing and overcoming one illusion at a time? Just as it is relatively innocent to play a computer game, where you work your way through different levels, then it is the same with the path on earth where everything in a sense is like a virtual environment that you see in a computer game. I am not saying thereby that there are not more serious consequences of what people do on earth than there is in a computer game. Nevertheless, you can avoid going into a negative reaction. I hope you get the point that there comes that level of the path where you need to stop taking the initiations so seriously that each step becomes a big burden and a big drama for you to go through.

What is truth?

Now, at this particular level of my retreat, what is the illusion we are dealing with? Well, there are many ascended master students (some who have studied our teachings for decades) who have adopted the belief – and it is an understandable belief – that our teachings are giving you the truth; the highest truth. You know, of course, that one aspect of the Fifth Ray is truth. As Pontius Pilate said to Jesus: "What is truth?" This is indeed a question that many students have not fully considered and that you need to consider at this level.

What is truth? Let us step back a moment and ask a different question: "Is there such a thing as truth?" Built into most people's concept of truth is that there is also an untruth, there is a lie. You have truth contrasted with a lie and what is that? Two opposites that are linked together, well, my beloved that is duality, is it not?

Now, I know, of course, that the dualistic mind can take any state and create a new situation where there are two opposites. We can say that there *is* such a thing as a non-dualistic truth. It is there. In the ascended realm, we know truth. I am on the Fifth Ray and I very well know what is truth because I experience truth as a living reality, as a spiritual flame, all the time. The truth that I experience at the ascended level does not have an opposite. It is not in contrast with an opposite. It is not in contrast with untruth or a lie.

What you need to recognize at this level of my retreat is that there is a difference between a non-dualistic truth and a dualistic truth. A dualistic truth has an opposite, and so you realize that what the vast majority of human beings on earth see as truth is indeed a dualistic concept because it has an opposite. You will see, for example, that the followers of most of the world's religions and most of the world's New Age gurus, think that their particular organization has the truth, the highest spiritual teaching, and all the others are lower or even the opposite of truth.

The difference between truth and The Truth

Well, my beloved, at this level there is no such thing as truth. You may think that if you look at all of the world's religions and spiritual philosophies, you can set them up on a scale and say some have a lower degree of truth and some have a higher degree of truth. I will not deny that this can be done because there are, of course, some philosophies out there that are more directly created by the fallen beings and therefore incorporate much more of their subtle illusions.

You need to recognize here that even a teaching that is entirely created by the fallen beings still has some concepts in it that most spiritual people would see as true. If there was no such thing, then people would not be fooled by the teaching. The fallen beings are not creating a teaching where everything is wrong or everything is a lie. They are creating a teaching where there is a high degree of what you might call truth, but there are some erroneous concepts mixed in. People accept the teaching because of what they recognize as being valid, and then they also accept the erroneous concepts and this takes them onto the false path.

Now, you see, my beloved, already from this (if you are paying attention) that even I, as an ascended master, find it difficult to use the word "truth" without going into a dualistic evaluation where you contrast it with something that is untruth. Let us put that aside for now. What I want to focus on here is that if you took all of these spiritual and religious philosophies and did create a scale of how much truth they contain, then ascended master students would tend to say that the teachings of the ascended masters, given through a sponsored messenger as dictations, have the highest degree of truth. Now, this is both true and untrue.

It is true, of course, that our teachings are given entirely for the purpose of setting you free. They do not contain any deliberate errors that can trip you up, as the teachings given by the fallen beings. Nevertheless, you need to recognize that even though what we are giving you is a true teaching, we are not giving you (and we are not attempting to give you) "The Truth." Let us make a distinction here, subtle as it may be, between *truth* and *The Truth*.

Truth is a general concept. Something can be more or less true. Floating around in the collective consciousness is the concept that there is something that is "The Truth." The idea is that there is a teaching that is the highest, that is an absolute truth. You will see, for example, that many Christians look at the Bible as the absolute infallible Word of God. To them, the Bible is "The Truth" the absolute highest revelation that could possibly be given on this planet.

10 | How to Stop Projecting out

The masters do not give The Truth

My beloved, the last thing that we of the ascended masters want is for our students to look at our teachings, even given through a sponsored messenger, the same way as fundamentalist Christians look at the Bible. If you do this, you will miss the entire point of our teachings. We are not attempting to give you "The Truth," an absolute highest teaching that therefore will be perfect and will stand for all time and will never need to be expounded upon or expanded. This is not our aim. What is our aim?

Our aim is to meet you at the level of consciousness where you are able to grasp our teaching (any aspect of our teaching), and then to offer you what helps you step up higher. We are not seeking to give a teaching that is an absolute, infallible and never-changing truth. We are always seeking to help you move on as an individual so that you can reach the 144th level and qualify for your ascension. We are also seeking to raise the collective consciousness, and you need to recognize a very simple fact. At the present level of the collective consciousness there is a limit to what we of the ascended masters can bring forth even through a sponsored messenger.

We do not have complete freedom to say absolutely anything because if we said something that was too high for the collective consciousness, very few people would be able to grasp it. We are not in this age seeking to reach only the few individuals. We are not seeking to reach everybody either, but we are seeking to reach a broader range of people than we have sought to reach previously. Even if you look at the organizations we have sponsored within the last century, you can see how, in the beginning, we brought forth a teaching that was very difficult to grasp, in a somewhat archaic language, and therefore it only appealed to a few people. Then, we have gradually brought forth teachings that are more easy to grasp and therefore can appeal to larger numbers of people. This, of course, we will continue to do as the collective consciousness is raised.

As the consciousness is raised, we can do two things. First of all, we can bring forth a higher teaching than we have brought forth before, but we can also, as the Omega aspect, bring forth a teaching that can reach a wider audience. We will, of course, continue to do both things as the collective consciousness is raised over the next decades or even centuries, as we move further and further into the Golden Age.

Consider your involvement with organizations

What you need to recognize at this level of my retreat is that it is not our goal to bring forth "The Truth." Everything we do has one purpose and that is to help people at a particular level of consciousness transcend that level of consciousness and move higher. It is important that you consider this with your conscious mind.

When you come to my retreat in your finer bodies, you cannot move on to the next level until you get this. It is important that this realization (which you can fairly easily get at the etheric level) filters down to your conscious mind. It is also important that you are willing, at the conscious level, to take a critical look at the involvement you have had with spiritual teachings up until this point.

I know that this can for some people be difficult, even painful. It is necessary that you go through the pain of looking at yourself and your approach to the path, making the necessary adjustments. When you make those adjustments, I can assure you that you will feel free—free from a burden that has been weighing you down all the time you have been walking the path. You will feel so much lighter, and then you will be ready to embrace an entirely new approach to the spiritual path.

Why there is no absolute truth

Now, my beloved, let us again look at the concept of "The Truth." I have said that we are not seeking to bring forth an absolute teaching because it could not reach people at their current level of consciousness and at the current level of the collective consciousness. This is only part of the reason we are not seeking to bring forth an absolute teaching. The other part of the reason is that we realize that it is impossible to bring forth an absolute teaching in an unascended sphere.

Earth is, of course, by no means the highest planet in your material universe. There are planets where the consciousness is much higher than it is on earth. Therefore, we can bring forth something that is a much higher form of truth than what could possibly be brought forth on earth. Still, as long as the sphere is unascended, it is not an absolute truth that will never change. In fact, you could say that there *is* no absolute truth that never changes because in the ascended realm there is also constant progress, constant growth, constant self-transcendence. As the entire universe is raising itself, transcending itself, truth keeps moving up. Truth is also transcendental and is transformed as the consciousness is raised. This goes on until you reach the level of the Creator Consciousness. What you need to do at the conscious level is to look at this and realize that if you have so far approached the spiritual path with a desire to find the absolute truth, then you need to let go of that desire because it is a millstone around your neck that will hold you back. It should not be, at this level, a goal for you to think that at some point the clouds will part and you will have this inner revelation of the absolute truth. The clouds may indeed part, and you may have an inner experience of the spiritual realm. As we have said many times, the Conscious you can actually step outside of your four lower bodies and experience the I AM Presence; experience higher levels of consciousness, even the spiritual realm. You can even experience the Creator itself as a state of pure Being. What you will recognize, if you have had such mystical experiences, is that they are beyond words. If you try to describe them with words, well, you degrade the experience.

Truth cannot be brought through words

We have used the example before that if you meet a person who has never tasted an apple, it is very difficult to describe the taste of an apple through words because it is a total experience. My point here is that it is impossible to bring forth, through words, The Truth.

You cannot bring forth an absolute truth through words. I have talked about planets that have a higher level of collective consciousness, but it also means that the people on those planets are not communicating through words, or at least not exclusively through words. This means that we can bring forth something that is a more holistic teaching that involves aspects that are non-verbal, and this allows us to give people more of an experience of truth.

You understand that what we would like to achieve is to bring you to a point where you have mystical experiences. You realize that there is a higher experience than could ever be communicated through words. We would like you to have that experience and this is our aim when you come to our retreats. It is also our hope that these books and the teachings and invocations will open your mind (the four levels of your mind) so you can have these experiences. Words are just a means to an end, the means to having the experience itself.

How to deal with mystical experiences

Now, of course, we come to another subtle illusion that you need to see. I have talked about fundamentalist Christians who believe the Bible is the Word of God. If you go into the minds of some of these people, you will see that there are indeed some people who are firmly convinced about this because they have had what you would call a mystical experience. They have had an experience where their consciousness was raised beyond their ordinary level and they suddenly "saw" that the Bible is the Word of God or that Jesus is the only road to salvation. They experienced this as a total inner experience that for them was overwhelming and that felt for them completely real.

How is it possible, my beloved, (when you know that the Bible is not the literal Word of God) to have an experience where you feel that the Bible is the Word of God and that this experience is completely real to you? Well, it is possible for the simple reason that you are at a certain level of consciousness on the scale of the 144 levels. As I said, on each level there is a certain illusion that is associated with that level. It is possible for you to step outside of that illusion to see something higher, and when you do this, what you see that is beyond the illusion will feel real to you. Throughout the ages, millions of people have had mystical experiences. These experiences, my beloved, have for the most part been genuine mystical experiences. They have shown people something that felt completely real to them. The reality of the matter is that it felt real to them because it reached beyond their current level of consciousness. It did not show them the absolute, highest reality that could ever be reached.

The illusion of an absolute truth in history

The problem is that at the lower levels of consciousness, you cannot see this. Serapis Bey did not tell you this in the same way I am telling you this because you were not ready to see this while you were attending his retreat. At the fourth level in my retreat, you are ready to see this and to see it with your conscious mind. That is why I am telling you this. You see, my beloved, right now you are holding on to a certain illusion, and it may very well be the illusion that there must be some highest truth. You are ready to see beyond this illusion.

Let us, as the next step, look at what this illusion has produced in world history. Right now, as I am speaking this, you have in the Middle East a movement called ISIS or IS. These are extremist Muslims who are feeling it completely justified to kill all non-Muslims, even to kill other Muslims that they do not consider to be following the only true path. Now, most people can, of course, see this as an expression of fanaticism. Many people in the West are wondering: How can these people believe in this, how can they act like this? You understand that most of the people who are acting like this do so because they have had an inner experience that for them felt completely real. This inner experience validated the beliefs that it is necessary to spread Islam, even with violence and that God will indeed reward them for doing so. Look throughout the history of the world and see how many times people have gone to war with this fanatical mindset of believing that a certain cause is so important that it justifies the killing of other human beings. My beloved, this has happened over and over and over again. Now, I know, of course, that you have risen above this level where you think it is justifiable to kill in order to promote a certain cause. What I am asking you to do now is to take that final step of letting go of the last seeds of this fanatical consciousness. This is where you, at the conscious level, realize and recognize that there is absolutely no cause on earth that justifies the killing of other human beings.

Truth, my beloved, is not worth dying for and it is not worth killing for. The reason for this is simple. Truth is a concept that is dependent on your current state of consciousness. As long as you are on earth, and indeed even in the ascended realm, it is always possible to raise your consciousness and grasp a higher expression of truth than what you can currently grasp.

Taking life (or even taking your own life by going into war with a fanatical mindset and getting yourself killed) is an absolute act in the sense that it permanently aborts the particular opportunity that an individual life represents. Sure, the soul does not die and can come back into embodiment, but it can never come back into embodiment in the exact same outer circumstances. Therefore, the particular opportunity represented by that life is permanently aborted when a person is killed. Truth on the other hand is not absolute, is not permanent, so you see: How can defending a non-permanent truth justify taking a permanent, absolute measure of killing someone?

Overcoming fanaticism

There are ascended master students who have held on to the belief for decades that somehow the ends can justify the means. Yes, they can see that during the Nazi times or during Communist times, those particular causes did not justify the killing. They still think that there might be some cause that is so important that it could justify the killing of other human beings. My beloved, this simply is not the case. You need to consciously see this, consciously let go of the illusion because, as I said, it is a millstone around your neck. It is an inroad for the fallen beings to manipulate you in very subtle ways. You just cannot go beyond this level of the path until you consciously let go of this belief.

Fanaticism has had some very obvious expressions on this planet. Of course, these clearly fanatical movements, such as Nazism or Communism, have been started by the fallen beings. As we have attempted to explain to you, there are different levels of fallen beings. Some are more primitive and some are indeed more subtle. You remember, of course, that even the Bible says that the serpent was the most subtle of the beasts. You see that fanaticism in a more obvious form, such as ISIS, Nazism or Communism, has always been started by the more primitive fallen beings. You can look at Hitler and you can see that even though he had great charisma, he was not really a great thinker. This is the case with, for example, Lenin, Marx or some of the other people who have started fanatical movements. They are not great thinkers, and they are not great thinkers because they fall prey to the fanatical mindset, which blinds you.

You see, my beloved, if you step back from these obvious expressions of fanaticism, there is a psychological mechanism behind them. It is this psychological mechanism that the more sophisticated fallen beings are very clever at making use of. When you have a very obvious expression of fanaticism, such as Nazism, then the subtle fallen beings will use this to say that this actually defines fanaticism. Other forms of human behavior or other belief systems that are not as extreme as Nazism, they are not fanatical. What I wish to do here is to expand your conscious recognition that fanaticism is far more subtle and far more widespread than you have ever imagined up until this point.

Falling in love with ideas

What is fanaticism? Well, the most common, the most widespread, form of fanaticism is being in love. When you are in love with another human being, what happens? Well, you have a clearly distorted view of the situation. You have a distorted view of the other person. You see only what validates your belief that this is the ideal partner for you and you refuse to see anything to the contrary. Well, this is, in its essence, the psychological mechanism that follows from being in love. You emphasize the things that validate your basic view of the situation and you ignore or reject the things that do not validate your view of the situation. This is the psychological mechanism behind fanaticism.

Now, we need to take this a step further and recognize that human beings have a tendency to fall in love with ideas. This is something you need to ponder very carefully with your conscious mind. When you are going through this initiation at my retreat, it is fairly easy for most people to get this at the level of their identity body. There are many people who find it difficult to let it filter through to the conscious mind because you have yourself been in love with an idea. It is very likely that most of the people who will read this book have followed the spiritual path up to this point because they have been in love with certain ideas.

Now, what did I start out by saying? At any level of the path there are certain illusions that are necessary. This is what defines that level. Again, there is nothing wrong with your approach up until this point. I am not trying to make you feel that what you have done so far has been completely wrong and that you therefore need to feel bad about this. On the contrary, I am simply trying to help you see that in order to go higher, there is another illusion that needs to be left behind. It needs to be left behind consciously in order for you to actually go to the next level. This is the case at any level of the path.

The real issue here is that the fallen beings have managed to insert this very idea into the collective consciousness. They have done this a very, very long time ago when they came to this planet. Before they came to this planet, they had done it on other planets, even in other spheres. Therefore, they themselves are firmly convinced that their approach is correct. You, of course, are a spiritual student. You are walking the path of self-mastery and if you are to master the self, you need to overcome this illusion.

The most dangerous illusion about ideas

What is the illusion? The illusion, my beloved, is that the universe functions according to ideas that can be grasped by the dualistic mind. The fallen beings have entered duality. They are not aware that they have entered duality. *Take care to listen to what I am saying.*

I have said that there are certain fallen beings that are very sophisticated, very subtle. If you were, even as an ascended master student, to encounter such a fallen being and start reasoning with it, you would find, as even Jesus had to admit, that you cannot out-reason the fallen beings. If you go into their line of reasoning, where they are using the linear, analytical, dualistic mind, you cannot out-reason them. They have such a long momentum on this that you cannot out-reason them. You cannot make them see that their reasoning is limited. They will always find some way to negate any argument you can come up with. If you try to out-reason them, you only involve yourself more and more in that mindset.

My point for bringing this up is to help you realize that there is no purpose in arguing about this. There is no point in reasoning about this, and the explanation for this is that every self-aware being has its own view of the world. A fallen being is looking at the world from a certain perspective. It sees the world through a certain perception filter, as I explained previously and as we have explained many times.

You may be able to present arguments to that fallen being, and to you, your arguments may seem entirely convincing. It may be completely obvious to you that the fallen being's arguments are wrong, contradictory and are not as good as your arguments. The reason this is obvious to you is that you are looking at the arguments through the filter of *your* consciousness, but the fallen being is not looking at the argument through the filter of your consciousness, it is looking at it through the filter of *its own* consciousness. Therefore, it does not see what you see.

It is futile to try to force other people to see what you see. You cannot ever force another being to see what you see because the being can never look at the situation from inside *your* mind. It will look at it from inside *its own* mind. Why do you need to understand this consciously? Because you need to take a look at your life and then you need to look at how you have possibly, during your life, attempted to force your ideas upon other people.

Forcing ideas upon other people

You will know that in the old days they were talking about a concept called the "evil eye." There were people who believed that certain people had the ability to look at another person and put a curse upon them, and then that person would experience some misfortune. There were times when there were people who were stoned or burned at the stake for putting the evil eye on someone. You can find many parts of the world where it is still believed that this is happening, and even parts of the world where people are still killed or ostracized from society because someone thinks they have put the evil eye on others.

There is some underlying reality here. I am not saying that these primitive people are entirely right or that it was justifiable to persecute others because of this. What I am saying is that all human beings have the ability, as I have said, to use vision as an active force where they are projecting their vision upon other people. This can be done with such psychic energy that it actually affects the identity, mental and emotional bodies of other people so that it also affects them at the physical level.

This, of course, is something that you need to stop doing at this point of the path. You need to be willing to take an honest look at your life and see if you have done this. Then, you need to be willing to admit this without putting yourself down for having done this. Again, what else could you do? What else can you do at these lower levels of consciousness on a planet like earth? It is not really a matter of what you have done. The real issue is: What are you going to do from this point forward? That is what I am interested in. I do not, at my retreat, take you into a room and confront you with everything you have done wrong in the past. I may give you a few insights into what you have done so you can see the necessity to transcend it, and so that you can begin to look for the underlying mechanism behind it.

What is the mechanism behind projecting a certain vision upon other people? Well, it is this consciousness introduced by the fallen beings of falling in love with ideas and beginning to think that the universe works according to your ideas. Or rather, the real issue is when you begin to think that the universe *should* work according to your ideas. This is what causes the fanatical mindset. People fall in love with an idea, they think that if only the universe worked according to that idea, everything would be harmony, everything would be paradise on earth. Then, they look at the reality of what is happening in the world and they see that currently the world is not functioning according to their idea.

Now at this point, my beloved, what ideally should happen is that people should say: "Wait a minute, if I can observe that the world is not working according to my idea, could it be that I need to revise my ideas so that they can explain how the world actually works instead of holding on to an ideal of how it *should* work?" Most people do not do this, and this is, again, a process created by the fallen beings over a very long period of time. People have been robbed of the idea, the concept, that they need to revise their idea when it does not conform to observation.

What do people do instead? They go into the fanatical mindset and they say: "The reason the world is not functioning according to my idea is that these other people are not behaving according to my idea. Therefore, it is my job to make those other people behave according to my idea and then we will have paradise on earth."

This is the essence of the fanatical mindset. It is not very far from the state that most people experience as being in love. It is *not* very far. You need to come to the point where you realize that you have had a tendency to approach the spiritual path based on this pattern. You have had a certain idea of how the spiritual path should work and you have attempted to force yourself to conform to this idea. You may also have attempted to force other people to conform to that idea.

This ends here

I am asking you to do two things at the conscious level. I am asking you, after you give the invocation associated with this chapter, to take some time to look at your life and say: "How have I attempted to force my idea of the spiritual path upon other people?" You can, of course, ask for my help to see this at the conscious level. I can assure you that you do this in your higher bodies at my retreat. In my retreat you are able to do this without any pain, without any resistance, without any reluctance.

I am sitting down with you and I am bringing you to a point where you are in a state of mind where you are ready to see this. Then, we look at it and then you see it. When you see it, you do not feel bad, you do not blame yourself. You simply say: "This ends here. *This ends here.* It ends right now. I see what I have been doing and I am not doing it anymore."

This is a shift, and when you can have that shift at the conscious level, then you have passed the initiation at this level of my retreat. The initiation at this level is really to stop projecting your vision of truth upon other people or the world outside of you. This is the initiation you are facing. I need you to consciously consider this because you cannot move on in this

10 | How to Stop Projecting out

course of self-mastery until you stop projecting your vision outside your own mind.

What the path is all about

You see, my beloved, what is the spiritual path all about? We have talked about an immersion phase and an awakening phase. What do you do when you immerse yourself? In order to take embodiment on earth, we have said that you start out at the 48th level of consciousness. What are you doing when you are first descending into embodiment on earth?

You are in the etheric realm, the identity realm. Your I AM Presence has generated the Conscious You out of itself. It is now sending you down to a point where you can take physical embodiment in an unascended sphere, on a planet with the density of matter that the earth had at the time.

What do you have to do to get to the point where you can actually enter a physical body? Well, the Conscious You cannot enter the physical body directly. It has to create a vehicle, which is the four lower bodies, the soul vehicle. How do you create this vehicle? Well, you first go to the 144th level. Then, you, so to speak, take on the illusion associated with that level. Then, you go to the 143rd level, take on the next illusion, then the 142nd level, take on the next illusion. You continue taking on illusion after illusion until you reach the 48th level.

What are the illusions you are taking on? They are illusions that make it seem believable that you are actually a human being in a physical body on earth. You see, there are all of these illusions necessary in order to give you the sense of reality that you are a human being.

I earlier talked about the fact that you can have a mystical experience where you see something beyond your present level of consciousness and this seems completely real to you. Well, when you are descending into embodiment, you are simply reversing that process. You are having an un-mystical experience that makes it seem completely real to you that you are a human being in embodiment on earth. This is the immersion phase; this is the immersion experience. The idea is, of course, that you immerse yourself in what life on earth has to offer. You have the kind of experiences you can have on this planet until you have had enough of this and begin to long for something more.

You start out at the 48th level of consciousness and you have the option to start going up from there or go down below the 48th level. When you go below the 48th level, what do you do? Well, you take on further illusions. As we have said before, the illusion you start to take on is that it is acceptable and justifiable that you use force. It is acceptable that you seek to force other people, that you seek to force the physical universe to comply with your ideas.

What does it take to awaken yourself? Well, it takes that you reverse the process and now (illusion by illusion) you start working your way back up. You shed one illusion, you reach a higher level of consciousness, then you shed the next illusion and so on.

You are following this course of self-mastery. You are not at the highest level of consciousness. You are not ready to ascend. Therefore, you have many illusions left that you need to shed before you can ascend. There is nothing unnatural about it. It is simply how life in an unascended sphere works.

You need to recognize this consciously so you can see that it is time, at this level, to stop projecting out your vision of truth; to stop projecting it on other people and to stop projecting it even on matter itself. You need to adopt the attitude consciously that you are willing to see beyond your current vision of truth. You are willing to see beyond your idea of how you think the world should work. You are willing to look at how the world actually works. When you see a difference between your idea of the world and the actual behavior of the world, you are willing to say: "Then I need to adjust my idea. It is my idea that is incomplete."

Seeking to make the world conform to ideas

Now, here we, of course, run into another subtlety. It is an extremely difficult subtlety to overcome for many people. The longer they have been on the spiritual path, the more difficult it tends to be to overcome this illusion. You, of course, think that as you have walked the spiritual path, as you have practiced various techniques, as you have studied spiritual teachings (even ascended master teachings) you have gradually raised your vision, your grasp of truth. You think that, therefore, what you see now is a much higher truth than what you could see ten or twenty years ago. This is true—of course it is. But it is not an ultimate truth, my beloved.

There is still a higher truth beyond what you see right now. What you need to accept consciously is that you are willing to see that higher truth. You will not hold on to your present truth. You will not seek to validate it, you will not seek confirmation of it.

You need to consciously decide that you will stop using the ascended masters' teachings (or other spiritual teachings) as a justification for your current vision of truth. You need to be willing to see that higher truth. In order to see it, you need to be willing to look at where the world does not validate your current vision. Then, you need to recognize that it is your vision that needs to change, not the world and not other people. Seeking to change the world and other people is simply nothing more than an excuse for not being willing to change yourself, to change your own vision. It is *that* simple, my beloved!

There comes a point – and it is right *now* – where you need to confront this reality consciously. You need to see this. You need to see that there is an aspect of your psychology (call it the ego or the dweller on the threshold or an internal spirit) that will not let you transcend this desperate grasp of wanting the world to validate your truth.

This is what the fallen beings do not want you to do. They do not want you to overcome this one point. They are potentially screaming at you right now, using every influence they have to make you reject what I am saying and grasp on to some idea that: "Of course, there is a highest vision of what the world should be like because obviously the world is not the way it should be right now." You see, my beloved, the world is *exactly* the way it should be right now.

Why the world is as it should be

This does not mean that I am saying that some of the conditions that are taking place on earth are justifiable, are right or are true according to a higher perspective, a non-dualistic perspective. Of course, they are dualistic, but you understand what we have been saying in our teachings and in this course?

The earth is a learning institution. There are two ways to learn. Either you listen for the higher direction from the ascended masters or you enter the School of Hard Knocks. When you enter the School of Hard Knocks, you cannot learn by listening to the ascended masters or any other spiritual teacher. You must learn by seeing physical conditions outpicture your state of consciousness until you have so many hard knocks that you become willing to say: "Oh, is it my consciousness that needs to change so that I can stop experiencing these hard knocks?"

Do you understand what I am saying? The world, and everything that is going on in the world, is an out-picturing of the collective consciousness. This is exactly what it should be. It should be outpicturing the imbalances in the collective consciousness, and, of course, it is because the cosmic mirror is reflecting back what people are collectively projecting into it.

What you need to do as a spiritual student is to recognize that the world is exactly as it should be right now because it is outpicturing people's consciousness. Therefore, you look at the many things that are going on out there and you say: "It is not my job to use force to make the world or other people comply with the vision I have. My job is to raise my individual consciousness and attain self-mastery. I do not attain self-mastery by forcing other people or the world. I do not even attain self-mastery by forcing myself. I attain self-mastery by letting go of the next illusion. When I continue to let go of illusion after illusion, I will reach a state of consciousness where I have self-mastery. In fact, for every step I take up, for every illusion I overcome, I attain a higher degree of self-mastery because it is the illusion that takes away my self-mastery, not a lack of mastery."

Why the path is not mechanical

Again, as I said before, there are people who think that the spiritual path is a mechanical process of attaining certain abilities. Self-mastery could easily be construed to be just another ability that you attain. It is like an athlete who needs to perform a certain exercise and therefore keeps training the muscles until they become harder and harder and they can do it better than the other person. That is *not* the spiritual path.

It is not a matter of using force and forcing yourself to have some mastery. This is what I have said is the false path pursued by the fallen beings. Your path is the path of self-mastery by giving up, by surrendering, by letting go of the illusions.

Why do you, at this point, need to let go of the illusion that causes you to project your vision out? It is because, my beloved, before you can project anything *out* of your mind, you must first have projected that something *into* your mind, upon yourself. You can only project upon others when you have first projected upon yourself.

The next initiation at my retreat will be where you start seeing what you have projected upon yourself and how you have attempted to jump through all kinds of hoops in order to force yourself to conform to your vision of what it means to be a good spiritual student. I am sure you have had all you can handle at the conscious level in this installment.

I will give you time to digest this lesson before we go into the very next lesson, which for many becomes even more difficult than the one of seeing the need to stop projecting out. Projecting in is so much more subtle and so much more difficult to see. Therefore, it is, indeed, a critical initiation. I am sure that when you are willing and when you have followed the course until this point, then you *can* and you *will* pass this initiation also.

Hilarion I AM.

11 | I INVOKE FREEDOM FROM PROJECTING OUT

In the name I AM THAT I AM, Jesus Christ, I call to my I AM Presence to flow through the I Will Be Presence that I AM and give this invocation with full power. I call to beloved Elohim Cyclopea and Virginia and Purity and Astrea, Archangel Raphael and Mother Mary and Gabriel and Hope, Hilarion and Serapis Bey to help me see how I have attempted to force my idea of the spiritual path upon other people. Help me see and surrender all patterns that block my oneness with Hilarion and with my I AM Presence, including …

[Make personal calls]

Part 1

1. It is a positive when I come to see that I have so far held on to an illusion. This sets me free to move to a higher level of the path.

Cyclopea so dear, the truth you reveal,
the truth that duality's ailments will heal,
your Emerald Light is like a great balm,
our emotional bodies are perfectly calm.

**Cyclopea so dear, in Emerald Sphere,
in raising perception we shall persevere,
as deep in our hearts your truth we revere,
to immaculate vision the earth does adhere.**

2. I need to rise to the 144th level before I am ready to ascend. At each level, there is a certain state of consciousness associated with that level. Built into this state of consciousness is a certain illusion.

Cyclopea so dear, with you we unwind,
all negative spirals clouding the mind,
we know pure awareness is truly our core,
the key to becoming the wide-open door.

**Cyclopea so dear, in Emerald Sphere,
in raising perception we shall persevere,
as deep in our hearts your truth we revere,
to immaculate vision the earth does adhere.**

3. Above the 48th level, the illusions are not aggressive or destructive illusions, and therefore there is no reason to feel negative about having them.

Cyclopea so dear, clear our inner sight,
empowered, we pierce the soul's fearful night,
we now see our life through your single eye,
beyond all disease we're ready to fly.

> **Cyclopea so dear, in Emerald Sphere,
> in raising perception we shall persevere,
> as deep in our hearts your truth we revere,
> to immaculate vision the earth does adhere.**

4. It is inevitable that at my current level of consciousness I cannot see through the illusion associated with that level. If I had seen through the illusion, I would have ascended to the next level up.

> Cyclopea so dear, life can only reflect,
> the images that the mind does project,
> the key to our healing is clearing the mind,
> from the images the ego is hiding behind.

> **Cyclopea so dear, in Emerald Sphere,
> in raising perception we shall persevere,
> as deep in our hearts your truth we revere,
> to immaculate vision the earth does adhere.**

5. The spiritual path is a process where I step-by-step come to see, and therefore let go of and overcome, certain illusions. This is what the path is all about.

> Cyclopea so dear, we want to aim high,
> to your healing flame we ever draw nigh,
> through veils of duality we now take flight,
> bathed in your penetrating Emerald Light.

> **Cyclopea so dear, in Emerald Sphere,
> in raising perception we shall persevere,
> as deep in our hearts your truth we revere,
> to immaculate vision the earth does adhere.**

6. I am not looking at this as a negative. I am not having any reluctance to see the illusion. I am open; I am willing to see the illusion. I am looking for what is the next illusion: "What is the illusion at this step that I need to overcome?"

> Cyclopea so dear, your Emerald Flame,
> exposes every subtle, dualistic power game,
> including the game of wanting to say,
> that truth is defined in only one way.
>
> **Cyclopea so dear, in Emerald Sphere,**
> **in raising perception we shall persevere,**
> **as deep in our hearts your truth we revere,**
> **to immaculate vision the earth does adhere.**

7. I see that the path can be approached as a kind of game. I no longer take the initiations so seriously that each step becomes a big burden and a big drama for me to go through.

> Cyclopea so dear, we're feeling the flow,
> as your Living Truth upon us you bestow,
> from all dual vision we are now set free,
> planet earth in immaculate matrix will be.
>
> **Cyclopea so dear, in Emerald Sphere,**
> **in raising perception we shall persevere,**
> **as deep in our hearts your truth we revere,**
> **to immaculate vision the earth does adhere.**

8. Is there such a thing as truth? Built into most people's concept of truth is that there is also an untruth, there is a lie. Truth contrasted with a lie, two opposites that are linked together. This is duality.

> Cyclopea so dear, the truth is now clear,
> we see higher purpose for which we are here
> we know truth transcends all systems below,
> immersed in your light, we continue to grow.
>
> **Cyclopea so dear, in Emerald Sphere,
> in raising perception we shall persevere,
> as deep in our hearts your truth we revere,
> to immaculate vision the earth does adhere.**

9. There is a non-dualistic truth in the ascended realm. This truth must be experienced as a living reality, as a spiritual flame. This truth does not have an opposite. It is not in contrast with an opposite. It is not in contrast with untruth or a lie.

> Cyclopea so dear, we're feeling your joy,
> as creative vision we now do employ,
> in lifting earth out of serpentine cage,
> to manifest Saint Germain's Golden Age.
>
> **Cyclopea so dear, in Emerald Sphere,
> in raising perception we shall persevere,
> as deep in our hearts your truth we revere,
> to immaculate vision the earth does adhere.**

Part 2

1. There is a difference between a non-dualistic truth and a dualistic truth. A dualistic truth has an opposite. What most people see as truth is a dualistic concept because it has an opposite.

Beloved Astrea, your heart is so true,
your Circle and Sword of white and blue,
cut all life free from dramas unwise,
on wings of Purity our planet will rise.

**Beloved Astrea, in oneness with you,
your circle and sword of electric blue,
with Purity's Light cutting right through,
raising the earth into all that is true.**

2. I give up the belief that a particular organization has the truth, the highest spiritual teaching, and all the others are lower or even the opposite of truth.

Beloved Astrea, in God Purity,
accelerate all of our life energy,
we're rising beyond every impurity,
as Purity's Light forever we see.

**Beloved Astrea, in oneness with you,
your circle and sword of electric blue,
with Purity's Light cutting right through,
raising the earth into all that is true.**

3. Even a teaching that is entirely created by the fallen beings still has some concepts in it that most spiritual people would see as true. If there was no such thing, then people would not be fooled by the teaching.

Beloved Astrea, from Purity's Ray,
send forth deliverance to all life today,
acceleration to Purity, we are now free
from all that is less than love's Purity.

11 | I Invoke Freedom from Projecting Out

**Beloved Astrea, in oneness with you,
your circle and sword of electric blue,
with Purity's Light cutting right through,
raising the earth into all that is true.**

4. The fallen beings are not creating a teaching where everything is wrong or everything is a lie. They are creating a teaching where there is a high degree of what we might call truth, but there are some erroneous concepts mixed in.

Beloved Astrea, accelerate us all,
as for your deliverance we fervently call,
set all life free from vision impure
beyond fear and doubt, we're rising for sure.

**Beloved Astrea, in oneness with you,
your circle and sword of electric blue,
with Purity's Light cutting right through,
raising the earth into all that is true.**

5. Even though the ascended masters are giving a true teaching, they are not giving "The Truth." There is a distinction between truth and The Truth.

Beloved Astrea, we're willing to see,
all of the lies that keep us unfree,
we surrender all lies causing the fall,
forever affirming the oneness of All.

**Beloved Astrea, in oneness with you,
your circle and sword of electric blue,
with Purity's Light cutting right through,
raising the earth into all that is true.**

6. I surrender any tendency to look at the teachings of the ascended masters the same way as fundamentalist Christians look at the Bible. The masters are not attempting to give us "The Truth," an absolute highest teaching that will never be expanded.

> Beloved Astrea, accelerate life
> beyond all duality's struggle and strife,
> consume all division between God and man,
> accelerate fulfillment of God's perfect plan.
>
> **Beloved Astrea, in oneness with you,**
> **your circle and sword of electric blue,**
> **with Purity's Light cutting right through,**
> **raising the earth into all that is true.**

7. The aim of the masters is to meet us at our current level of consciousness and offer us what helps us step up higher.

> Beloved Astrea, we lovingly call,
> break down separation's invisible wall,
> raising our minds into true unity
> with the Masters of love in Infinity.
>
> **Beloved Astrea, in oneness with you,**
> **your circle and sword of electric blue,**
> **with Purity's Light cutting right through,**
> **raising the earth into all that is true.**

8. At the present level of the collective consciousness, there is a limit to what the ascended masters can bring forth even through a sponsored messenger.

> Beloved Astrea, help all of us find,
> the secret that we create with the mind,
> and thus what in ignorance we decreate,
> in knowledge we easily can recreate.
>
> **Beloved Astrea, in oneness with you,**
> **your circle and sword of electric blue,**
> **with Purity's Light cutting right through,**
> **raising the earth into all that is true.**

9. Everything the masters do has one purpose and that is to help people at a particular level of consciousness transcend that level of consciousness and move higher. I am willing to consider this with my conscious mind.

> Beloved Astrea, we all do aspire,
> to learning to use your purity's fire,
> to raise every form in infamy sown,
> as Saint Germain makes this planet his own.
>
> **Beloved Astrea, in oneness with you,**
> **your circle and sword of electric blue,**
> **with Purity's Light cutting right through,**
> **raising the earth into all that is true.**

Part 3

1. I am willing to take a critical look at the involvement I have had with spiritual teachings up until this point. I am willing to make the necessary adjustments and feel free from a burden that has been weighing me down as long as I have been walking the path.

> Raphael Archangel, your light so intense,
> raise us beyond all human pretense.
> Mother Mary and you have a vision so bold,
> to see that our highest potential unfold.
>
> **Raphael Archangel, for vision we pray,**
> **Raphael Archangel, show us the way,**
> **Raphael Archangel, your emerald ray,**
> **Raphael Archangel, our lives a new day.**

2. It is impossible to bring forth an absolute teaching in an unascended sphere. There is no absolute truth that never changes because in the ascended realm there is also constant self-transcendence.

> Raphael Archangel, in emerald sphere,
> to immaculate vision we always adhere.
> Mother Mary enfolds us in her Sacred Heart,
> from Mother's true love, we're never apart.
>
> **Raphael Archangel, for vision we pray,**
> **Raphael Archangel, show us the way,**
> **Raphael Archangel, your emerald ray,**
> **Raphael Archangel, our lives a new day.**

3. Truth is transcendental and is transformed as the consciousness is raised. This goes on until we reach the level of the Creator Consciousness.

> Raphael Archangel, all ailments you heal,
> each cell in our bodies in light now you seal.
> Mother Mary's immaculate concept we see,
> perfection of health our new reality.
>
> **Raphael Archangel, for vision we pray,**
> **Raphael Archangel, show us the way,**
> **Raphael Archangel, your emerald ray,**
> **Raphael Archangel, our lives a new day.**

4. I surrender all tendency to approach the spiritual path with a desire to find the absolute truth or to think that at some point the clouds will part and I will have this inner revelation of the absolute truth.

> Raphael Archangel, your light is so real,
> the vision of Christ in us you reveal.
> Mother Mary now helps us to truly transcend,
> in emerald light with you we ascend.
>
> **Raphael Archangel, for vision we pray,**
> **Raphael Archangel, show us the way,**
> **Raphael Archangel, your emerald ray,**
> **Raphael Archangel, our lives a new day.**

5. A mystical experience is beyond words. If I try to describe it with words, I degrade the experience. It is impossible to bring forth an absolute truth through words.

Raphael Archangel, diseases are done,
as you help us see that all life is One,
we no longer do your true love reject,
immaculate vision on all we project.

**Raphael Archangel, for vision we pray,
Raphael Archangel, show us the way,
Raphael Archangel, your emerald ray,
Raphael Archangel, our lives a new day.**

6. I am open to having a mystical experience, and I realize that there is a higher experience than could ever be communicated through words. Words are just a means to an end, the means to having the experience itself.

Raphael Archangel, we're healing the earth,
in immaculate vision we give her rebirth,
a new era has on this day begun,
your emerald light now shines like a sun.

**Raphael Archangel, for vision we pray,
Raphael Archangel, show us the way,
Raphael Archangel, your emerald ray,
Raphael Archangel, our lives a new day.**

7. For each of the 144 levels, there is a certain illusion that is associated with that level. It is possible to step outside of that illusion to see something higher. When we do this, what we see will feel real to us.

11 | I Invoke Freedom from Projecting Out

Raphael Archangel, the fall is behind,
as all of earth's people the Christ path do find,
we call now to you all people to heal,
as four lower bodies in love you do seal.

Raphael Archangel, for vision we pray,
Raphael Archangel, show us the way,
Raphael Archangel, your emerald ray,
Raphael Archangel, our lives a new day.

8. A mystical experience feels real because it reaches beyond our current level of consciousness. It does not show us the absolute, highest reality that could ever be reached. I surrender the illusion that there must be some highest truth. I am ready to see beyond this illusion.

Raphael Archangel, as you bring the light,
the forces of darkness swiftly take flight,
their day is now done as we claim the earth,
spreading to all an innocent mirth.

Raphael Archangel, for vision we pray,
Raphael Archangel, show us the way,
Raphael Archangel, your emerald ray,
Raphael Archangel, our lives a new day.

9. I am letting go of the last seeds of the fanatical consciousness. At the conscious level, I realize and recognize that there is absolutely no cause on earth that justifies the killing of other human beings.

Raphael Archangel, our vision set free,
as we can now see God's reality,
as Saint Germain's vision is manifest here,
the earth is now sealed in immaculate sphere.

Raphael Archangel, for vision we pray,
Raphael Archangel, show us the way,
Raphael Archangel, your emerald ray,
Raphael Archangel, our lives a new day.

Part 4

1. Truth is not worth dying for and it is not worth killing for.

    Gabriel Archangel, your light we revere,
    immersed in your Presence, nothing we fear.
    Disciples of Christ, we do leave behind,
    the ego's desire for responding in kind.

    Gabriel Archangel, of this we are sure,
    Gabriel Archangel, Christ light is the cure.
    Gabriel Archangel, intentions so pure,
    Gabriel Archangel, in you we're secure.

2. Truth is a concept that is dependent on our current state of consciousness. It is always possible to raise our consciousness and grasp a higher expression of truth than what we can currently grasp.

11 | I Invoke Freedom from Projecting Out

Gabriel Archangel, we fear not the light,
in purifications' fire, we delight.
With your hand in ours, each challenge we face,
we follow the spiral to infinite grace.

Gabriel Archangel, of this we are sure,
Gabriel Archangel, Christ light is the cure.
Gabriel Archangel, intentions so pure,
Gabriel Archangel, in you we're secure.

3. Taking life is an absolute act in the sense that it permanently aborts the particular opportunity that an individual life represents.

Gabriel Archangel, your fire burning white,
ascending with you, out of the night.
The ego has nowhere to run and to hide,
in ascension's bright spiral, with you we abide.

Gabriel Archangel, of this we are sure,
Gabriel Archangel, Christ light is the cure.
Gabriel Archangel, intentions so pure,
Gabriel Archangel, in you we're secure.

4. Truth is not absolute, is not permanent. Defending a non-permanent truth cannot justify taking a permanent, absolute measure of killing someone.

Gabriel Archangel, your trumpet we hear,
announcing the birth of Christ drawing near.
In lightness of being, we now are reborn,
rising with Christ on bright Easter morn.

> **Gabriel Archangel, of this we are sure,**
> **Gabriel Archangel, Christ light is the cure.**
> **Gabriel Archangel, intentions so pure,**
> **Gabriel Archangel, in you we're secure.**

5. I surrender the belief that there might be some cause that is so important that it could justify the killing of other human beings. I consciously let go of the illusion because it is a millstone around my neck, an inroad for the fallen beings to manipulate me.

> Gabriel Archangel, the earth is now free,
> embracing a nondual reality,
> the judgment of Christ upon forces so dark,
> who deny that all have a spiritual spark.

> **Gabriel Archangel, of this we are sure,**
> **Gabriel Archangel, Christ light is the cure.**
> **Gabriel Archangel, intentions so pure,**
> **Gabriel Archangel, in you we're secure.**

6. There is a psychological mechanism behind fanaticism. It is to think that the obvious expressions of fanaticism define fanaticism. Other forms of human behavior or other belief systems that are not as extreme, are not fanatical.

> Gabriel Archangel, with angels so white,
> raising our planet out of the dark night,
> as we now intone the Word of the Lord,
> the beings who fell are bound by your sword.

**Gabriel Archangel, of this we are sure,
Gabriel Archangel, Christ light is the cure.
Gabriel Archangel, intentions so pure,
Gabriel Archangel, in you we're secure.**

7. Fanaticism is far more subtle and widespread than I have ever imagined. Fanaticism is the mindset in which we emphasize the things that validate our basic view of a situation and we ignore or reject the things that do not validate our view of the situation.

Gabriel Archangel, we call now to you,
the astral plane your light burning through,
entities, demons, discarnates are bound,
as you and we intone Sacred Sound.

**Gabriel Archangel, of this we are sure,
Gabriel Archangel, Christ light is the cure.
Gabriel Archangel, intentions so pure,
Gabriel Archangel, in you we're secure.**

8. Human beings have a tendency to fall in love with ideas. I am willing to see where I am in love with an idea and how it has influenced my spiritual path.

Gabriel Archangel, what glorious day,
your radiant angels have come here to stay,
your purifications fire burning white,
intentions so pure, our hearts taking flight.

**Gabriel Archangel, of this we are sure,
Gabriel Archangel, Christ light is the cure.
Gabriel Archangel, intentions so pure,
Gabriel Archangel, in you we're secure.**

9. The fallen beings have created the illusion that the universe functions according to ideas that can be grasped by the dualistic mind.

Gabriel Archangel, our planet so pure,
in our bright new future we do feel secure,
with your band of light encircling the earth,
Saint Germain's Golden Age is now given birth.

**Gabriel Archangel, of this we are sure,
Gabriel Archangel, Christ light is the cure.
Gabriel Archangel, intentions so pure,
Gabriel Archangel, in you we're secure.**

Part 5

1. It is futile to try to force other people to see what I see. I cannot ever force another being to see what I see because the being can never look at the situation from inside *my* mind. It will look at it from inside *its own* mind.

Hilarion, on emerald shore,
we're free from all that's gone before.
Hilarion, we let all go,
that keeps us out of sacred flow.

11 | I Invoke Freedom from Projecting Out

**Hilarion, with light so green,
we see behind the matter screen,
immaculate our inner sight,
we see the earth is taking flight.**

2. I am willing to take a look at my life and see how I have attempted to force my ideas upon other people.

Hilarion, the secret key,
is wisdom's own reality.
Hilarion, all life is healed,
the ego's face no more concealed.

**Hilarion, with light so green,
we see behind the matter screen,
immaculate our inner sight,
we see the earth is taking flight.**

3. I am willing to take an honest look at my life and see if I have projected psychic energy at other people in order to get them to validate my vision.

Hilarion, your love for life,
helps us surrender inner strife.
Hilarion, your loving words,
thrill our hearts like song of birds.

**Hilarion, with light so green,
we see behind the matter screen,
immaculate our inner sight,
we see the earth is taking flight.**

4. I am willing to admit this without putting myself down for having done this. I will simply stop doing it from this point forward.

> Hilarion, invoke the light,
> your sacred formulas recite.
> Hilarion, your secret tone,
> philosopher's most sacred stone.
>
> **Hilarion, with light so green,**
> **we see behind the matter screen,**
> **immaculate our inner sight,**
> **we see the earth is taking flight.**

5. The mechanism behind projecting a certain vision upon other people is the consciousness of falling in love with ideas and beginning to think that the universe does or should work according to our ideas.

> Hilarion, with love you greet,
> us in your temple over Crete.
> Hilarion, your emerald light,
> the third eye sees with Christic sight.
>
> **Hilarion, with light so green,**
> **we see behind the matter screen,**
> **immaculate our inner sight,**
> **we see the earth is taking flight.**

6. I surrender all aspects of the fanatical mindset, of thinking that if only the universe worked according to a certain idea, everything would be paradise on earth.

11 | I Invoke Freedom from Projecting Out

Hilarion, you give us fruit,
of truth that is so absolute.
Hilarion, all stress decrease,
as our ambitions we release.

**Hilarion, with light so green,
we see behind the matter screen,
immaculate our inner sight,
we see the earth is taking flight.**

7. If I can observe that the world is not working according to my idea, then I need to revise my ideas so that they can explain how the world actually works instead of holding on to an ideal of how it should work.

Hilarion, our chakras clear,
as we let go of subtlest fear.
Hilarion, we are sincere,
as freedom's truth we do revere.

**Hilarion, with light so green,
we see behind the matter screen,
immaculate our inner sight,
we see the earth is taking flight.**

8. The fanatical mindset causes people to say: "The reason the world is not functioning according to my idea, is that these other people are not behaving according to my idea. Therefore, it is my job to make those other people behave according to my idea and then we will have paradise on earth."

Hilarion, you balance all,
the seven rays upon our call.
Hilarion, you keep us true,
as we remain all one with you.

**Hilarion, with light so green,
we see behind the matter screen,
immaculate our inner sight,
we see the earth is taking flight.**

9. I am willing to see where I have a tendency to approach the spiritual path based on this pattern. I surrender my ideas of how the spiritual path should work and my attempts to force myself or other people to conform to this idea.

Hilarion, your Presence here,
filling up the inner sphere.
Life is now a sacred flow,
God Vision we on all bestow.

**Hilarion, with light so green,
we see behind the matter screen,
immaculate our inner sight,
we see the earth is taking flight.**

Part 6

1. I am willing to look at my life and say: "How have I attempted to force my idea of the spiritual path upon other people?"

11 | I Invoke Freedom from Projecting Out

Serapis Bey, what power lies,
behind your purifying eyes.
Serapis Bey, it is a treat,
to enter your sublime retreat.

**Serapis Bey, we call to you,
to help us dual lies see through,
come purify our inner sight,
we see the earth in your great light.**

2. As I see this, I say: "This ends here. *This ends here.* It ends right now. I see what I have been doing and I am not doing it anymore."

Serapis Bey, what wisdom found,
your words are always most profound.
Serapis Bey, we tell you true,
our minds have room for naught but you.

**Serapis Bey, we call to you,
to help us dual lies see through,
come purify our inner sight,
we see the earth in your great light.**

3. I choose to consciously stop projecting my vision of truth upon other people or the world outside of me.

Serapis Bey, what love beyond,
our hearts do leap, as we respond.
Serapis Bey, your life a poem,
that calls us to our starry home.

> **Serapis Bey, we call to you,**
> **to help us dual lies see through,**
> **come purify our inner sight,**
> **we see the earth in your great light.**

4. In order to take embodiment on earth, I have to create a soul vehicle. As I do this, I start at the 144th level and I take on illusion after illusion until I reach the 48th level.

> Serapis Bey, your guidance sure,
> our base is clear and white and pure.
> Serapis Bey, no longer trapped,
> by soul in which the self was wrapped.

> **Serapis Bey, we call to you,**
> **to help us dual lies see through,**
> **come purify our inner sight,**
> **we see the earth in your great light.**

5. The illusions I am taking on make it seem believable that I am actually a human being in a physical body on earth. The illusions are necessary in order to give me the sense of reality that I am a human being immersed in an external universe.

> Serapis Bey, what healing balm,
> in mind that is forever calm.
> Serapis Bey, our thoughts are pure,
> your discipline we shall endure.

> **Serapis Bey, we call to you,**
> **to help us dual lies see through,**
> **come purify our inner sight,**
> **we see the earth in your great light.**

6. Descending into embodiment is having an un-mystical experience that makes it seem completely real that I am a human being in embodiment on earth. This is the immersion experience.

> Serapis Bey, what secret test,
> for egos who want to be best.
> Serapis Bey, expose the "me,"
> that takes away our harmony.
>
> **Serapis Bey, we call to you,**
> **to help us dual lies see through,**
> **come purify our inner sight,**
> **we see the earth in your great light.**

7. In order to awaken myself, I have to reverse the process and start working my way back up. I shed one illusion, I reach a higher level of consciousness, then I shed the next illusion and so on.

> Serapis Bey, what moving sight,
> the self ascends to sacred height.
> Serapis Bey, forever free,
> in sacred synchronicity.
>
> **Serapis Bey, we call to you,**
> **to help us dual lies see through,**
> **come purify our inner sight,**
> **we see the earth in your great light.**

8. I have many illusions left that I need to shed before I can ascend. There is nothing unnatural about it. It is simply how life in an unascended sphere works.

Serapis Bey, you balance all,
the seven rays upon our call.
Serapis Bey, in space and time,
the pyramid of self, we climb.

**Serapis Bey, we call to you,
to help us dual lies see through,
come purify our inner sight,
we see the earth in your great light.**

9. It is time to stop projecting out my vision of truth; to stop projecting it on other people and to stop projecting it on matter itself. I adopt the attitude consciously that I am willing to see beyond my current vision of truth. I am willing to see beyond my idea of how I think the world *should* work.

Serapis Bey, your Presence here,
filling up the inner sphere.
Life is now a sacred flow,
God Purity we do bestow.

**Serapis Bey, we call to you,
to help us dual lies see through,
come purify our inner sight,
we see the earth in your great light.**

11 | I Invoke Freedom from Projecting Out

Part 7

1. I am willing to look at how the world actually works. When I see a difference between my idea of the world and the actual behavior of the world, I am willing to say: "Then I need to adjust my idea. It is my idea that is incomplete."

> Divine Director, I now see,
> the world is unreality,
> in my heart I now truly feel,
> the Spirit is all that is real.

> **Divine Director, send the light,**
> **from blindness clear my inner sight,**
> **my vision free, my vision clear,**
> **your guidance is forever here.**

2. I surrender the tendency to think that as I have walked the spiritual path, as I have practiced various techniques, as I have studied spiritual teachings, I have gradually raised my vision and can now see some absolute truth.

> Divine Director, vision give,
> in clarity I want to live,
> I now behold my plan Divine,
> the plan that is uniquely mine.

> **Divine Director, send the light,**
> **from blindness clear my inner sight,**
> **my vision free, my vision clear,**
> **your guidance is forever here.**

3. There is still a higher truth beyond what I see right now. I accept consciously that I am willing to see that higher truth. I will not hold on to my present truth. I will not seek to validate it, I will not seek confirmation of it.

> Divine Director, show in me,
> the ego games, and set me free,
> help me escape the ego's cage,
> to help bring in the golden age.
>
> **Divine Director, send the light,**
> **from blindness clear my inner sight,**
> **my vision free, my vision clear,**
> **your guidance is forever here.**

4. I consciously decide that I will stop using spiritual teachings as a justification for my current vision of truth. I am willing to see that higher truth, and in order to see it, I am willing to look at where the world does not validate my current vision. It is my vision that needs to change, not the world and not other people.

> Divine Director, I'm with you,
> my vision one, no longer two,
> as karma's veil you do disperse,
> I see a whole new universe.
>
> **Divine Director, send the light,**
> **from blindness clear my inner sight,**
> **my vision free, my vision clear,**
> **your guidance is forever here.**

5. Seeking to change the world and other people is nothing more than an excuse for not being willing to change myself, to change my own vision.

> Divine Director, I go up,
> electric light now fills my cup,
> consume in me all shadows old,
> bestow on me a vision bold.

> **Divine Director, send the light,**
> **from blindness clear my inner sight,**
> **my vision free, my vision clear,**
> **your guidance is forever here.**

6. I am willing to confront this reality consciously. I am willing to see this. I am willing to see that there is an aspect of my psychology that will not let me transcend this desperate grasp of wanting the world to validate my truth.

> Divine Director, heart of gold,
> my sacred labor I unfold,
> o blessed Guru, I now see,
> where my own plan is taking me.

> **Divine Director, send the light,**
> **from blindness clear my inner sight,**
> **my vision free, my vision clear,**
> **your guidance is forever here.**

7. The fallen beings want me to believe that there is a highest vision of what the world should be like because the world is not the way it should be right now. Yet the world is exactly the way it should be right now.

Divine Director, by your grace,
in grander scheme I find my place,
my individual flame I see,
uniqueness God has given me.

**Divine Director, send the light,
from blindness clear my inner sight,
my vision free, my vision clear,
your guidance is forever here.**

8. The earth is a learning institution. Some people learn by seeing physical conditions outpicture their state of consciousness. The world is an out-picturing of the collective consciousness. This is exactly what it should be. I recognize that the world is exactly as it should be because it is outpicturing people's consciousness.

Divine Director, vision one,
I see that I AM God's own Sun,
with your direction so Divine,
I am now letting my light shine.

**Divine Director, send the light,
from blindness clear my inner sight,
my vision free, my vision clear,
your guidance is forever here.**

9. I say: "It is not my job to use force to make the world or other people comply with the vision I have. My job is to raise my individual consciousness and attain self-mastery. I do not attain self-mastery by forcing other people or the world. I do not even attain self-mastery by forcing myself. I attain self-mastery by letting go of the next illusion. When I continue to let go of illusion after illusion, I will reach a state of consciousness where I have self-mastery. In fact, for every step I take up, for every illusion I overcome, I attain a higher degree of self-mastery because it is the illusion that takes away my self-mastery, not a lack of mastery."

> Divine Director, what a gift,
> to be a part of Spirit's lift,
> to raise mankind out of the night,
> to bask in Spirit's loving sight.
>
> **Divine Director, send the light,**
> **from blindness clear my inner sight,**
> **my vision free, my vision clear,**
> **your guidance is forever here.**

Sealing:

In the name of the Divine Mother, I fully accept that the power of these calls is used to set free the River of Life, so it can outpicture the perfect vision of Christ for my own life, for all people and for the planet. In the name I AM THAT I AM, it is done! Amen.

12 | HOW TO STOP PROJECTING IN

I AM the Ascended Master Hilarion. What do you encounter at the fifth level of my retreat? Well, as I have already said, you encounter the need to take a look at what you are projecting in at yourself.

Let us begin by looking at the fact that most of the people that follow this course will have been on the spiritual path for some time. You have probably studied several spiritual teachings, maybe been part of several organizations or followed several gurus. You have probably read many books that are maybe popular out there among spiritual people. What has happened as a result of this process? Well, what has happened is that you have taken in certain ideas, certain very subtle beliefs, and you have used them to create an image in your mind of what it means to be a spiritual student, what it means to follow the spiritual path. Many people have followed ascended master teachings for decades and they have built an image of what it means to be a good ascended master student.

Your image of a good spiritual student

Now again, what have I said several times? There is nothing wrong with this because you can do nothing else at a certain level of the path. It is not that what you have been doing is wrong. It is not that I am here to tell you that this was wrong. What I am here to tell you is that it is now time to take a look at this and realize that you need to let go of at least some of these ideas. As you complete this course of self-mastery, I can assure you that you will have to let go of *all* of your ideas.

How can I say this? You may have followed an ascended master teaching that talks about what it takes to walk the spiritual path. Is it not natural that you use such a teaching to build an image of what a spiritual student should be like? Yes, my beloved, it *is* natural that you do this, but are you not beginning to understand that the path of self-mastery means overcoming the outer self, the separate self? Do you not realize that in order to attain self-mastery, it is not a matter of forcing the outer self or giving the outer self some special abilities?

The goal of the path to self-mastery is not to somehow make the outer self acceptable in the eyes of God so that he will let it into the kingdom of heaven. This is what the fallen beings would like to see happen and what they are projecting out there through the false teachers in or out of embodiment. You will *not* attain self-mastery by perfecting the outer self, the separate self—it cannot be perfected.

You will attain self-mastery by coming to the point where you are able to exercise your creative power without having it be affected by the outer self. You are free of the outer self so that you are not the "doer" but your I AM Presence is the doer through the Conscious You and your four lower bodies. This is, again, subtle because rising to the 96th level does not mean that you have no desires at all. It *does* mean that your desires at the personal level are in alignment with the desires in your Divine plan, the desires that you yourself chose before you came into embodiment. They are also in alignment with the individuality built into your I AM Presence, the individuality that you have partly built through your past embodiments.

Creativity and the separate self

What you need to recognize here is that as you have walked the spiritual path up until this point, you have taken in certain ideas and you have used them to formulate an image in your mind of what you should be like as a spiritual student. This means, among other things, how you should express your creativity, given that you are a spiritual student. The reason you need to look at this is very simple. At each stage of the path, at each level of the path, you have (as I said) certain illusions. It is inevitable that when you build an image of what you should be like as a spiritual person, then that image will incorporate the illusions you still have, the illusions you have not let go of.

Again, this is not wrong, it is simply the mechanics of how the path works in an atmosphere as dense as earth. I have said to you that as you climb towards the 144th level, for each level of consciousness there is an illusion you need to overcome. This means that when you reach the 96th level and have completed the course of self-mastery, you have still not overcome all illusions. You have, ideally and hopefully, come to a certain point where you have overcome the illusions that cause you to express your creativity through the separate self.

This may not seem all that important to you at your current level, but it will become increasingly clear and increasingly important as we go higher in this course. The Chohans above me will explain this and help you become more and more free of these subtle images that you have. I am not expecting that, at the fifth level of my retreat, you can let go of all the images you have of what it means to be a spiritual student. There is one aspect of this image that I would like you to become conscious of at this level. In fact, you need to become conscious of it in order to pass the initiation at this level and rise to the next level.

What should you be?

Now, I want you to do this consciously at the conscious level of the mind as you are reading or hearing this. Of course, I have already had you go through this at my retreat, but I am seeking to help you filter this down to the conscious awareness. I want you to calm the mind, to relax the mind and to focus within, to focus on your heart chakra. Then, I want you, as you are hearing or reading this, to have no preconceived opinions or beliefs, but I want you to be aware of your first reaction to what I will say next. What is your first reaction when I say: "As a good spiritual student, I should be..." What comes to your mind? There are two aspects of this. You may have a concrete idea of what you should be, but what I am really seeking to make you aware of is that when I say: "As a good spiritual student, I should be"... there is a pull on you. Something is pulling you. In other words there is an aspect of your vision of what it means to be a spiritual student that is based on a sense that you *should* be a certain way.

This is, of course, not surprising when you look at the history of this planet. Just look at the religions that you see on earth and how many of them have prescribed certain outer rules for how you should behave when you are a member of that religion. You will see how some religions have taken this to an extreme where almost every aspect of people's lives is determined by some rule defined by their religion. This entire idea is released by the fallen beings because the idea is very simple. It is that by living up to conditions in the *material* realm, you can qualify to enter the *spiritual* realm.

Now, again, there is a subtlety here, my beloved. I am not saying that it is completely wrong to have certain rules for how people should live. You will see that Jesus, for example, in the Sermon on the Mount and other teachings gave certain general rules for how people should behave, how they should treat each other. You understand that such rules are primarily for people below the 48th level of consciousness?

When you are below the 48th level, you are in a state of consciousness where you are very focused on the separate self and you are willing to use force to protect the separate self or fulfill the desires of the separate self. There may be varying degrees of force you are willing to use but you are willing to use force. This, of course, means that practically everything you do with force makes karma for yourself. It has been necessary, for people at this state of consciousness, to give certain general rules so that if they follow these rules, they will make less karma for themselves. You understand that anything that is given on this planet, the fallen beings will attempt to pervert it? What they have done with this is they have said that these outer rules are not just for people below the 48th level of consciousness, they are for *all* people and all people should follow them. Then, the fallen beings have put out the idea that following these outer rules (which usually means obeying a power elite of fallen beings in embodiment, such as the priesthood or a secular ruler) guarantees that you will qualify to go to heaven. This is precisely the lie.

You will not go to heaven

There are many levels of this lie. My beloved, you will not go to heaven. Think about this statement. You will not *go* to heaven. There are two reasons for this. Number one is that the "you" that you are right now is not qualified to ascend. As you rise towards the 144th level of consciousness, the "you" that you have right now will die. The next "you" that you take on will also die. You will continue to let one "you" at a time die until you are at the 144th level and can let the last remnants of the separate self die and you ascend into oneness. The other aspect of this is that you will never enter heaven if you think you have to go somewhere else different from where you are.

As you go towards the 144th level, it is not that you get closer and closer to heaven. It is that you gradually overcome the illusion that there is a distance between you and heaven. You come to the point where, at the 144th level, you are not so much entering heaven as accepting that you are there. Do you see that there comes this point – and the point is now – where in order to attain self-mastery, you need to consciously recognize this?

You need to recognize that even on the spiritual path, you can use a spiritual teaching to solidify the separate self. When you do this, there will come a point where this actually stops your progress. I said in my last discourse that we have many examples of people who have followed an ascended master teaching for decades but their growth has stopped and this is the reason. They have not been aware of the need to look at the image they have imposed upon themselves of what it means to be an ascended master student—a *good* ascended master student.

It is not necessarily that all aspects of this image are wrong. You need to be aware that you need to gradually let go of this until you come to a point where you have no image of what you should be like. You have overcome the very sense that as a spiritual student you should *be anything*.

Do you not see that even if you are studying a spiritual teaching, my beloved, that teaching presents ideas that are coming to you from without? The purpose of the teaching (if it is a genuine spiritual teaching coming from the ascended masters) is to take you towards the point where you are the open door for your I AM Presence. It may be constructive that in order to get to that point, you for a time adopt a certain image of what it means to be a spiritual student and you seek to live up to that image. Can you not see that by doing this, you are still reinforcing a certain aspect of the outer self and this aspect will prevent you from being the open door for your I AM Presence?

Conforming to an idea in the mind

I am asking you here to step back and consider the mechanism of what you are doing psychologically when you have the idea that as a spiritual student you should be such and such. This mechanism is the very essence of the outer self. It is (as I said in my last discourse) the attempt to make the universe conform to an idea in the mind, the outer mind, the separate self. Instead of seeking to make the *universe* conform, you are seeking to make *yourself* conform.

What is the self you are seeking to make conform? Well, it is partly the outer self. Of course, the outer self is accepting an image of what it means to be the perfect spiritual student. The outer self is often very eager to live up to this image because it believes that if it does, then it must be acceptable to the ascended masters and we will let it into the ascended realm.

What is also being forced to live up to this image is the Conscious You and what have we said over and over again? The Conscious You is pure awareness. The Conscious You is *not* the outer self, it never has been and it never will be. The Conscious You did not descend with the outer self. It needs the outer self to express itself in this world, but you do not need the outer self to ascend, to re-enter the spiritual realm. In fact, you need to let go of the outer self in order to enter.

You see here that the outer self can only be a hindrance to your spiritual progress? Ideally, the Conscious You is the open door for the I AM Presence, nothing less, nothing more. Therefore, when you are forcing the Conscious You to comply with an image created by the outer self, you are not being the open door for your I AM Presence.

The entire trick of the fallen beings, my beloved, is to get you to believe that you *cannot* be an open door for the I AM Presence. You are not *allowed* to be an open door for the I AM Presence, it is *wrong* to be an open door for the I AM Presence, it is *wrong* to express your spiritual light, it is *wrong* to be creative because you should always follow rules. The trick of the fallen beings is to get you to believe that instead of being creative and expressing the creativity of the I AM Presence, you have to allow the creative flow to go through the filter of the outer self. That filter is, of course, created based on conditions in the material realm. This means that if you allow your creativity to flow through this filter, there will be certain conditions in the material realm that you will never go beyond. You will never dare to express anything that challenges or transcends those limitations.

Going beyond people's perception of what is possible

Why do you think Jesus, 2,000 years ago, had to perform certain miracles? They are called miracles officially but they were not miracles. Jesus simply allowed his I AM Presence to act through him; he was the open door. The I AM Presence can do anything it wants in the material world, or rather it can go beyond what Serapis Bey called the secondary laws of nature. The secondary laws of nature are not limitations for your I AM Presence, and this is what Jesus was attempting to demonstrate by performing what people called miracles.

He did something that broke people's perception of what was possible. Now, we are in a different day and age and therefore it is no longer time to do these kind of miracles. It is time to help people see their own inner power and this means something entirely different in this age. The point I want to get to here is that the fallen beings have defined the secondary laws of nature and they have done so for two reasons. Partly, because it gives themselves certain powers when they attain what I call the "outer mastery" where they can master the secondary laws of nature. They have also defined these laws because it limits all other people and therefore it allows the fallen beings to have power over others.

You will see, if you take a closer look, that there has never been a fallen being who demonstrated great power in the physical world without taking advantage of other people. I earlier talked about certain billionaires that have been able to manifest the exact outer conditions that they want. They always do so because they are getting other people to do most of the work for them, either by forcing them or by buying their services. They are not manifesting these conditions exclusively by their own power but only by controlling other people. This is partly what the secondary laws of nature are defined to do so that people believe that they have no power beyond a certain level. Can you see that if you have come to see yourself as having to live up to a certain image of what it means to be a spiritual student, then you cannot be a completely open door for the creative power of your I AM Presence?

My beloved, this messenger followed an ascended master teaching for many years. It was a valid teaching. It was at the time a vibrant organization and he benefited in many ways from it. If he had completely accepted the image given by that organization of what it means to be an ascended master student, then he would never have dared to be today a messenger for the ascended masters. He would have remained a student. This is not what was in his Divine plan. You have your own Divine plan, and my only concern is that you are not allowing your image of what it means to be a good spiritual student to stand in the way of the fulfillment of your Divine plan.

How important is your Divine plan?

You, of course, at this point need to consciously decide what is most important for you. I know that at this point you may not see clearly what is your Divine plan. You may see very clearly what you think it means to be a good spiritual student. Obviously, it is easier to choose a clear vision over an unclear vision. Nevertheless, the essence of the spiritual path is that you are willing to take the next step even if you do not see clearly where it is going to lead you. I am asking you to consider here what is most important: That you fulfill your Divine

12 | How to Stop Projecting in

plan (which you and your ascended teachers defined before you came into embodiment), or that you continue to live up to your current image of what it means to be a good spiritual student? You see, my beloved, you cannot do both.

You may think that if you have a valid vision of what it means to be a good spiritual student, then if you keep living up to that image, one day you will magically fulfill your Divine plan, but this is not the case. You will *not* fulfill your Divine plan by holding on to your current image of how you should behave. You *cannot* fulfill your Divine plan by seeking to force yourself to live up to an image defined in this world. You need to come to the point where you are completely open to letting your I AM Presence express what it wants through you.

My beloved, let me take you back to what I said earlier, namely that behind the reaction of thinking that you have to be a certain way as a spiritual student, there is the mechanism where you feel you should live up to some image. What I need you to see at this point is that whenever you have this feeling that you *should* be something you *should* do something, you *should* behave a certain way, then this comes from the separate self, the outer self, the ego, the dweller on the threshold. It is a pull that opens you to the fallen beings.

I know very well that there are many ascended master students who see us, the ascended masters, as wanting to impose something on you, as making demands on you, as almost threatening you into complying with our teachings. What have I said throughout these previous discourses about perception filters? My beloved, we are the ascended masters; we are who we are. We know very well that when a student finds our teachings, that student has a certain perception filter and therefore cannot see us for who we are. We therefore allow students to gradually shed their perception filters until they begin to see us as we are.

At this point in my retreat, you need to come to the realization that we are not seeking to force you to do anything. The idea that we are seeking to force you is an idea that comes from the fallen beings. It has been promoted through many religions in this world and through many spiritual or New Age ideas and philosophies.

Overcoming a fear-based culture

We have in previous ascended master organizations seen how people came in with this fear-based view of spiritual teachers. They have, in certain organizations, created a fear-based culture that actually promoted this view that we are so strict disciplinarians, we are so demanding, we are appealing to your fear, to your doubt, to your shame, to your guilt. There have been organizations that were sponsored by us and who were bringing forth genuine dictations, but nevertheless the students in those organizations built this fear-based, guilt-based culture. Do you know what was the most devastating effect of this culture? It was that it caused those who entered that culture to doubt their intuitive promptings from their I AM Presences. They attempted to conform to the outer culture instead of following their intuition.

It is, incidentally, the quickest way to make karma when you cause another human being to doubt his or her intuition. Again, I am not seeking to promote fear here. What I am seeking to point out is that you can have a genuine messenger of the ascended masters who is bringing forth genuine dictations and has created an organization that is sponsored by us, and yet the people in the organization can build a fear-based culture. Again, this is not wrong in some epic sense because it is understandable that people come in with the perception filters they had. This is based on the long history of the fallen beings projecting this idea into the collective mind. There is, of course, a reason why there can be a limit to how long we can sponsor an organization that has such a fear-based culture and will not let go of it. That is why what I am seeking to do here is to have you realize that it is time for you to let go of this fear-based image of what you should be like as a spiritual student.

Continuity versus creativity

This, my beloved, brings up a very subtle point, a very subtle topic. The entire idea behind the secondary laws of nature is that they give continuity, that they are constant over time. The dream of the fallen beings is to create a mechanical universe. You understand what they actually want to do, even though most of them are not even conscious of this? What they want to do is to create a mechanical path to salvation so they can enter the ascended realm without giving up all remnants of the separate self, all remnants of the fallen consciousness. They want to cheat or force their way into heaven.

Now, this, of course, cannot be done. Nevertheless, in order for the Law of Free Will to outplay itself, we have allowed a limited number of planets to reach the density of matter where it seems that there are certain secondary laws of nature that are constant over time. This has been allowed because it gives not only the fallen beings but also other beings the opportunity to live out that desire for control until they come to the point where they realize either that it is futile or where they simply have had enough of it.

Now, there are many spiritual students who have used a genuine spiritual teaching to reinforce the very subtle belief that in order to qualify for their ascension (or attain enlightenment or whatever the goal was), you need to follow certain mechanical steps. In a sense, you could say that anything we give you can be used for this. We have given you the concept of the 144 levels of consciousness. We have given you a structured course of self-mastery that takes you from one step to the next. You may use this to reinforce the mechanical mindset where you think it is just a matter of performing certain steps. Have we not said several times (if you really pay attention) that this course is *not* a mechanical course?

You can, of course, follow this course in a mechanical way. You can go down and start with the first book and read the dictation for the first step, for the 48th to the 49th level of consciousness. You can perform the invocation based on that step every day for nine or 33 days or however many days you want to do it. This does not mean that you automatically rise from one step to the next.

We have said all along that this course is a *creative* course. It requires you to come to a certain insight and it requires you to make a certain decision. At the very minimum, you need to accept the insight and thereby let go of the illusion that is replaced by the insight. This is not a mechanical process.

The dream of the fallen beings

The path of walking up through the 144 levels of consciousness requires you to gradually let go of aspects of the separate self. What the fallen beings want to do is that they want to enter heaven without letting go of the separate self. Their dream is, my beloved, that if they can cheat their way into heaven, they would suddenly get all this power and therefore they can express that power through the separate self and take complete control over the world.

12 | How to Stop Projecting in

This, of course, can never happen because as long as you have any intent of forcing any other being or forcing the world, well, you cannot ascend, my beloved. You need to be completely non-aggressive, non-violent, in order to enter the spiritual realm. The fallen beings are on an impossible quest and you need to recognize here at this level that it is impossible.

You need to come to that point (whatever it takes for you consciously) where you truly see this consciously and you feel how something in you lets go. It is not enough to see this intellectually and with the linear, intellectual mind decide that you will overcome this illusion. You need to work on this, study this lesson, study my previous lessons, give the invocation, look at it from different angles, ask for my help so that you feel that this is not an outer decision. It is not made with the outer mind; it comes to you spontaneously from within. There is a decision, but it is not a *willful* decision, it is a *spontaneous* decision. It is not a *fear-based* decision; it is a *love-based* decision. You see that you no longer want to follow this false path, you no longer want to live your entire life based on this outer idea of what you *should* be. You want to be who you are at any moment.

Survival of the outer self

You see, my beloved, the outer self has a desperate need to survive. It knows it is mortal but it wants to create the impression that it can become immortal. It thinks that in order to become immortal, it must remain constant over time. Do you not see that this is the dream behind the fallen beings and their secondary laws of nature? They try to create something that is permanent, that can remain constant over time. What does it mean, my beloved, to be an open door for the I AM Presence?

Does this mean that you are always the same? Nay, it means that you are *never* the same because whatever the I AM Presence wants to express through you in a given situation on earth, you allow this to happen. When Jesus walked the earth 2,000 years ago, he did not go around with his outer mind thinking: "I am the Living Christ, I have to behave according to this standard in everything I do." When he encountered a certain situation, he did not think with the outer mind: "How am I supposed to act in this situation" and then he forced himself to act that way.

No, he was there in the situation. His outer mind was completely neutralized, whatever remnants of the outer mind he had were completely neutralized. What he did in that outer situation was that he went into his inner space and was simply completely neutral, completely open. Then, the Presence could act through him freely. Now, you may see that Jesus (if you could have followed him) may meet one person that had a certain handicap, such as a withered arm, and Jesus healed that person. Two weeks later he met another person with a withered arm, and if you are applying the fallen consciousness, you would say: "Well, then Jesus should heal the second person also just as he did with the first."

Every situation is very complex

What you cannot know with the outer mind is all of the complexities involved in a given situation. Jesus' I AM Presence was aware of all of the complicated karmic circumstances of the first person with the withered arm. Therefore, it could see that it was constructive for the overall progression of the planet and of the person that the arm be healed. Likewise, the I AM Presence could see that for the second person this was not constructive.

12 | How to Stop Projecting in

Now, if you were to really look at these situations and analyze every aspect of them, you could come up with an evaluation, with an analysis, that could be what scientists are attempting to do and would explain why the first person was healed and the second person was not. The problem is, my beloved, that this explanation would be so complex that it would take you a very long time to fathom it. Do you see what I am trying to say here?

You are going through life and you are meeting many different situations. Let us say you come across a certain situation and you want to know with the outer mind exactly how you should act in that situation and why. Well, let us say that you were given this explanation written down in a book that was 1500 pages so it would take you several days to read through the entire book. Of course, by the time you had read through the book and understood with the outer mind how you should act, the situation had changed and now it was too late to act.

If you want to put it to the extreme, let us say that you are walking through the jungle and you hear some noise in the underbrush. You want to understand the situation with your outer mind and it takes you five minutes to understand the situation. By that time, the lion has already jumped upon you and killed you.

You can see this is not what it means to be a Christed being. It does not mean that you have an explanation with the outer mind of how you should act in every situation. It does not mean that you know everything, every aspect of a situation. What it means to be a Christed being is that you are always tuned in to the I AM Presence and you follow the impulse from the I AM Presence in every situation.

You are not seeking to force yourself to act the same way in this situation as you did in the past. You are not imposing any *should* upon a given situation. You are not seeking to be *constant* in your actions. You are seeking to be *spontaneous* in every action. This is what Christhood is.

Being spontaneous without analyzing

There are students who have built the idea that the spiritual path is about coming to know and understand more and more with the outer mind, the linear mind, the intellectual mind. They think that you finally come to a point where you know everything and you can explain everything. Therefore, in every situation, you can know that this is the right thing to do.

Then, you also have these same students who, when they act in a certain situation, will analyze what they did afterwards in great detail and often, so to speak, "beat themselves up" whatever the result was because it is never good enough. You see, my beloved, when you act based on the idea that you should be a certain way, what will inevitably happen? After you have acted and you are faced with the result of your action, you must judge yourself and the outcome of the action.

Did it live up to this perfect image that you *should* have followed? How many times does your action live up to the perfect image? You go into this whole process of having to deal with the pain of not having lived up to the perfect image, having to explain it in some way, having to analyze it, having to at look it as a learning experience and force yourself to try to learn from it.

You understand that as you go towards Christhood, this mechanism falls away? You do not analyze because you know that you were tuned in to the Presence. This is what the Presence wanted to do in that situation and regardless of the outcome, this was the best that could happen in that situation. This does not mean that as a Christed being you will always do something that has the ideal or the perfect consequences. If you look at the life of Jesus, you will see that there were times where he did not get the best result out of a situation. The reason for this was that the other people involved in the situation did not react in the highest possible way. Jesus did what he could by being attuned to his I AM Presence. He gave the other people an opportunity to transcend their level of consciousness and come up higher, but they chose not to take that opportunity and therefore the outcome was less than ideal. Nevertheless, Jesus did not go within and analyze and beat himself up over this because he knew that a situation is not fixed in time. Life is a process that continually moves on. It is not the goal of a Christed being to produce a specific outer result and to maintain that result over time.

Christhood and permanency

A Christed being is not seeking to create permanency, constancy, ongoingness. A Christed being is always seeking to move the process of life along. He or she knows that life is a river that is constantly flowing. If you have one situation, regardless of the outcome, the river moves on. It is not a matter of analyzing a certain outcome of what it should or should not have been. It is a matter of saying: "Now that the outcome was this, what is the next step? How can we now move the situation further so that we get onward in the process of life?"

The fallen beings are constantly working towards a result that they envision. A Christed being has no end result, except perhaps the ascension of a planet or the ascension of all people on it. Really, the Christed being sees this as moving along the river, helping people constantly transcend their current situation, their current state of consciousness, and move forward.

Do you not see that what the fallen beings have done with the secondary laws of nature is that they have attempted to stop the River of Life from flowing? They have attempted to create a situation where they can maintain a certain state over time. For example, you will see how they have had these dreams of creating a civilization, such as the Roman Empire or the Soviet Union or even today the capitalist part of the world, where they can maintain a certain state indefinitely. It is always a state, my beloved, where the fallen beings are the leaders and all other people are their slaves. They are in control, they have a position of power and privilege. *Constancy* is what the fallen beings want.

Transcendence is what the ascended masters want. Constant self-transcendence is what we want. You see, my beloved, that at this point of your path I am asking you to consider: What does the image you have of yourself say about the goal you are working towards? What is your vision of where the spiritual path leads? What is the end goal you are working towards?

Do you have a fixed image in your mind of what goal you should reach when you complete this course of self-mastery and attain the 96th level of consciousness? Do you have a fixed image of what it means to be a Christed being? Do you have a fixed image of what it means to be an ascended master? Then, what I am asking you to consider consciously is that these images are out of touch with reality because the path is ongoing self-transcendence. It never ends, my beloved.

Being dissatisfied with yourself

If you are striving towards a fixed goal, I can assure you that you will never get there and that means you will be dissatisfied with yourself indefinitely. I do not want you to be dissatisfied with yourself and your progress. I want you to be feeling and accepting that you are exactly where you need to be at this point. I want you to feel completely at peace with knowing that you are where you need to be. You will also move on to the next level and then you will be content there. Why should you be dissatisfied with yourself for your entire lifetime?

Can you see, my beloved, that many of you were more content, more at peace with your lives, before you found the spiritual path than after? Ever since you found the path, you have had a goal that you felt you had to strive towards. You have known you were not there and therefore you have felt this gap, this emptiness. Well, I know that you are not quite ready to overcome this emptiness at this point. I know that you *are* ready to have the idea planted in your mind that there will come to a point where you are ready to confront it and overcome it. It is not necessary, but it is an inevitable product of having the idea that you *should* be something.

Can you, my beloved, see the image you are imposing upon yourself right now of what it means to be a spiritual student? Can you see it? If not, ask me to help you and I will, as you continue to work with this lesson. When you can see it, can you let it go and be more and allow yourself to be more than that image?

I AM the Ascended Master Hilarion. I am more now than when I started giving this dictation. Are you more now that you have heard or read it?

13 | I INVOKE FREEDOM FROM PROJECTING IN

In the name I AM THAT I AM, Jesus Christ, I call to my I AM Presence to flow through the I Will Be Presence that I AM and give this invocation with full power. I call to beloved Elohim Cyclopea and Virginia, Archangel Raphael and Mother Mary and Hilarion to help me see and surrender all images I have of what it means to be a spiritual student or the Living Christ. Help me see and surrender all patterns that block my oneness with Hilarion and with my I AM Presence, including …

[Make personal calls]

Part 1

1. As a result of following the spiritual path for a time, I have taken in ideas and subtle beliefs, and I have used them to create an image in my mind of what it means to be a spiritual student, what it means to follow the spiritual path.

> Cyclopea so dear, the truth you reveal,
> the truth that duality's ailments will heal,
> your Emerald Light is like a great balm,
> our emotional bodies are perfectly calm.
>
> **Cyclopea so dear, in Emerald Sphere,**
> **in raising perception we shall persevere,**
> **as deep in our hearts your truth we revere,**
> **to immaculate vision the earth does adhere.**

2. I am willing to take a look at my image and let go of some of these ideas. I see that the course of self-mastery requires me to let go of *all* of my ideas.

> Cyclopea so dear, with you we unwind,
> all negative spirals clouding the mind,
> we know pure awareness is truly our core,
> the key to becoming the wide-open door.
>
> **Cyclopea so dear, in Emerald Sphere,**
> **in raising perception we shall persevere,**
> **as deep in our hearts your truth we revere,**
> **to immaculate vision the earth does adhere.**

13 | I Invoke Freedom from Projecting In

3. The path of self-mastery means overcoming the outer self, the separate self. In order to attain self-mastery, it is not a matter of forcing the outer self or giving the outer self some special abilities.

> Cyclopea so dear, clear our inner sight,
> empowered, we pierce the soul's fearful night,
> we now see our life through your single eye,
> beyond all disease we're ready to fly.

> **Cyclopea so dear, in Emerald Sphere,**
> **in raising perception we shall persevere,**
> **as deep in our hearts your truth we revere,**
> **to immaculate vision the earth does adhere.**

4. The goal of the path to self-mastery is not to make the outer self acceptable in the eyes of God so that he will let it into the kingdom of heaven. This is what the fallen beings are projecting out there through the false teachers.

> Cyclopea so dear, life can only reflect,
> the images that the mind does project,
> the key to our healing is clearing the mind,
> from the images the ego is hiding behind.

> **Cyclopea so dear, in Emerald Sphere,**
> **in raising perception we shall persevere,**
> **as deep in our hearts your truth we revere,**
> **to immaculate vision the earth does adhere.**

5. I will not attain self-mastery by perfecting the separate self—it cannot be perfected. I will attain self-mastery by exercising my creative power without having it be affected by the outer self.

> Cyclopea so dear, we want to aim high,
> to your healing flame we ever draw nigh,
> through veils of duality we now take flight,
> bathed in your penetrating Emerald Light.
>
> **Cyclopea so dear, in Emerald Sphere,**
> **in raising perception we shall persevere,**
> **as deep in our hearts your truth we revere,**
> **to immaculate vision the earth does adhere.**

6. The goal is that I am free of the outer self so that I am not the "doer" but my I AM Presence is the doer through the Conscious You and my four lower bodies.

> Cyclopea so dear, your Emerald Flame,
> exposes every subtle, dualistic power game,
> including the game of wanting to say,
> that truth is defined in only one way.
>
> **Cyclopea so dear, in Emerald Sphere,**
> **in raising perception we shall persevere,**
> **as deep in our hearts your truth we revere,**
> **to immaculate vision the earth does adhere.**

7. This does not mean that I have no desires at all. It means that my desires at the personal level are in alignment with the desires in my Divine plan, the desires that I myself chose before I came into embodiment.

13 | I Invoke Freedom from Projecting In

Cyclopea so dear, we're feeling the flow,
as your Living Truth upon us you bestow,
from all dual vision we are now set free,
planet earth in immaculate matrix will be.

**Cyclopea so dear, in Emerald Sphere,
in raising perception we shall persevere,
as deep in our hearts your truth we revere,
to immaculate vision the earth does adhere.**

8. As I have walked the spiritual path up until this point, I have taken in certain ideas and I have used them to formulate an image in my mind of how I should express my creativity, given that I am a spiritual student.

Cyclopea so dear, the truth is now clear,
we see higher purpose for which we are here
we know truth transcends all systems below,
immersed in your light, we continue to grow.

**Cyclopea so dear, in Emerald Sphere,
in raising perception we shall persevere,
as deep in our hearts your truth we revere,
to immaculate vision the earth does adhere.**

9. At each stage of the path, I have certain illusions. It is inevitable that when I build an image of what I *should* be like as a spiritual person, then that image will incorporate the illusions I still have, the illusions I have not let go of.

> Cyclopea so dear, we're feeling your joy,
> as creative vision we now do employ,
> in lifting earth out of serpentine cage,
> to manifest Saint Germain's Golden Age.
>
> **Cyclopea so dear, in Emerald Sphere,**
> **in raising perception we shall persevere,**
> **as deep in our hearts your truth we revere,**
> **to immaculate vision the earth does adhere.**

Part 2

1. There is an aspect of my vision of what it means to be a spiritual student that is based on a sense that I *should* be a certain way.

> Cyclopea so dear, the truth you reveal,
> the truth that duality's ailments will heal,
> your Emerald Light is like a great balm,
> our emotional bodies are perfectly calm.
>
> **Cyclopea so dear, in Emerald Sphere,**
> **in raising perception we shall persevere,**
> **as deep in our hearts your truth we revere,**
> **to immaculate vision the earth does adhere.**

2. Most religions on earth have prescribed outer rules for how I should behave when I am a member of that religion. The idea behind this is that by living up to conditions in the material realm, I can qualify to enter the spiritual realm. This is a lie.

13 | I Invoke Freedom from Projecting In

> Cyclopea so dear, with you we unwind,
> all negative spirals clouding the mind,
> we know pure awareness is truly our core,
> the key to becoming the wide-open door.
>
> **Cyclopea so dear, in Emerald Sphere,**
> **in raising perception we shall persevere,**
> **as deep in our hearts your truth we revere,**
> **to immaculate vision the earth does adhere.**

3. I *will not* go to heaven. The "you" that I am right now is not qualified to ascend. As I rise towards the 144th level of consciousness, the "you" I have right now will die. I will continue to let one "you" at a time die until I am at the 144th level and can let the last remnants of the separate self die and I ascend into oneness.

> Cyclopea so dear, clear our inner sight,
> empowered, we pierce the soul's fearful night,
> we now see our life through your single eye,
> beyond all disease we're ready to fly.
>
> **Cyclopea so dear, in Emerald Sphere,**
> **in raising perception we shall persevere,**
> **as deep in our hearts your truth we revere,**
> **to immaculate vision the earth does adhere.**

4. I will never enter heaven if I think I have to go somewhere different from where I am. I need to gradually overcome the illusion that there is a distance between me and heaven. I am not so much entering heaven as accepting that I am there.

Cyclopea so dear, life can only reflect,
the images that the mind does project,
the key to our healing is clearing the mind,
from the images the ego is hiding behind.

**Cyclopea so dear, in Emerald Sphere,
in raising perception we shall persevere,
as deep in our hearts your truth we revere,
to immaculate vision the earth does adhere.**

5. Even on the spiritual path, I can use a spiritual teaching to solidify the separate self. When I do this, there will come a point where this stops my progress.

Cyclopea so dear, we want to aim high,
to your healing flame we ever draw nigh,
through veils of duality we now take flight,
bathed in your penetrating Emerald Light.

**Cyclopea so dear, in Emerald Sphere,
in raising perception we shall persevere,
as deep in our hearts your truth we revere,
to immaculate vision the earth does adhere.**

6. I am willing to gradually let go of this image until I come to a point where I have no image of what I should be like. I have overcome the sense that as a spiritual student I should be anything.

Cyclopea so dear, your Emerald Flame,
exposes every subtle, dualistic power game,
including the game of wanting to say,
that truth is defined in only one way.

13 | I Invoke Freedom from Projecting In

> **Cyclopea so dear, in Emerald Sphere,**
> **in raising perception we shall persevere,**
> **as deep in our hearts your truth we revere,**
> **to immaculate vision the earth does adhere.**

7. A spiritual teaching presents ideas that are coming to me from without. The purpose of the teaching is to take me towards the point where I am the open door for my I AM Presence.

> Cyclopea so dear, we're feeling the flow,
> as your Living Truth upon us you bestow,
> from all dual vision we are now set free,
> planet earth in immaculate matrix will be.

> **Cyclopea so dear, in Emerald Sphere,**
> **in raising perception we shall persevere,**
> **as deep in our hearts your truth we revere,**
> **to immaculate vision the earth does adhere.**

8. When I have the idea that as a spiritual student I should be such and such, the mechanism behind it is the very essence of the outer self. I am seeking to make myself conform to an idea in the outer mind.

> Cyclopea so dear, the truth is now clear,
> we see higher purpose for which we are here
> we know truth transcends all systems below,
> immersed in your light, we continue to grow.

> **Cyclopea so dear, in Emerald Sphere,**
> **in raising perception we shall persevere,**
> **as deep in our hearts your truth we revere,**
> **to immaculate vision the earth does adhere.**

9. The self I am seeking to make conform is partly the outer self, which will gladly conform. I am also forcing the Conscious You, and the Conscious You is not the outer self, it never has been and it never will be.

> Cyclopea so dear, we're feeling your joy,
> as creative vision we now do employ,
> in lifting earth out of serpentine cage,
> to manifest Saint Germain's Golden Age.

> **Cyclopea so dear, in Emerald Sphere,**
> **in raising perception we shall persevere,**
> **as deep in our hearts your truth we revere,**
> **to immaculate vision the earth does adhere.**

Part 3

1. The Conscious You did not descend with the outer self. It needs the outer self to express itself in this world, but I do not need the outer self to ascend, to re-enter the spiritual realm. I need to let go of the outer self in order to enter.

> Raphael Archangel, your light so intense,
> raise us beyond all human pretense.
> Mother Mary and you have a vision so bold,
> to see that our highest potential unfold.

**Raphael Archangel, for vision we pray,
Raphael Archangel, show us the way,
Raphael Archangel, your emerald ray,
Raphael Archangel, our lives a new day.**

2. When I am forcing the Conscious You to comply with an image created by the outer self, I am not being the open door for my I AM Presence.

Raphael Archangel, in emerald sphere,
to immaculate vision we always adhere.
Mother Mary enfolds us in her Sacred Heart,
from Mother's true love, we're never apart.

**Raphael Archangel, for vision we pray,
Raphael Archangel, show us the way,
Raphael Archangel, your emerald ray,
Raphael Archangel, our lives a new day.**

3. The entire trick of the fallen beings is to get me to believe that I cannot be an open door for the I AM Presence, that it is wrong to express my spiritual light, it is wrong to be creative because I should always follow rules.

Raphael Archangel, all ailments you heal,
each cell in our bodies in light now you seal.
Mother Mary's immaculate concept we see,
perfection of health our new reality.

**Raphael Archangel, for vision we pray,
Raphael Archangel, show us the way,
Raphael Archangel, your emerald ray,
Raphael Archangel, our lives a new day.**

4. The trick of the fallen beings is to get me to believe that instead of being creative and expressing the creativity of the I AM Presence, I have to allow the creative flow to go through the filter of the outer self.

> Raphael Archangel, your light is so real,
> the vision of Christ in us you reveal.
> Mother Mary now helps us to truly transcend,
> in emerald light with you we ascend.
>
> **Raphael Archangel, for vision we pray,**
> **Raphael Archangel, show us the way,**
> **Raphael Archangel, your emerald ray,**
> **Raphael Archangel, our lives a new day.**

5. If I allow my creativity to flow through this filter, there will be certain conditions in the material realm that I will never go beyond, I will never dare to express anything that challenges or transcends those limitations.

> Raphael Archangel, diseases are done,
> as you help us see that all life is One,
> we no longer do your true love reject,
> immaculate vision on all we project.
>
> **Raphael Archangel, for vision we pray,**
> **Raphael Archangel, show us the way,**
> **Raphael Archangel, your emerald ray,**
> **Raphael Archangel, our lives a new day.**

6. The secondary laws of nature are defined so that people believe that they have no power beyond a certain level. If I have come to see myself as having to live up to a certain image of what it means to be a spiritual student, then I cannot be a completely open door for the creative power of my I AM Presence.

> Raphael Archangel, we're healing the earth,
> in immaculate vision we give her rebirth,
> a new era has on this day begun,
> your emerald light now shines like a sun.

> **Raphael Archangel, for vision we pray,**
> **Raphael Archangel, show us the way,**
> **Raphael Archangel, your emerald ray,**
> **Raphael Archangel, our lives a new day.**

7. I have my Divine plan, and I will not allow my image of what it means to be a good spiritual student to stand in the way of the fulfillment of my Divine plan.

> Raphael Archangel, the fall is behind,
> as all of earth's people the Christ path do find,
> we call now to you all people to heal,
> as four lower bodies in love you do seal.

> **Raphael Archangel, for vision we pray,**
> **Raphael Archangel, show us the way,**
> **Raphael Archangel, your emerald ray,**
> **Raphael Archangel, our lives a new day.**

8. I am willing to take the next step even if I don't see clearly where it is going to lead me. It is more important to fulfill my Divine plan than to live up to my current image of what it means to be a good spiritual student.

Raphael Archangel, as you bring the light,
the forces of darkness swiftly take flight,
their day is now done as we claim the earth,
spreading to all an innocent mirth.

Raphael Archangel, for vision we pray,
Raphael Archangel, show us the way,
Raphael Archangel, your emerald ray,
Raphael Archangel, our lives a new day.

9. I cannot fulfill my Divine plan by seeking to force myself to live up to an image defined in this world. I want to be completely open to letting my I AM Presence express what it wants through me.

Raphael Archangel, our vision set free,
as we can now see God's reality,
as Saint Germain's vision is manifest here,
the earth is now sealed in immaculate sphere.

Raphael Archangel, for vision we pray,
Raphael Archangel, show us the way,
Raphael Archangel, your emerald ray,
Raphael Archangel, our lives a new day.

Part 4

1. Whenever I have a feeling that I should *be* something, I should *do* something, I should behave a certain way, then this comes from the separate self. It is a pull that opens me to the fallen beings.

> Raphael Archangel, your light so intense,
> raise us beyond all human pretense.
> Mother Mary and you have a vision so bold,
> to see that our highest potential unfold.
>
> **Raphael Archangel, for vision we pray,**
> **Raphael Archangel, show us the way,**
> **Raphael Archangel, your emerald ray,**
> **Raphael Archangel, our lives a new day.**

2. The ascended masters are not seeking to force me to do anything, they are not appealing to my fear, to my doubt, to my shame, to my guilt.

> Raphael Archangel, in emerald sphere,
> to immaculate vision we always adhere.
> Mother Mary enfolds us in her Sacred Heart,
> from Mother's true love, we're never apart.
>
> **Raphael Archangel, for vision we pray,**
> **Raphael Archangel, show us the way,**
> **Raphael Archangel, your emerald ray,**
> **Raphael Archangel, our lives a new day.**

3. A fear-based organizational culture causes me to doubt my intuitive promptings from my I AM Presence. I surrender all fear-based images of what I should be like as a spiritual student.

> Raphael Archangel, all ailments you heal,
> each cell in our bodies in light now you seal.
> Mother Mary's immaculate concept we see,
> perfection of health our new reality.
>
> **Raphael Archangel, for vision we pray,**
> **Raphael Archangel, show us the way,**
> **Raphael Archangel, your emerald ray,**
> **Raphael Archangel, our lives a new day.**

4. The fallen beings want to create a mechanical path to salvation so they can enter the ascended realm without giving up all remnants of the separate self, all remnants of the fallen consciousness. They want to cheat or force their way into heaven.

> Raphael Archangel, your light is so real,
> the vision of Christ in us you reveal.
> Mother Mary now helps us to truly transcend,
> in emerald light with you we ascend.
>
> **Raphael Archangel, for vision we pray,**
> **Raphael Archangel, show us the way,**
> **Raphael Archangel, your emerald ray,**
> **Raphael Archangel, our lives a new day.**

5. I surrender the subtle belief that in order to qualify for my ascension, I need to follow certain mechanical steps. I accept that the path is a creative process because it requires me to see an illusion and decide to let go of it.

13 | I Invoke Freedom from Projecting In

Raphael Archangel, diseases are done,
as you help us see that all life is One,
we no longer do your true love reject,
immaculate vision on all we project.

**Raphael Archangel, for vision we pray,
Raphael Archangel, show us the way,
Raphael Archangel, your emerald ray,
Raphael Archangel, our lives a new day.**

6. As long as I have any intent of forcing any other being or forcing the world, I cannot ascend. I need to be completely non-aggressive, non-violent, in order to enter the spiritual realm.

Raphael Archangel, we're healing the earth,
in immaculate vision we give her rebirth,
a new era has on this day begun,
your emerald light now shines like a sun.

**Raphael Archangel, for vision we pray,
Raphael Archangel, show us the way,
Raphael Archangel, your emerald ray,
Raphael Archangel, our lives a new day.**

7. The fallen beings are on an impossible quest. I consciously and intuitively see that I no longer want to follow this false path, I no longer want to live my entire life based on this outer idea of what I should be. I want to be who I am at any moment.

Raphael Archangel, the fall is behind,
as all of earth's people the Christ path do find,
we call now to you all people to heal,
as four lower bodies in love you do seal.

Raphael Archangel, for vision we pray,
Raphael Archangel, show us the way,
Raphael Archangel, your emerald ray,
Raphael Archangel, our lives a new day.

8. The outer self knows it is mortal but it wants to create the impression that it can become immortal. It thinks that in order to become immortal, it must remain constant over time.

Raphael Archangel, as you bring the light,
the forces of darkness swiftly take flight,
their day is now done as we claim the earth,
spreading to all an innocent mirth.

Raphael Archangel, for vision we pray,
Raphael Archangel, show us the way,
Raphael Archangel, your emerald ray,
Raphael Archangel, our lives a new day.

9. The dream behind the fallen beings and their secondary laws of nature is to create something that is permanent, that can remain constant over time.

Raphael Archangel, our vision set free,
as we can now see God's reality,
as Saint Germain's vision is manifest here,
the earth is now sealed in immaculate sphere.

Raphael Archangel, for vision we pray,
Raphael Archangel, show us the way,
Raphael Archangel, your emerald ray,
Raphael Archangel, our lives a new day.

Part 5

1. Being an open door for my I AM Presence does not mean that I am *always* the same. It means that I am *never* the same because whatever the I AM Presence wants to express through me in a given situation, I allow this to happen.

Hilarion, on emerald shore,
we're free from all that's gone before.
Hilarion, we let all go,
that keeps us out of sacred flow.

Hilarion, with light so green,
we see behind the matter screen,
immaculate our inner sight,
we see the earth is taking flight.

2. I am willing to neutralize my outer mind and go into my inner space so I can be completely open to my I AM Presence.

Hilarion, the secret key,
is wisdom's own reality.
Hilarion, all life is healed,
the ego's face no more concealed.

> Hilarion, with light so green,
> we see behind the matter screen,
> immaculate our inner sight,
> we see the earth is taking flight.

3. I cannot know with the outer mind all of the complexities involved in a given situation. An analysis of a situation would be so complex that it would take me a very long time to fathom it with the conscious mind.

> Hilarion, your love for life,
> helps us surrender inner strife.
> Hilarion, your loving words,
> thrill our hearts like song of birds.

> Hilarion, with light so green,
> we see behind the matter screen,
> immaculate our inner sight,
> we see the earth is taking flight.

4. By the time I understood with the outer mind how I should act, the situation would have changed and now it was too late to act. Being a Christed being does not mean that I have an explanation with the outer mind of how I should act in every situation. It does not mean that I know every aspect of a situation.

> Hilarion, invoke the light,
> your sacred formulas recite.
> Hilarion, your secret tone,
> philosopher's most sacred stone.

**Hilarion, with light so green,
we see behind the matter screen,
immaculate our inner sight,
we see the earth is taking flight.**

5. What it means to be a Christed being is that I am always tuned in to the I AM Presence and I follow the impulse from the I AM Presence in every situation.

Hilarion, with love you greet,
us in your temple over Crete.
Hilarion, your emerald light,
the third eye sees with Christic sight.

**Hilarion, with light so green,
we see behind the matter screen,
immaculate our inner sight,
we see the earth is taking flight.**

6. I am not seeking to force myself to act the same way in this situation as I did in the past. I am not imposing any *should* upon a given situation. I am not seeking to be *constant* in my actions. I am seeking to be *spontaneous* in every action.

Hilarion, you give us fruit,
of truth that is so absolute.
Hilarion, all stress decrease,
as our ambitions we release.

**Hilarion, with light so green,
we see behind the matter screen,
immaculate our inner sight,
we see the earth is taking flight.**

7. I surrender the idea that the spiritual path is about coming to know and understand more and more with the outer mind, the linear mind, the intellectual mind.

> Hilarion, our chakras clear,
> as we let go of subtlest fear.
> Hilarion, we are sincere,
> as freedom's truth we do revere.

> **Hilarion, with light so green,**
> **we see behind the matter screen,**
> **immaculate our inner sight,**
> **we see the earth is taking flight.**

8. I surrender the idea that I will finally come to a point where I know everything and I can explain everything. Therefore, in every situation, I can know what is the right thing to do.

> Hilarion, you balance all,
> the seven rays upon our call.
> Hilarion, you keep us true,
> as we remain all one with you.

> **Hilarion, with light so green,**
> **we see behind the matter screen,**
> **immaculate our inner sight,**
> **we see the earth is taking flight.**

9. I surrender the tendency to analyze my actions in great detail and "beat myself up" because the result is never good enough.

Hilarion, your Presence here,
filling up the inner sphere.
Life is now a sacred flow,
God Vision we on all bestow.

**Hilarion, with light so green,
we see behind the matter screen,
immaculate our inner sight,
we see the earth is taking flight.**

Part 6

1. When I act based on the idea that I should be a certain way, I inevitably must judge myself and the outcome of the action. An action never lives up to the perfect image.

Hilarion, on emerald shore,
we're free from all that's gone before.
Hilarion, we let all go,
that keeps us out of sacred flow.

**Hilarion, with light so green,
we see behind the matter screen,
immaculate our inner sight,
we see the earth is taking flight.**

2. I surrender the tendency to go into a process of dealing with the pain of not having lived up to the perfect image, having to explain it in some way, having to analyze it, having to look at it as a learning experience and force myself to try to learn from it.

Hilarion, the secret key,
is wisdom's own reality.
Hilarion, all life is healed,
the ego's face no more concealed.

**Hilarion, with light so green,
we see behind the matter screen,
immaculate our inner sight,
we see the earth is taking flight.**

3. As I go towards Christhood, this mechanism falls away. I don't analyze because I know that I was tuned in to the Presence. This is what the Presence wanted to do in that situation and regardless of the outcome, this was the best that could happen in that situation.

Hilarion, your love for life,
helps us surrender inner strife.
Hilarion, your loving words,
thrill our hearts like song of birds.

**Hilarion, with light so green,
we see behind the matter screen,
immaculate our inner sight,
we see the earth is taking flight.**

4. I accept that as a Christed being I will not always do something that has the ideal or the perfect consequences. The reason is that I will never override the free will of others.

13 | I Invoke Freedom from Projecting In

Hilarion, invoke the light,
your sacred formulas recite.
Hilarion, your secret tone,
philosopher's most sacred stone.

**Hilarion, with light so green,
we see behind the matter screen,
immaculate our inner sight,
we see the earth is taking flight.**

5. I am here to give other people an opportunity to transcend their level of consciousness and come up higher, but I never seek to force their choices and thus I do not worry about the outcome being less than ideal.

Hilarion, with love you greet,
us in your temple over Crete.
Hilarion, your emerald light,
the third eye sees with Christic sight.

**Hilarion, with light so green,
we see behind the matter screen,
immaculate our inner sight,
we see the earth is taking flight.**

6. I do not go within and analyze and beat myself up over this because I know that a situation is not fixed in time. Life is a process that continually moves on. It is not the goal of a Christed being to produce a specific outer result and to maintain that result over time.

Hilarion, you give us fruit,
of truth that is so absolute.
Hilarion, all stress decrease,
as our ambitions we release.

**Hilarion, with light so green,
we see behind the matter screen,
immaculate our inner sight,
we see the earth is taking flight.**

7. A Christed being is not seeking to create permanency, constancy, ongoingness. A Christed being is always seeking to move the process of life along.

Hilarion, our chakras clear,
as we let go of subtlest fear.
Hilarion, we are sincere,
as freedom's truth we do revere.

**Hilarion, with light so green,
we see behind the matter screen,
immaculate our inner sight,
we see the earth is taking flight.**

8. I know life is a river that is constantly flowing. It is not a matter of analyzing a certain outcome of what it should or should not have been. It is a matter of saying: "Now that the outcome was this, what is the next step? How can we now move the situation further so that we get onward in the process of life?"

Hilarion, you balance all,
the seven rays upon our call.
Hilarion, you keep us true,
as we remain all one with you.

Hilarion, with light so green,
we see behind the matter screen,
immaculate our inner sight,
we see the earth is taking flight.

9. The fallen beings are constantly working towards a result that they envision. A Christed being has no end result, but is seeking to move along the river, helping people constantly transcend their current situation, their current state of consciousness, and move forward.

Hilarion, your Presence here,
filling up the inner sphere.
Life is now a sacred flow,
God Vision we on all bestow.

Hilarion, with light so green,
we see behind the matter screen,
immaculate our inner sight,
we see the earth is taking flight.

Part 7

1. What the fallen beings have done with the secondary laws of nature is that they have attempted to stop the River of Life from flowing. They have attempted to create a situation where they can maintain a certain state over time.

> Divine Director, I now see,
> the world is unreality,
> in my heart I now truly feel,
> the Spirit is all that is real.
>
> **Divine Director, send the light,**
> **from blindness clear my inner sight,**
> **my vision free, my vision clear,**
> **your guidance is forever here.**

2. Transcendence is what the ascended masters want, constant self-transcendence.

> Divine Director, vision give,
> in clarity I want to live,
> I now behold my plan Divine,
> the plan that is uniquely mine.
>
> **Divine Director, send the light,**
> **from blindness clear my inner sight,**
> **my vision free, my vision clear,**
> **your guidance is forever here.**

3. I am willing to look at what the image I have of myself says about the goal I am working towards, my vision of where the spiritual path leads.

> Divine Director, show in me,
> the ego games, and set me free,
> help me escape the ego's cage,
> to help bring in the golden age.

> **Divine Director, send the light,**
> **from blindness clear my inner sight,**
> **my vision free, my vision clear,**
> **your guidance is forever here.**

4. I am willing to see any fixed images I have of what is the end goal of the spiritual path, what it means to be a Christed being, what it means to be an ascended master.

> Divine Director, I'm with you,
> my vision one, no longer two,
> as karma's veil you do disperse,
> I see a whole new universe.

> **Divine Director, send the light,**
> **from blindness clear my inner sight,**
> **my vision free, my vision clear,**
> **your guidance is forever here.**

5. All such fixed images are out of touch with reality because the path is ongoing self-transcendence. It never ends.

> Divine Director, I go up,
> electric light now fills my cup,
> consume in me all shadows old,
> bestow on me a vision bold.
>
> **Divine Director, send the light,**
> **from blindness clear my inner sight,**
> **my vision free, my vision clear,**
> **your guidance is forever here.**

6. If I am striving towards a fixed goal, I will never get there and that means I will be dissatisfied with myself indefinitely. I do not want to be dissatisfied with myself and my progress.

> Divine Director, heart of gold,
> my sacred labor I unfold,
> o blessed Guru, I now see,
> where my own plan is taking me.
>
> **Divine Director, send the light,**
> **from blindness clear my inner sight,**
> **my vision free, my vision clear,**
> **your guidance is forever here.**

7. I want to be feeling and accepting that I am exactly where I need to be at this point. I want to feel completely at peace with knowing that I am where I need to be. I will also move on to the next level and then I will be content there.

> Divine Director, by your grace,
> in grander scheme I find my place,
> my individual flame I see,
> uniqueness God has given me.

13 | I Invoke Freedom from Projecting In

**Divine Director, send the light,
from blindness clear my inner sight,
my vision free, my vision clear,
your guidance is forever here.**

8. I surrender the sense that I have a goal and that I am not there, and the emptiness that follows. I am ready and willing to confront it and overcome it.

Divine Director, vision one,
I see that I AM God's own Sun,
with your direction so Divine,
I am now letting my light shine.

**Divine Director, send the light,
from blindness clear my inner sight,
my vision free, my vision clear,
your guidance is forever here.**

9. Hilarion, I am ready for you to help me see the image I am imposing upon myself right now of what it means to be a spiritual student. When I can see it, I will let it go and be more and allow myself to be more than that image.

Divine Director, what a gift,
to be a part of Spirit's lift,
to raise mankind out of the night,
to bask in Spirit's loving sight.

**Divine Director, send the light,
from blindness clear my inner sight,
my vision free, my vision clear,
your guidance is forever here.**

Sealing:

In the name of the Divine Mother, I fully accept that the power of these calls is used to set free the River of Life, so it can outpicture the perfect vision of Christ for my own life, for all people and for the planet. In the name I AM THAT I AM, it is done! Amen.

14 | BEING A TRUE HEALER

I AM the Ascended Master Hilarion. When you reach the sixth level of my retreat, you face an initiation that at the conscious level will be ongoing. This does not prevent you from moving on in the course, but it does mean that the initiation you face here is something you will have to work on for a time. It is meant to take you beyond the very subtle and very persistent programming that you have been exposed to, most likely for many lifetimes, in many cases for the entire time you have been in embodiment on earth.

Now, you see, my beloved: What have I done in these last lessons? I have talked to you about the need to see that you are using the power of vision to project an image outside yourself. You have an image of what you want the world to be like, or what the world *is* like, and you are projecting this outside your mind. In the last lesson I took you through the realization that you also have an image of what *you* should be like as a spiritual person, or as a human being, and you are projecting this vision in upon yourself.

Seeing the world as it is

When you begin to clear these visions that you are projecting, when you begin to stop projecting with the mind, you can move on to a phase where, instead of seeing the world as you think it is or as you want it to be, you can see the world as it *is*. Philosophers have for centuries been aware of the influence of perception upon what human beings see. Unfortunately, Western philosophers have not been willing to look at the mind itself and therefore they have not discovered the relatively simple truths we have given you about the four levels of the mind. If one is a philosopher and wants to understand what human beings can and cannot see, then one would think one would want to examine one's own subconscious mind before one starts making grandiose conclusions about how the universe functions.

Nevertheless, it is not my intent here to give a philosophy lesson, but to help you see that it is possible to see the world in a different way than the way you were brought up to see it and the way the vast majority of human beings see the world. We have talked about the secondary laws of nature and how the fallen beings have attempted to create something that functions in mechanical ways so that they can get control over it without changing the fundamental mindset of separation. Separation, therefore, is the essence of the fallen mindset.

What you need to come to recognize here is that the universe allows you to do many things but there is always a price to be paid. The fallen beings have been able to change how the universe works in the energetic realm of planet earth because they have been able to densify matter. The more dense matter becomes, the more it functions according to laws that are, if not eternal and never-changing, then at least ongoing for a long time. The laws of nature, that scientists currently see, have been in operation on this planet for a very long timespan compared to the lifespan of a human being. They have, however, not been in operation forever on this planet.

Circumventing the laws of nature

What you need to recognize is that when the fallen beings managed to get humankind at large to go into the duality consciousness, the collective consciousness started creating these secondary laws of nature that are an effect of the densification of matter. What you also need to recognize is that the fallen beings themselves become subject to these laws.

Now, they think they have found ways to circumvent these laws and to, for example, gather great power and riches around one person. This, as I said, can be done on a temporary basis. What the fallen beings do not recognize, is that the basic mindset that has allowed the creation of these secondary laws of nature is something that they are subject to because they cannot see beyond it. Even though they have been able to manipulate matter in a certain way, they cannot go beyond a certain limit. They cannot do what you saw, for example, Jesus do: walk on water, heal the withered hand and other things like that. This is not within their capability with the level of vision they have.

You can create a condition like what you have on earth where matter is more dense than is natural, but how do you create this condition? You create it by projecting a limited vision upon the Ma-ter Light. How do you project this vision? Well, only when you have this vision in your mind. How long can you have this vision in your mind when you are reborn over several lifetimes, without actually coming to be so identified with it that you think it is the only true vision? You cannot see beyond it because there is nothing beyond it to see. This is what has happened to the fallen beings on earth; this is what has happened to the vast majority of humankind.

You have, over several lifetimes, projected a vision of matter being so dense (and therefore setting certain limitations for what you can do) that you have come to believe in this vision. The vast majority of human beings believe that matter is dense, matter does set limitations for their creative ability and the only way to really get beyond those limitations is to use some kind of force-based technology to manipulate and force matter into compliance.

How fallen beings control matter

Well, my beloved, let us look at the example of a person who has gathered to himself great riches. He has started a company that employs thousands of people and that sells some kind of product. How has he gathered those riches to himself? Well, he has partly used his own power of mind, which is the power to control other people. You see, my beloved, the fallen beings in general have not worked on the power to control matter directly. They have worked on their power to control other people and get them to work for them. This is what I, in earlier lessons, talked about as the false self-mastery that the fallen beings have attained.

This rich person has been able to manipulate other people to work for him, at a wage that is far less than the value they actually produce with their labor. He can reap the majority of the fruits of the people's labor and therefore concentrate wealth in his own hands instead of sharing it with his employees. You see, this wealth is created through the work, the physical work, of the employees. Many, many people have done this physical work in order to create, generate, concentrate the wealth in the hands of this one person.

The alternative would have been that if the person really wanted to experience having great wealth, then that person could have focused on expanding the abilities of his mind to bring this wealth forth in a more direct manner by bringing energy from the spiritual realm into the material frequency spectrum. You understand that there are two ways to bring about wealth? The one is, as I described, that you accept conditions as they are in the material universe and then you get other people to work for you and you take the wealth that they produce. The other way to bring forth wealth, other than working with matter and creating something more out of matter, is to work with the mind's ability to be an open door for spiritual light to be brought down through the four levels until it is expressed in the material.

You can actually manifest wealth through the powers of the mind alone, but this is not what the fallen beings have done. They have been trapped by their desire to have power over other people, or even have power over the universe, or even thinking they have power over God. They have accepted that matter has a certain density. That is why they will do everything they can to make sure that nobody challenges this. That is why they are working against anybody who starts to manifest a degree of Christhood, trying to in all ways manipulate you into not daring to accept what Christhood is about and that Christhood can give you the mastery of mind over matter.

How to be a true healer

Now, my beloved, one aspect of the Fifth Ray is that of healing. I know that some of you have been waiting for me to speak about healing, but perhaps you are not quite aware that I have been speaking about healing all along, even though I have not been using the word. How do you heal, my beloved? Well, through the power of vision.

If you cannot free your vision from the illusions of the fallen beings, you cannot heal. It is very simple. What did I say? The universe allows you to do certain things, such as densify matter, but everything has a price. When you densify matter, you densify the bodies you are wearing and those denser bodies will be subject to certain laws. What you do not realize is that when you start creating these secondary laws of nature, then the Law of Free Will allows you to do this. The price you pay is that your creation becomes subject to what we have often referred to as the second law of thermodynamics. This says that if you create something that is set aside from the primary laws of nature, then whatever you create will begin to break down. As soon as you create something, there is an in-built force in your creation that will break it down over time. This is done as a safety mechanism so you cannot create a condition that traps you for eternity in your own creation.

The hope is always that you will have enough of a certain experience so that you will feel a desire from inside yourself to have more and therefore you will be willing to expand your mind. If people do not come to that point, then what we call the second law of thermodynamics (or even the wrath of Shiva) begins to break down what you have created. That is the primary reason you have diseases in the human body. Matter is so dense that anything that is created at this level of density will have built-in forces that break it down. That is why your body ages; that is why diseases manifest.

Now, my beloved, what the fallen beings want you to believe is that there is nothing you can do about this. They want you to believe that matter is matter and matter has a certain density. Matter is functioning under these secondary laws of nature and you cannot go beyond it. That is why they want you to believe that your physical body is an entirely material creation. It functions according to certain mechanical, material laws. Your body is a biological mechanism, it is a chemical factory or whatever they want you to believe.

They want you to believe that once a disease has manifested, that disease must have a physical cause and therefore, there may be or there may not be, some physical cure that can be devised and executed. If there is no physical cure that has been discovered, then there is nothing you can do about the disease, other than hope that in the future, the materialistic scientists will come up with a cause and a cure.

Now, as we have explained to you many times, you have four lower bodies. What manifests in the physical body is a projection of the conditions in your three higher bodies. A physical disease starts in the emotional, mental and identity realms and is then projected upon the physical body. Obviously, any cure must start there as well.

What I need you to come to realize here is that the fallen beings actually have a point when they say that you cannot change certain conditions in matter. I need to explain this in a sort of roundabout way because it is a subtle point.

Why some people cannot heal with the mind

We may say, my beloved, that if the Conscious You is entirely focused at the physical level (where you truly believe that you are a human being, that you are limited to the powers of the body and what technology can be created), then you cannot change matter, you cannot go beyond the secondary laws of nature. In a sense, we could say that if you are functioning at that level, then the fallen beings are right: You are trapped in the material universe and you are subject to its laws.

Therefore, you cannot heal a physical disease through the powers of the mind. You can only seek to find some physical means to destroy the disease or change the course of the disease. Can you not see that this is an extremely primitive view of healing? The primary view that seems to be penetrating the medical establishments in the modern world is that there is a state of normal health. Once in a while, a disease manifests that is abnormal. This is an abnormal condition. It is caused by something that is abnormal, such as a bacteria. Then, we need to discover what the bacteria is and we need to find a way to kill the bacteria. If we can do that, we can cure the disease.

Something is destroying your body, and in order to cure you, we need to destroy that something. Can you see that you are seeking to cure destruction with another form of destruction and this can only lead to further problems in the long run? Destruction cannot overcome destruction. You cannot overcome a problem with the same mindset that created the problem.

This now ties in to my attempts to help you see that you need to stop projecting with the mind. What is it you need to stop projecting? Well, the first layer of projections that you have is projections that involve some kind of judgment based on what should or should not be taking place, what is right or wrong, for example. When you look at a disease, you immediately go into a mindset that this is wrong, that this should not be happening.

Now, what is the mindset behind the medical establishment in the modern world? It is, my beloved, that when something goes wrong with the body, then we need to find the cause and destroy the cause at a physical, mechanical level. What is the deeper mindset behind this? It is an unwillingness to look at the mind itself, to look at consciousness, to look beyond the physical level.

You are looking for a cause only at the physical level, but, as we have said, the physical level is simply the tip of the iceberg, a projection from the three higher levels. The fallen beings are not willing to do this in themselves and they do not want anyone below them to do so. They realize that if people start looking at their higher bodies, then they can free themselves from the limitations of the physical level and therefore the power that the fallen beings have over them. You are not going to be a slave of somebody on earth when you know you are a spiritual being and that you can take command over your reactions. You do not need to fear anyone on earth.

What is the real mindset behind the modern approach to healing? It is, my beloved, that you look at the disease as something that has gone wrong with the body. Then, you want to remove the symptom of this without looking at the person's mind and changing the person's mind. You want to continue doing what you are doing without changing yourself. You want to change the world without changing yourself. This is the hallmark of the fallen beings.

I have said that some of them have been willing to look at certain aspects of their minds and gain a certain "mastery," as we might call it, over their minds. They have not been willing to go very deep and look at their intentions, their sense of separation, their desire to gain power for themselves at the expense of other people. They have not been willing to overcome this self-centeredness, this basic sense that they are separate beings and that they can have power as separate beings. This, they are not willing to deal with.

This is the mindset that has filtered down to the approach to healing in the modern world. You are not asking people to look at their state of mind when they go to the doctor.

The doctor looks for a physical cause and then seeks to deal with that physical cause. How often does the doctor sit down and say: "Maybe you should look at your lifestyle, maybe you should look at your state of mind, maybe you should go to a psychologist, maybe you should this, maybe you should that?"

You see here: If you are trapped in this mindset, if this is your approach to your physical body and to healing, then you cannot attain the powers to heal with the mind. It cannot be done.

How we look at things

Now, I want to explain this in a slightly different way because we need to go to an even deeper level of how you look at matter. I have said that the first level of judgment is that there are certain things that are right and certain things that are wrong. Having good health is right, having a disease is wrong. There is an even deeper level and that is where you accept things as being things, as being unchangeable, as being beyond the powers of the mind to change.

I would like you to envision that in front of you is a table and upon the table sits a rock. You can pick up the rock; you can feel that it is hard. It is rounded but hard. You cannot crush that rock; you cannot mold it with your hands. It is unchangeable by normal means. You can, of course, create a machine that can grind the rock or smoothen it out. Nevertheless, with the power of your hands, there is little you can do with it. There is less you can do with it with the power of the mind, or so you have been brought up to think.

What I want you to become aware of here is that when you are looking at a simple thing like a rock, there is a program in your mind (and it actually starts in the visual cortex) that immediately categorizes and labels this as a rock. You have now projected upon this thing that it is a rock and you have certain characteristics associated in your mind with a rock. It is not just about what the rock is, but also what you *can* and *cannot* do with a rock.

You realize that there is a certain level of your mind where you are labeling everything based on certain categories? You are labeling everything as things. My beloved, when you look at this rock, do you not realize that the word "rock" is just a word that has been chosen (or perhaps unconsciously chosen) and it has been associated with the thing you call a rock? You might as well call it an apple. If from ancient times, people had used the word "apple" about rocks, then today you would be calling rocks "apples." It does not mean that you would think that a rock was something soft you could eat. What I am trying to help you see is that "rock" is just a word. When you begin to realize that "rock" is just a word, then you can say: "But what else is there about a rock that is just characteristics that we have chosen with the mind?"

You see that human beings with their minds came up with the word rock and associated it with the thing. They could as well have chosen a different word. They also came up with the characteristics of a rock. It is hard, it is difficult to change, you cannot mold it with your hands—all of these things. These are also just characteristics that are defined in the mind—*by* the mind. They are just one way to look at a rock.

Seeing beyond things

Is there a different way to look at a rock, perhaps? Could you use your power of vision to go behind, to go beyond, the vision that most people have when they see a rock? Well, let me take you on a journey based on what you actually learned in science class in school. Is a rock just a rock? Well, you know (because you learned in school) that a rock is made out of molecules that are small units that you cannot see with your physical eyes. It is possible to look at a rock in a different way than at the level of the thing. You could look at the rock as simply a collection of molecules.

You know, for example, that you can take many small rocks and mix them with some glue and you can put them together so they form a ball. Now you have a ball that may be as big as the big rock, but it is made out of much smaller units. You could even take sand, grains of sand, put them together into a ball, but you can see that this is not one big rock, one solid rock. It is made of smaller pieces and it could actually be taken apart. It could be given a different shape, if you could just make those smaller pieces move in relation to each other.

What I am helping you see here is that beyond your perception of the rock as a solid object, it is possible to go to a deeper level where you see that the rock is made out of smaller units that have simply been combined and put together into this shape that you call a rock—and which you see as one coherent thing that cannot be easily changed.

Now, you know of course (also from science) that molecules are made of smaller units, called atoms. What you may or may not have learned in school (but what you may have read later), is that atoms are even made of smaller units, called elementary particles. If you have studied a little bit of quantum physics, you will realize that these elementary particles have a dual nature, or at least this is how scientists currently see it. An elementary particle will sometimes behave like a traditional particle (that is a solid object) and sometimes it will behave like a wave, an energy wave that vibrates. You see that even if you take what science currently recognizes, there is a different way to look at a rock? You can start at the level of the thing, the rock. At this point, you see it as a coherent unit. If you go to deeper and deeper levels, you see that it is not coherent because it is made out of smaller units. Why is it that at the level of the thing, you see it as a coherent unit? Where does the coherence come from? Well, it comes entirely from your mind. It is a mental image projected by your mind.

A rock is not coherent at all. It is made out of molecules that are made out of atoms, that are made out of elementary particles, that are really energy waves. Not only is there a lack of coherence in the rock, but when you go to deeper levels of perception, you also see that the rock seems less and less solid. The "rock" is a solid unit because your mind sees it as solid. When you go to the level of the molecules, you realize it is made out of smaller units that could potentially be moved around in relation to each other, or some of them could be taken away.

Can you see that, at the level of the rock, it seems impossible to manipulate the rock and to change the rock—or at least very difficult? If your mind could go to the level of the molecules and start manipulating the molecules, then it might be very much easier for your mind to manipulate these smaller units than the rock itself. Well, what if you could go to the level of atoms that are even smaller? They might be even easier to manipulate if you could find out how. Now, what if you could go to the level of the elementary particles that are really, actually energy waves?

The mind can manipulate energy waves

My beloved, I agree that your mind cannot manipulate a rock, but why is it that the mind cannot manipulate a rock? It is because the rock is a mental concept created by the mind, and the mind cannot go beyond the concept that it itself has imposed upon the rock. As long as you believe in this concept, as long as you have not questioned it, as long as you see it as inevitable, as unchangeable, then your mind cannot manipulate the rock.

What is your mind, my beloved? Is it not an energy field? What is the rock? It is made of molecules that are made of atoms that are made of elementary particles that are truly energy waves. If your mind is an energy field, why should it not be possible for your mind to manipulate the energy fields that make up the elementary particles that make up the atoms that make up the molecules that make up the rock?

If you can go to a deep enough level with the mind, why couldn't you manipulate the rock with the mind? Or why couldn't you heal your physical body with the mind when you realize that your body is also made up of smaller units? Not only are there organs inside the body but everything in the body is made out of molecules. Everything is made out of atoms. Everything is made out of elementary particles that are truly energy waves.

Your mind is an energy wave. Your body is an energy wave. Why could not the mind attain the mastery of being able to manipulate the basic energy waves that make up your body and thereby change the body even at the physical level? You see, you cannot do this as long as your mind is fixated on this "thing," this image that you have imposed on the physical body. You see the body as a thing, as a coherent unit. You may realize it has parts, such as organs and cells and this and that, but, nevertheless, most people see their bodies as a coherent unit.

Then, something goes wrong with the body and they immediately, my beloved, accept that something has gone wrong with the body. If something has gone wrong with the physical body at the physical level, then their minds are also accepting that it can only be corrected at the physical level. If the cause is not physical (because the body is a projection of the three higher bodies), then why could you not change what is in the three higher bodies and thereby change the physical manifestation?

This, my beloved is simple logic. It is not so simple when your mind is fixated on wanting to see "things." As long as you see your body as a thing, as a coherent unit, you cannot heal the body with the powers of the mind. The mind cannot change the thing concept that the mind itself is imposing upon the body. Do you understand this? Do you grasp how significant this is?

It is the mind itself that has imposed the image of a thing upon the body. As long as the mind has not questioned this image, has not seen it for what it is, namely just an image and has not seen beyond it, then the mind cannot heal the body. If you could free your mind from the tendency to see things as things, then it is indeed possible that you can begin to heal your body through the powers of the mind. This, my beloved, is, of course, what I desire to see for you.

The immaculate concept

It is clear that you have a Divine plan. You have things you need to do. It is clear that in some cases having a disease and dealing with that disease can be part of your Divine plan. In other cases, having a healthy body will be part of your Divine plan. Of course, I want you to be able to come to the point where you either know if a disease is part of your Divine plan, or you know how to transcend the disease and get on with your Divine plan. For you to get to this point, you need to come to certain realizations.

Now, there is a concept, which we have used for some time, and it is originally brought out by Mother Mary. It is the concept of holding the immaculate concept. It is, of course, a play on the idea of the "immaculate conception" where Jesus was supposedly conceived immaculately without the intercession of a human element. In other words, there was no man who gave his sperm to fertilize the egg—it was done by the Holy Spirit. This, of course, is (as we have explained) not truly how it happened.

The point is that Mother Mary has developed this idea that there is an immaculate concept that she can hold. She has explained how she herself held the immaculate concept for Jesus from the moment he was born and until he grew up. My beloved, now look at the situation more closely.

Here is a woman who gives birth to a son. Now, however, he was conceived and whatever her vision may have been of this son, is it not likely that she would have had normal motherly feelings for her son based on her culture? Look at what happens to this son, Jesus. He grows up to be a healthy and capable young man but at the prime of his life he is captured by the authorities, tortured, nailed to a cross and dies. Is this likely to have been the vision that a normal mother would have for her son?

When you look at this, you realize that if Mother Mary was holding the immaculate concept for Jesus, this probably did not mean that from his birth she had the vision that he would one day be captured, tortured and executed. What did it mean that she held the immaculate concept for Jesus? She realized that he was not a normal son, he would not have a normal life, but what was the concept she was holding? Well, she was holding the concept, first of all, that Jesus would continue to grow in consciousness and transcend his consciousness until he reached the level of Christhood that would allow him to fulfill his mission. There are two aspects of the immaculate concept. There is the vision of the continued growth and then the vision that each person has a mission, a Divine plan and holding the vision that the person fulfills that Divine plan.

This is, of course, what you can do for yourself. If you are holding the immaculate concept for yourself, you are holding this Alpha and Omega perspective. First of all, you realize that life is about growth, is about self-transcendence. You are holding the immaculate concept that you will continue to grow, pass your initiations and reach the highest possible level of consciousness in this embodiment. Then, you are holding the vision that there is something you are here to do in this embodiment. You hold the vision that you will fulfill the elements of your Divine plan. Now, this is where you need to step back and realize that if you are holding the immaculate concept for yourself, as I have just explained, then the vision you are holding for yourself is very likely to be dramatically different from the way most people see a normal human life. It may even be dramatically different from the way *you* have seen your life so far.

There is nothing that should not happen

Do you not realize, my beloved, that as you are growing up in modern society, you are having projected upon you from so many sources what your life should or should not be like? It may be parents, siblings, friends, teachers—every person you meet, society itself, the fallen beings and the dark forces and this and that. You have so many projections coming at you throughout your life of what life should or should not be. At this point what I am saying is: If you really want to move on with your life, you need to take a look at this and say: "How many ideas do I have about what should or should not happen to me?"

Then, you need to ask yourself: "Have I so far been thinking that holding the immaculate concept for myself means that my life follows this path that I have taken on from without of what should or should not happen to me? Do I think that holding the immaculate concept is evaluating every situation, based on what should or should not happen and then immediately judging when something happens that I think should not happen, judging it as wrong? Is this how I have been looking at holding the immaculate concept? Is this how I have been looking at my life?"

You see, this is, again, what you have received as you grew up. These projections were based at the level of things, namely that certain things *should* happen in a normal life, certain things *should not* happen. There are certain things you should do and certain things you should not do. This is at the level of things. Your Divine plan involves that you grow in consciousness. In order to transcend a certain level of consciousness, you have to come to see that consciousness.

What you realize here is that, as a human being in embodiment, seeing a certain limitation is a very tricky, very subtle, thing. There are certain instances where you can read a spiritual book and you can come to see: "Oh yes, this is a limitation in my mind and I need to let go of it." We have all (who have been in embodiment) realized that you cannot learn everything this way. There are certain instances where the only way to see something is to experience a certain outer situation. We are simply that way when we are in a dense environment like earth. Sometimes, we can be awakened by a teaching given by words but other times we must be awakened by a direct experience that involves all of the senses, the body, the mind. You see, my beloved, you have to have a certain amount of experiences in life.

What can you do now? You can look at your life and say: "Is it really constructive to evaluate my life based on this standard that has been imposed upon me, of what should or should not happen? Is it not possible to step back and look at my life and say: 'There is no should and there is no should not. Everything that has happened in my life has happened because somehow the universe is trying to show me something, to teach me something, to awaken me from an illusion.'"

What is the message?

Now, instead of resisting the thing that is happening, instead of trying to change the symptoms of it at the physical level, you can start thinking: "What is the message here? What is it that I have not gotten so far?" Let us speak of disease again. You have been brought up to think that normal health is natural and that when a disease happens, this is wrong. You should therefore look at it as something wrong and you should go to a doctor and see if he can find a physical cause and destroy that physical cause.

Now, I am not saying you should not go to a doctor to save your life, my beloved. What I am saying is: What actually prevents you from stepping back and taking a different approach where you say: "Might there be a message in this disease? Is the universe trying to teach me something? Is the disease trying to show me a certain illusion, a certain consciousness, that I need to transcend? Could doing this possibly help me move closer to fulfilling my Divine plan?" Now, as I said, in some cases, you have chosen to have a certain disease because you wanted to demonstrate to other people that you can be a happy, fulfilled and peaceful human being even though you have this limitation. Some of you have also chosen to take on a disease in order to demonstrate that you can overcome that disease, that you can be healed from it, that you can transcend it.

You see, if you have chosen to take on a disease because either you want to show something to others, you want to overcome it or it is part of your Divine plan because you are trying to help yourself see a certain consciousness, then what sense does it make to resist it? Why are you allowing your mind to be fixated at the level of things where you think your body is a thing and now this thing has happened to the body and you need to destroy the thing? Why can you not go beyond this and look at it in a different way? Is there anything that prevents you from doing this? Nay, of course there is not—other than the fallen consciousness that says the last thing you should do is look at yourself.

Transcendence of consciousness

You realize what holding the immaculate concept for yourself really means? What the fallen beings do not want to do is change themselves. What *you* want to do (as a spiritual person who has created a Divine plan in cooperation with the ascended masters) is, of course, to change yourself. The backbone of your Divine plan is centered around changing yourself, transcending levels of consciousness and coming up as many steps (on the 144 levels) that you can do in this lifetime. This is the backbone of your Divine plan: your growth in consciousness.

The very essence of life, the very essence of the spiritual path for you is the transcendence of consciousness. The very essence of what the fallen beings are resisting is the transcendence of consciousness. When you see this, you can say: "Why should I live my life based on the mindset of the fallen ones? I want to live my life based on the mindset of the ascended masters: constant self-transcendence." This is the shift you can make, and many people have come to this level and have not made this shift consciously. Therefore, they are still trapped in this seeing only at the level of things, seeing only at the level of concepts, and judging everything based on what should or should not happen.

Making peace with your life

My beloved, in this lesson and at this level of my retreat, I really desire to see you free yourself from these judgments based at the level of the things (that are just concepts that your mind and the collective mind is imposing upon everything that happens in the universe). I would truly like you to be able to look at your life and be free of all judgments of what should or should not have happened.

I know that many of you have had very difficult lives, very difficult childhoods. You have grown up in very difficult family situations. This is the case for many, many people who are on the spiritual path. You chose those situations for a reason. It is part of your Divine plan. Is there anything there that happened that should not have happened? Was it not an opportunity for you to see something in yourself and for you to demonstrate to others that you can grow up in a difficult situation but rise above it? Can you not come to a point where you can look at your life and say: "Might there be a different way to look at my life than to look at it at the level of the event itself and to judge it based on the should and should not consciousness?" I told you that a rock can be seen as having different components.

Cannot also a situation in life be seen as having different components? Instead of looking at the situation just at the level of things, based on the judgment of what should and should not have happened, you can step back and see a more nuanced, more sophisticated view of the situation. Perhaps your difficult childhood was the quickest way to balance karma from a past life that you had with parents and siblings? Perhaps you could realize that by learning your lesson and taking control over your reactions to the situation, you will have balanced that karma and now you will be free to move on, not only from these people but from the consciousness they represent? Perhaps you chose to be in a very difficult situation because you needed to learn the lesson that you cannot change other people, you can only change yourself? Therefore, when you focus on changing yourself, and when you forgive the other people and allow them to simply be who they are and outplay the consciousness they are outplaying, then you can be free to move on to other aspects of your Divine plan.

Making peace with other people

You see, my beloved, when we are in embodiment, we are all growing up around other people and they have a great impact on our lives. An integral part of the course of self-mastery is that you come to the point where you can see that if you stop judging your interactions with other people based on the should or should not consciousness, then you can be at peace with how that interaction unfolded. You can come to a point where you can see that, as *your* actions are a product of your state of consciousness, *their* actions were a product of their state of consciousness. You can also see that they have complete free will. It is not your job to change another human being. It may be part of your Divine plan that you gave this person an opportunity to see that there is a different way to *act,* there is a different way to *react,* there is a different way to look at life.

You see, my beloved, your job was to give that person the opportunity by demonstrating a different approach. Your job was *not* to force that person to make the choice to accept the lesson. This is why you need to disassociate your view of the situation from the idea that they should have gotten the lesson and they should have learned what you think they should learn. There is no should or should not. Your job was to give them an opportunity to choose, *not* to choose for them.

When you have given the opportunity, you have done your job. That means you can now be free of the situation, but you cannot be free of the situation if you are judging them based on what they should or should not have done. Then you will tie yourself to them again and create a new round of karma for yourself. This means you may have to come back in another lifetime with these same people until you can finally be free and set them free to be who they are. You set yourself free to be who you are regardless of what they choose.

You see that if you look at all of your current interactions and involvements with other human beings, they can be dealt with based on this approach? You look at: What is it going to take for me to come to a point in my mind where I am completely free of this person? It is not a matter of changing the other person because your freedom does not depend on the actions or the state of mind of the other person. It depends on *your* state of mind.

You will be free when you are free in your mind. This is what I have been telling you throughout these previous lessons and especially in this one. You are looking at your relationship to other people as a thing because you are looking at it based on this level of vision that sees everything as things. You often look at other people and think: Oh, he is such and such and there is nothing that can be done about it. Then you think that your relationship to that person could not change until the person changes, but since he is not going to change, you cannot see how the relationship can change. Well, this is taking power away from yourself.

When you take back your power, then you realize that it does not matter how the other person is or whether the other person changes. What matters is that *you* change the way you look at that person so the person no longer has any hold on you. Jesus said: "The prince of this world comes and has nothing in me." Well, you can look at it that any person you encounter can be a tool for the prince of this world. He is simply trying to find some way to get you to react in a negative, fear-based way so that the devil has a hold on you.

Being embroiled in human conflicts

What is the simplest way, my beloved, to prevent you from getting on with the positive aspects of your Divine plan? It is to keep you embroiled with some kind of conflict with another human being that eats up all of your time, attention and energy. Well, you cannot go beyond a certain level of the spiritual path as long as you are embroiled in these very draining personal relationships.

There simply needs to come a point where you look beyond the level of things and you say: "I have a Divine plan and part of my Divine plan is that I transcend a certain level of consciousness, a certain level of illusion. Could it be that this person, who is annoying me so much, is annoying me precisely because he or she is taking advantage of this illusion that I have not seen in myself? Could it therefore be that this person, who is annoying me terribly, is actually a Divine messenger? He has been sent to try to point out to me what I haven't seen so far and what I need to overcome in myself so that I can move to a higher level of consciousness and start doing the positive aspects of my Divine plan—giving my gift?"

It is also part of your Divine plan that you overcome your limitations but this is usually not the fun part of your Divine plan. The fun part of your Divine plan is when you have a positive gift to bring to this earth and you get on with doing it. Why would you allow these petty struggles with other people to keep you from doing the fun aspect of your Divine plan, when all it takes is to shift your vision and say: "What is the lesson here? What do I need to learn from my involvement with this person? What does it show about the attachments that I have to how certain things should or should not be?"

If you analyze any relationship where you are having less than harmony, you will see that the other person is annoying you because you have a certain image that people should not be doing this or behaving like this or saying these kind of things to each other. If you go behind that, you will see that any should or should not that you have in your mind will prevent you from fulfilling your Divine plan. It will also prevent you from attaining the vision that I have been guiding you towards.

Attaining a non-dual vision

I have been guiding you towards a vision that is not dualistic, that is not based on a judgment with two polar opposites. It is a pure vision, a clear vision, where you see things for what they are. You can come to a point where you see every situation without any judgments. This, my beloved, is when you can begin to lock in to what we have called the River of Life where you can see that your life is an ongoing flow.

Consider how most people look at situations in life. They think: "Here is my relationship to this person who is annoying me and this stops me from growing. This stops me from doing what I want to do in life." You see that most people have this stop-and-go view of life. They want to go somewhere in life but there is always something that stops them from going there.

When you shift your vision, you can get away from the stop-and-go vision and you can start seeing that every situation you encounter is just a way to move on with your life. When you look at a river that is flowing, there may be cliffs on the side of the river and maybe a rock in the river. When the water hits it, does the water stop? Does the water stand there and say: "This rock shouldn't be here, someone needs to move this rock so that we can move on?" No, the water just flows around. Yes, the course of the water is changed by the rock, but it is not stopped. The water just moves beyond and soon it has moved beyond the rock and now the water is back as if there had never been a rock. This is how you should look at situations in your life. I apologize for using the word "should," but this is how you can come to look at life when you attain this higher vision I am talking about.

You can come to the point where you see that anything that happens in life is not an obstacle to your progress. It simply is a message that actually shows you how you can get around the obstacle and move on. When you do this, you have made progress.

Letting the mind become like water

It is then that you can come to the realization that the fallen beings do not want you to have, and it is that the mind is like water. Water is an amazing substance, my beloved. You can take the biggest hammer you can lift, and you can slam it into a river. You can make a big splash but what happens in a few seconds? The water just moves on and it is as if there was never anything that impacted the river. Well, your mind has that ability. You can come to see that anything that has happened in your life, even if it made a big splash, your mind can flow on. When you forgive, when you let go, then your mind will flow on, the water will come together again, your mind will be whole and you will be flowing on as if this never happened.

I want you, at this point of my retreat, to come to the conscious realization that it is possible for you to liquefy your mind. I am not saying you can fully attain the liquefaction of your mind at this point. What I want you to realize is that it is possible, and it is a necessary goal to set for yourself. You liquefy the mind and, in order to truly attain this, you need to be willing to look at your life and see: Where is there an event that has solidified my mind around either a certain trauma, a certain pain, or a certain view that this should not have happened? Where has my mind solidified around the view that either other people should change or the universe should change or other people should not be this way or the universe should not be this way? Where has my mind solidified?

Then, you realize that every instance that has solidified your mind some time in your past, in your journey on this planet, is holding you back from moving on with your Divine plan. It is preventing you from flowing with the River of Life. This is when you get a new motivation to look at these illusions that you have come to accept. This is when you can come to a point where you realize that there really is nothing that should or should not happen.

Now, you would see that there really is nothing that should or should not happen anywhere in the universe, but it is especially important to have this attitude on a planet as dense as earth. You are on a very difficult planet where there are fallen beings in embodiment, there are fallen beings in the three higher realms. They have set people up against each other so you have all of these groups of people that are in constant conflict with each other. It is a very difficult environment to grow up in. It is a very, very difficult planet to embody on for many lifetimes. What I am trying to point out to you here is that the only way to really be on a planet like earth, and to not be embroiled in all of these petty squabbles that are tying up your attention, is to liquefy the mind so that you never allow it to solidify anywhere in the past. You keep your mind with you as a mass of water that is flowing with the River of Life.

Maintaining the flow

This, my beloved, is not an easy goal to attain. I am not saying that you should attain this right now or in five minutes. My beloved, you *can* attain it, and it does not have to take the rest of your lifetime to attain this. It really can be attained in one dramatic shift where you then gradually do the cleanup work by giving the invocations to consume the energies that are tied up in past events. You may also need to look at specific situations and other people and see: "What is the lesson I need to learn here so that I can forgive that person, so I can let go of my sense of what should or should not happen."

There may be a lot of cleanup work to do, but you can make the shift very quickly and come to this realization that your mind is liquid. Your mind is like water. There is an obstacle. Well, what is the way to get around the obstacle and get back to flowing with the River of Life, unhindered, unobstructed, unaffected by anything?

You can come to a point, my beloved, where you are not constantly waiting for the next crisis, the next hindrance, the next obstacle. You are not attached to any particular situation where you are struggling against other people or against the universe. You are constantly flowing and you are simply looking for how you can maintain the flow. There is an obstacle but you are not looking at the obstacle and whether it should or should not be there. You are looking at: "How do I flow around it? What is on the other side?" Then, *you* are on the other side and you are flowing, and it is as if the obstacle was never there. You may have learned a lesson from the obstacle but now the lesson is integrated and you do not need to think about it anymore. Now, you move on to the next lesson.

Do you understand, my beloved? You can look at a situation and many spiritual people do this and say: "What is the lesson? What do I need to learn?" You understand that when you have fully learned the lesson, when you have fully transcended a certain state of consciousness, a certain level of consciousness, then you do not need to worry about it anymore? You do not need to think back to it. You just flow on and now you look for the next lesson or the next service you can give.

Life can become a process where you are free from the judgment of what should or should not happen. There is no should, there is no should not. There is just the joy of knowing that you are flowing with the River of Life. You are moving constantly towards that point where you can unify with your spiritual source – with your I AM Presence – in this glorious ritual that we call the ascension.

Hilarion I AM, and I am gratified that you are with me at this level of my retreat. I look forward to giving you the last lesson that I have to give you.

15 | INVOKING TRUE HEALING

In the name I AM THAT I AM, Jesus Christ, I call to my I AM Presence to flow through the I Will Be Presence that I AM and give this invocation with full power. I call to beloved Elohim Cyclopea and Virginia and Peace and Aloha, Archangel Raphael and Mother Mary and Uriel and Aurora, Hilarion and Nada to help me transcend the tendency to look at life based on the level of "things." Help me see the underlying energetic interactions behind everything. Help me see and surrender all patterns that block my oneness with Hilarion and with my I AM Presence, including …

[Make personal calls]

Part 1

1. I want to stop projecting with the mind, I want to move on to a phase where, instead of seeing the world as I think it is or as I want it to be, I can see the world as it *is*.

> Cyclopea so dear, the truth you reveal,
> the truth that duality's ailments will heal,
> your Emerald Light is like a great balm,
> our emotional bodies are perfectly calm.
>
> **Cyclopea so dear, in Emerald Sphere,**
> **in raising perception we shall persevere,**
> **as deep in our hearts your truth we revere,**
> **to immaculate vision the earth does adhere.**

2. I want to see the world in a different way than the way I was brought up to see it and the way the vast majority of human beings see the world.

> Cyclopea so dear, with you we unwind,
> all negative spirals clouding the mind,
> we know pure awareness is truly our core,
> the key to becoming the wide-open door.
>
> **Cyclopea so dear, in Emerald Sphere,**
> **in raising perception we shall persevere,**
> **as deep in our hearts your truth we revere,**
> **to immaculate vision the earth does adhere.**

3. The universe allows me to do many things but there is always a price to be paid. When I project a vision out, I also begin to believe in that vision and thereby it limits me.

> Cyclopea so dear, clear our inner sight,
> empowered, we pierce the soul's fearful night,
> we now see our life through your single eye,
> beyond all disease we're ready to fly.

**Cyclopea so dear, in Emerald Sphere,
in raising perception we shall persevere,
as deep in our hearts your truth we revere,
to immaculate vision the earth does adhere.**

4. I have, over several lifetimes, projected a vision of matter being so dense, and therefore setting certain limitations for what I can do, that I have come to believe in this vision.

> Cyclopea so dear, life can only reflect,
> the images that the mind does project,
> the key to our healing is clearing the mind,
> from the images the ego is hiding behind.

**Cyclopea so dear, in Emerald Sphere,
in raising perception we shall persevere,
as deep in our hearts your truth we revere,
to immaculate vision the earth does adhere.**

5. I have been brought up to believe that matter is dense, matter sets limitations for my creative ability and the only way to get beyond those limitations is to use force-based technology to manipulate and force matter into compliance.

Cyclopea so dear, we want to aim high,
to your healing flame we ever draw nigh,
through veils of duality we now take flight,
bathed in your penetrating Emerald Light.

**Cyclopea so dear, in Emerald Sphere,
in raising perception we shall persevere,
as deep in our hearts your truth we revere,
to immaculate vision the earth does adhere.**

6. The fallen beings have accepted that matter has a certain density. They are working against anybody who starts to manifest a degree of Christhood, trying to in all ways manipulate me into not daring to accept what Christhood is about and that Christhood can give me the mastery of mind over matter.

Cyclopea so dear, your Emerald Flame,
exposes every subtle, dualistic power game,
including the game of wanting to say,
that truth is defined in only one way.

**Cyclopea so dear, in Emerald Sphere,
in raising perception we shall persevere,
as deep in our hearts your truth we revere,
to immaculate vision the earth does adhere.**

7. I heal through the power of vision. In order to heal, I need to free my vision from the illusions of the fallen beings.

Cyclopea so dear, we're feeling the flow,
as your Living Truth upon us you bestow,
from all dual vision we are now set free,
planet earth in immaculate matrix will be.

> Cyclopea so dear, in Emerald Sphere,
> in raising perception we shall persevere,
> as deep in our hearts your truth we revere,
> to immaculate vision the earth does adhere.

8. The universe allows us to densify matter, but everything has a price. When we densify matter, we densify the bodies we are wearing and those denser bodies will be subject to certain laws.

> Cyclopea so dear, the truth is now clear,
> we see higher purpose for which we are here
> we know truth transcends all systems below,
> immersed in your light, we continue to grow.

> Cyclopea so dear, in Emerald Sphere,
> in raising perception we shall persevere,
> as deep in our hearts your truth we revere,
> to immaculate vision the earth does adhere.

9. When we start creating the secondary laws of nature, then the Law of Free Will allows us to do this. The price we pay is that our creation becomes subject to the second law of thermodynamics.

> Cyclopea so dear, we're feeling your joy,
> as creative vision we now do employ,
> in lifting earth out of serpentine cage,
> to manifest Saint Germain's Golden Age.

> Cyclopea so dear, in Emerald Sphere,
> in raising perception we shall persevere,
> as deep in our hearts your truth we revere,
> to immaculate vision the earth does adhere.

Part 2

1. If we set something aside from the primary laws of nature, then whatever we create will begin to break down. There is an in-built force in our creation that will break it down over time.

> O Elohim Peace, in Unity's Flame,
> there is no more room for duality's game,
> we know that all form is from the same source,
> empowering us to plot a new course.
>
> **O Elohim Peace, through your tranquility,**
> **we are free from the chaos of duality,**
> **in oneness with God a new identity,**
> **we are raising the earth into Infinity.**

2. This is the primary reason we have diseases in the human body. Matter is so dense that anything that is created at this level of density will have built-in forces that break it down. That is why the body ages; that is why diseases manifest.

> O Elohim Peace, the bell now you ring,
> causing all atoms to vibrate and sing,
> we give up the sense of a separate "me,"
> we're crossing Samsara's turbulent sea.
>
> **O Elohim Peace, through your tranquility,**
> **we are free from the chaos of duality,**
> **in oneness with God a new identity,**
> **we are raising the earth into Infinity.**

15 | Invoking True Healing

3. I surrender the illusion of the fallen beings that there is nothing I can do about this. I surrender the illusion that my physical body is an entirely material creation that functions according to certain mechanical, material laws.

> O Elohim Peace, you help us to know,
> that Jesus has come your Flame to bestow,
> upon all who are ready to give up the strife,
> by following Christ into infinite life.

> **O Elohim Peace, through your tranquility,**
> **we are free from the chaos of duality,**
> **in oneness with God a new identity,**
> **we are raising the earth into Infinity.**

4. I surrender the illusion that once a disease has manifested, that disease must have a physical cause and therefore it can only be cured through some physical cure.

> O Elohim Peace, through your eyes we see,
> that only in oneness will we ever be free,
> we now see that there is no separate thing,
> to the ego-based self we no longer cling.

> **O Elohim Peace, through your tranquility,**
> **we are free from the chaos of duality,**
> **in oneness with God a new identity,**
> **we are raising the earth into Infinity.**

5. I surrender the illusion that if no physical cure has been discovered, then there is nothing I can do about the disease.

O Elohim Peace, you show us the way,
for clearing the mind from duality's fray,
you pierce the illusions of both time and space,
separation consumed by your Infinite Grace.

**O Elohim Peace, through your tranquility,
we are free from the chaos of duality,
in oneness with God a new identity,
we are raising the earth into Infinity.**

6. What manifests in the physical body is a projection of the conditions in my three higher bodies. A physical disease starts in the emotional, mental and identity realms and is then projected upon the physical body. Any cure must start in the three higher bodies.

O Elohim Peace, what beauty your name,
consuming within us duality's shame,
the earth is set free from burden of fear,
accepting your peace is now manifest here.

**O Elohim Peace, through your tranquility,
we are free from the chaos of duality,
in oneness with God a new identity,
we are raising the earth into Infinity.**

7. I surrender the illusion that there is a state of normal health and that a disease is an abnormal condition that has a physical cause and must be cured by destroying the physical cause.

15 | Invoking True Healing

O Elohim Peace, with Christ at our side,
no force of duality can evermore hide,
It was through the vibration of your Golden Flame,
that Christ the illusion of death overcame.

**O Elohim Peace, through your tranquility,
we are free from the chaos of duality,
in oneness with God a new identity,
we are raising the earth into Infinity.**

8. I surrender the illusion that if something is destroying my body, I need to destroy that something. I surrender the illusion that I must cure destruction with another form of destruction. Destruction cannot overcome destruction. I cannot overcome a problem with the same mindset that created the problem.

O Elohim Peace, you bring now to earth,
the unstoppable flame of Cosmic Rebirth,
we give up the sense that something is "mine,"
allowing your Light through our beings to shine.

**O Elohim Peace, through your tranquility,
we are free from the chaos of duality,
in oneness with God a new identity,
we are raising the earth into Infinity.**

9. I am willing to stop projecting with the mind. The first layer of projections that I have is projections that involve a judgment based on what should or should not be taking place.

O Elohim Peace, as peace now we feel,
all records of war you totally heal,
the earth is now free from forces of war,
restoring her purity known from before.

**O Elohim Peace, through your tranquility,
we are free from the chaos of duality,
in oneness with God a new identity,
we are raising the earth into Infinity.**

Part 3

1. I surrender the tendency to look at a disease by going into a mindset that this is wrong, that this should not be happening. I am willing to look beyond the physical level.

Raphael Archangel, your light so intense,
raise us beyond all human pretense.
Mother Mary and you have a vision so bold,
to see that our highest potential unfold.

**Raphael Archangel, for vision we pray,
Raphael Archangel, show us the way,
Raphael Archangel, your emerald ray,
Raphael Archangel, our lives a new day.**

2. I am willing to start looking at my higher bodies and freeing myself from the limitations of the physical level and therefore the power that the fallen beings have over me.

15 | Invoking True Healing

Raphael Archangel, in emerald sphere,
to immaculate vision we always adhere.
Mother Mary enfolds us in her Sacred Heart,
from Mother's true love, we're never apart.

**Raphael Archangel, for vision we pray,
Raphael Archangel, show us the way,
Raphael Archangel, your emerald ray,
Raphael Archangel, our lives a new day.**

3. I am not going to be a slave of somebody on earth because I know I am a spiritual being and that I can take command over my reactions. I do not need to fear anyone on earth.

Raphael Archangel, all ailments you heal,
each cell in our bodies in light now you seal.
Mother Mary's immaculate concept we see,
perfection of health our new reality.

**Raphael Archangel, for vision we pray,
Raphael Archangel, show us the way,
Raphael Archangel, your emerald ray,
Raphael Archangel, our lives a new day.**

4. I surrender the tendency to look at a disease as something that has gone wrong with the body, wanting to remove the symptom of this without looking at my mind and changing my mind.

Raphael Archangel, your light is so real,
the vision of Christ in us you reveal.
Mother Mary now helps us to truly transcend,
in emerald light with you we ascend.

**Raphael Archangel, for vision we pray,
Raphael Archangel, show us the way,
Raphael Archangel, your emerald ray,
Raphael Archangel, our lives a new day.**

5. I surrender the desire to continue doing what I am doing without changing myself. Wanting to change the world without changing oneself is the hallmark of the fallen beings.

Raphael Archangel, diseases are done,
as you help us see that all life is One,
we no longer do your true love reject,
immaculate vision on all we project.

**Raphael Archangel, for vision we pray,
Raphael Archangel, show us the way,
Raphael Archangel, your emerald ray,
Raphael Archangel, our lives a new day.**

6. I am willing to overcome all self-centeredness, the basic sense that I am a separate being and that I can have power as a separate being.

Raphael Archangel, we're healing the earth,
in immaculate vision we give her rebirth,
a new era has on this day begun,
your emerald light now shines like a sun.

**Raphael Archangel, for vision we pray,
Raphael Archangel, show us the way,
Raphael Archangel, your emerald ray,
Raphael Archangel, our lives a new day.**

15 | Invoking True Healing

7. I surrender the illusion that causes me to accept things as being things, as being unchangeable, as being beyond the powers of the mind to change.

> Raphael Archangel, the fall is behind,
> as all of earth's people the Christ path do find,
> we call now to you all people to heal,
> as four lower bodies in love you do seal.
>
> **Raphael Archangel, for vision we pray,**
> **Raphael Archangel, show us the way,**
> **Raphael Archangel, your emerald ray,**
> **Raphael Archangel, our lives a new day.**

8. When I look at a thing, there is a program in my mind that categorizes and labels it as having certain characteristics. It also labels what I can and cannot do with the thing.

> Raphael Archangel, as you bring the light,
> the forces of darkness swiftly take flight,
> their day is now done as we claim the earth,
> spreading to all an innocent mirth.
>
> **Raphael Archangel, for vision we pray,**
> **Raphael Archangel, show us the way,**
> **Raphael Archangel, your emerald ray,**
> **Raphael Archangel, our lives a new day.**

9. There is a level of my mind where I am labeling everything based on categories. I am labeling things with certain characteristics, such as being difficult to change or impossible to change with the mind.

Raphael Archangel, our vision set free,
as we can now see God's reality,
as Saint Germain's vision is manifest here,
the earth is now sealed in immaculate sphere.

Raphael Archangel, for vision we pray,
Raphael Archangel, show us the way,
Raphael Archangel, your emerald ray,
Raphael Archangel, our lives a new day.

Part 4

1. I am willing to use my power of vision to go behind, to go beyond, the vision that most people have when they look at the body.

Uriel Archangel, immense is the power,
of angels of peace, all war to devour.
The demons of war, no match for your light,
consuming them all, with radiance so bright.

Uriel Archangel, use your great sword,
Uriel Archangel, consume all discord,
Uriel Archangel, we're of one accord,
Uriel Archangel, we walk with the Lord.

2. My body is made out of smaller units, such as molecules, cells, atoms and subatomic particles.

15 | Invoking True Healing

> Uriel Archangel, intense is the sound,
> when millions of angels, their voices compound.
> They build a crescendo, piercing the night,
> life's glorious oneness revealed to our sight.
>
> **Uriel Archangel, use your great sword,**
> **Uriel Archangel, consume all discord,**
> **Uriel Archangel, we're of one accord,**
> **Uriel Archangel, we walk with the Lord.**

3. I am willing to go to a deeper level where I see that my body is made out of smaller units that have been combined into something that I see as one coherent thing that cannot be easily changed.

> Uriel Archangel, from out the Great Throne,
> your millions of trumpets, sound the One Tone.
> Consuming all discord with your harmony,
> the sound of all sounds will set all life free.
>
> **Uriel Archangel, use your great sword,**
> **Uriel Archangel, consume all discord,**
> **Uriel Archangel, we're of one accord,**
> **Uriel Archangel, we walk with the Lord.**

4. My body is made from elementary particles, but they can be seen as both waves and particles. The level of the elementary particles is the borderline where energy from the three higher levels enters the physical spectrum.

Uriel Archangel, all war is now done,
for you bring a message, from heart of the One.
The hearts of all men, now singing in peace,
the spirals of love, forever increase.

**Uriel Archangel, use your great sword,
Uriel Archangel, consume all discord,
Uriel Archangel, we're of one accord,
Uriel Archangel, we walk with the Lord.**

5. When I go to deeper and deeper levels, I see that my body is not coherent because it is made out of smaller units. Coherence comes entirely from my mind. It is a mental image projected by my mind.

Uriel Archangel, your infinite peace,
from all warring beings our planet release,
war is a prison from which we are free,
embracing the peace of true unity.

**Uriel Archangel, use your great sword,
Uriel Archangel, consume all discord,
Uriel Archangel, we're of one accord,
Uriel Archangel, we walk with the Lord.**

6. My body is not coherent at all. It is made out of molecules that are made out of atoms, that are made out of elementary particles, that are really energy waves. When I go to deeper levels of perception, my body seems less and less solid.

15 | Invoking True Healing

> Uriel Archangel, we send forth the call,
> reveal now the oneness that unifies all,
> help us the vision of peace now to see,
> so we from all conflicts and struggles are free.
>
> **Uriel Archangel, use your great sword,**
> **Uriel Archangel, consume all discord,**
> **Uriel Archangel, we're of one accord,**
> **Uriel Archangel, we walk with the Lord.**

7. At the level of the body, it seems impossible to manipulate the body with my mind. When I go to the level of the elementary particles that are actually energy waves, it is entirely possible that the energy waves of my mind could change the energy waves of the body.

> Uriel Archangel, in service to life,
> you give us release from struggle and strife,
> forgetting the self is truly the key,
> to living a life in true harmony.
>
> **Uriel Archangel, use your great sword,**
> **Uriel Archangel, consume all discord,**
> **Uriel Archangel, we're of one accord,**
> **Uriel Archangel, we walk with the Lord.**

8. My mind cannot manipulate the body, but only because "body" is a mental concept created by the mind, and the mind cannot go beyond the concept that it itself has imposed upon the body.

Uriel Archangel, the earth now you raise,
out of duality's death-bringing haze,
we call now upon your great Flame of Peace,
commanding that all petty squabbles do cease.

Uriel Archangel, use your great sword,
Uriel Archangel, consume all discord,
Uriel Archangel, we're of one accord,
Uriel Archangel, we walk with the Lord.

9. I surrender my concept of "my body" as a solid thing that is beyond change. I am willing to question this concept and recognize that my mind can indeed manipulate the energy waves that make up the body.

Uriel Archangel, as peace is the norm,
to your higher vision the earth does conform,
as people have found your peace from within,
a Golden Age is the prize that we win.

Uriel Archangel, use your great sword,
Uriel Archangel, consume all discord,
Uriel Archangel, we're of one accord,
Uriel Archangel, we walk with the Lord.

Part 5

1. My mind is an energy field. My body is made of molecules that are made of atoms that are made of elementary particles that are truly energy waves. Because my mind is an energy field, it is entirely possible for my mind to manipulate the energy fields that make up the elementary particles that make up the atoms that make up the molecules that make up my body.

> Hilarion, on emerald shore,
> we're free from all that's gone before.
> Hilarion, we let all go,
> that keeps us out of sacred flow.
>
> **Hilarion, with light so green,**
> **we see behind the matter screen,**
> **immaculate our inner sight,**
> **we see the earth is taking flight.**

2. When I go to a deep enough level with the mind, I can manipulate the body with the mind. I can heal my physical body with the mind when I realize that my body is made up of smaller units that are truly energy waves.

> Hilarion, the secret key,
> is wisdom's own reality.
> Hilarion, all life is healed,
> the ego's face no more concealed.

> **Hilarion, with light so green,**
> **we see behind the matter screen,**
> **immaculate our inner sight,**
> **we see the earth is taking flight.**

3. My mind is an energy wave. My body is an energy wave. I can attain the mastery of being able to manipulate the basic energy waves that make up my body and thereby change the body even at the physical level.

> Hilarion, your love for life,
> helps us surrender inner strife.
> Hilarion, your loving words,
> thrill our hearts like song of birds.

> **Hilarion, with light so green,**
> **we see behind the matter screen,**
> **immaculate our inner sight,**
> **we see the earth is taking flight.**

4. I cannot do this as long as my mind is fixated on this "thing," this image that I have imposed on the physical body. I surrender the tendency to see the body as a thing, as a coherent unit.

> Hilarion, invoke the light,
> your sacred formulas recite.
> Hilarion, your secret tone,
> philosopher's most sacred stone.

> **Hilarion, with light so green,**
> **we see behind the matter screen,**
> **immaculate our inner sight,**
> **we see the earth is taking flight.**

5. I surrender the tendency to think that when something goes wrong with the body, it can only be corrected at the physical level. I see that the cause is not physical because the body is a projection of the three higher bodies. By changing what is in the three higher bodies, I can change the physical manifestation.

> Hilarion, with love you greet,
> us in your temple over Crete.
> Hilarion, your emerald light,
> the third eye sees with Christic sight.
>
> **Hilarion, with light so green,**
> **we see behind the matter screen,**
> **immaculate our inner sight,**
> **we see the earth is taking flight.**

6. As long as I see my body as a thing, as a coherent unit, I cannot heal the body with the powers of the mind. The mind cannot change the thing concept that the mind itself is imposing upon the body. I grasp how significant this is.

> Hilarion, you give us fruit,
> of truth that is so absolute.
> Hilarion, all stress decrease,
> as our ambitions we release.
>
> **Hilarion, with light so green,**
> **we see behind the matter screen,**
> **immaculate our inner sight,**
> **we see the earth is taking flight.**

7. It is the mind itself that has imposed the image of a thing upon the body. I am willing to question this image, to see it for what it is, namely just an image. I am willing to see beyond it, and then the mind can indeed heal the body.

> Hilarion, our chakras clear,
> as we let go of subtlest fear.
> Hilarion, we are sincere,
> as freedom's truth we do revere.
>
> **Hilarion, with light so green,**
> **we see behind the matter screen,**
> **immaculate our inner sight,**
> **we see the earth is taking flight.**

8. I am freeing my mind from the tendency to see things as things. Therefore, it is indeed possible that I can begin to heal my body through the powers of the mind.

> Hilarion, you balance all,
> the seven rays upon our call.
> Hilarion, you keep us true,
> as we remain all one with you.
>
> **Hilarion, with light so green,**
> **we see behind the matter screen,**
> **immaculate our inner sight,**
> **we see the earth is taking flight.**

9. I am also willing to see if having a disease and dealing with that disease can be part of my Divine plan or if having a healthy body is part of my Divine plan.

15 | Invoking True Healing

> Hilarion, your Presence here,
> filling up the inner sphere.
> Life is now a sacred flow,
> God Vision we on all bestow.

> **Hilarion, with light so green,**
> **we see behind the matter screen,**
> **immaculate our inner sight,**
> **we see the earth is taking flight.**

Part 6

1. I want to know if a disease is part of my Divine plan. If not, I want to know how to transcend the disease and get on with my Divine plan.

> Master Nada, beauty's power,
> unfolding like a sacred flower.
> Master Nada, so sublime,
> a will that conquers even time.

> **Master Nada, peace you give,**
> **forevermore in peace we live,**
> **our planet has a peaceful morn,**
> **the Golden Age is hereby born.**

2. I want to hold the immaculate concept for myself, and I see that means holding the vision that I will continue to grow in consciousness and transcend my consciousness until I reach the level of Christhood that will allow me to fulfill my mission.

> Master Nada, you bestow,
> upon us wisdom's rushing flow.
> Master Nada, mind so strong
> rising on your wings of song.
>
> **Master Nada, peace you give,**
> **forevermore in peace we live,**
> **our planet has a peaceful morn,**
> **the Golden Age is hereby born.**

3. There are two aspects of the immaculate concept. There is the vision of the continued growth and then the vision that I have a mission, a Divine plan, and holding the vision that I fulfill that Divine plan.

> Master Nada, precious scent,
> your love is truly heaven-sent.
> Master Nada, kind and soft
> on wings of love we rise aloft.
>
> **Master Nada, peace you give,**
> **forevermore in peace we live,**
> **our planet has a peaceful morn,**
> **the Golden Age is hereby born.**

4. Life is about growth, is about self-transcendence. I am holding the immaculate concept that I will continue to grow, pass my initiations and reach the highest possible level of consciousness in this embodiment.

Master Nada, mother light,
our hearts are rising like a kite.
Master Nada, from your view,
all life is pure as morning dew.

Master Nada, peace you give,
forevermore in peace we live,
our planet has a peaceful morn,
the Golden Age is hereby born.

5. I am holding the vision that there is something I am here to do in this embodiment. I hold the vision that I will fulfill the joyful elements of my Divine plan.

Master Nada, truth you bring,
as morning birds in love do sing.
Master Nada, we now feel,
your love that all four bodies heal.

Master Nada, peace you give,
forevermore in peace we live,
our planet has a peaceful morn,
the Golden Age is hereby born.

6. When I am holding the immaculate concept for myself, it is likely to be dramatically different from the way most people see a normal human life. It may even be dramatically different from the way *I* have seen my life so far.

Master Nada, serve in peace,
as all emotions we release.
Master Nada, life is fun,
the solar plexus is a sun.

**Master Nada, peace you give,
forevermore in peace we live,
our planet has a peaceful morn,
the Golden Age is hereby born.**

7. As I am growing up in modern society, I am having projected upon me from so many sources what my life should or should not be like.

Master Nada, love is free,
conditions we no longer see.
Master Nada, rise above,
all human forms of lesser love.

**Master Nada, peace you give,
forevermore in peace we live,
our planet has a peaceful morn,
the Golden Age is hereby born.**

8. I want to move on with my life, so I am willing to take a look the ideas I have about what should or should not happen to me.

Master Nada, balance all,
the seven rays upon our call.
Master Nada, rise and shine,
your radiant beauty most divine.

**Master Nada, peace you give,
forevermore in peace we live,
our planet has a peaceful morn,
the Golden Age is hereby born.**

9. I surrender the illusion that holding the immaculate concept for myself means that my life follows the path I have taken on from without of what should or should not happen to me.

> Nada Dear, your Presence here,
> filling up the inner sphere.
> Life is now a sacred flow,
> God Peace we do on all bestow.

> **Master Nada, peace you give,**
> **forevermore in peace we live,**
> **our planet has a peaceful morn,**
> **the Golden Age is hereby born.**

Part 7

1. I surrender the illusion that holding the immaculate concept means evaluating every situation, based on what should or should not happen and then immediately judging something I think should not happen as wrong.

> O Jesus, blessed brother mine,
> I walk the path that you outline,
> a great example to us all,
> I follow now your inner call.

> **O Jesus, let the Fire of Joy,**
> **consume the devil's subtle ploy,**
> **transfigured is our planet earth,**
> **the golden age is given birth.**

2. My Divine plan involves that I grow in consciousness. In order to transcend a certain level of consciousness, I have to come to see that consciousness. I may need certain experiences in order to see a certain state of consciousness.

> O Jesus, open inner sight,
> the ego wants to prove it's right,
> but this I will no longer do,
> I want to be all one with you.
>
> **O Jesus, let the Fire of Joy,**
> **consume the devil's subtle ploy,**
> **transfigured is our planet earth,**
> **the golden age is given birth.**

3. It is not constructive to evaluate my life based on this standard that has been imposed upon me, of what should or should not happen. I surrender this standard and I say: "There is no should and there is no should not. Everything that has happened in my life has happened because the universe is trying to awaken me from an illusion."

> O Jesus, I now clearly see,
> the Key of Knowledge given me,
> my Christ self I hereby embrace,
> as you fill up my inner space.
>
> **O Jesus, let the Fire of Joy,**
> **consume the devil's subtle ploy,**
> **transfigured is our planet earth,**
> **the golden age is given birth.**

15 | Invoking True Healing

4. Instead of resisting what is happening, instead of trying to change the symptoms at the physical level, I will start looking at what might be the message here. What is it that I have not gotten so far?

> O Jesus, show me serpent's lie,
> expose the beam in my own eye,
> as Christ discernment you me give,
> in oneness I forever live.

> **O Jesus, let the Fire of Joy,**
> **consume the devil's subtle ploy,**
> **transfigured is our planet earth,**
> **the golden age is given birth.**

5. I am willing to consider whether there might be a message in a disease. Is the universe trying to teach me something? Is the disease trying to show me a certain illusion, a certain consciousness, that I need to transcend? Could doing this possibly help me move closer to fulfilling my Divine plan?

> O Jesus, I am truly meek,
> and thus I turn the other cheek,
> when the accuser attacks me,
> I go within and merge with thee.

> **O Jesus, let the Fire of Joy,**
> **consume the devil's subtle ploy,**
> **transfigured is our planet earth,**
> **the golden age is given birth.**

6. Have I chosen to have a disease in order to demonstrate to other people that I can be a happy, fulfilled and peaceful human being even though I have this limitation?

> O Jesus, ego I let die,
> surrender ev'ry earthly tie,
> the dead can bury what is dead,
> I choose to walk with you instead.

> **O Jesus, let the Fire of Joy,**
> **consume the devil's subtle ploy,**
> **transfigured is our planet earth,**
> **the golden age is given birth.**

7. Have I chosen to take on a disease in order to demonstrate that I can overcome that disease, that I can be healed from it, that I can transcend it?

> O Jesus, help me rise above,
> the devil's test through higher love,
> show me separate self unreal,
> my formless self you do reveal.

> **O Jesus, let the Fire of Joy,**
> **consume the devil's subtle ploy,**
> **transfigured is our planet earth,**
> **the golden age is given birth.**

8. Holding the immaculate concept for myself means knowing that my Divine plan is centered around changing myself, transcending levels of consciousness and coming up as many steps as I can in this lifetime.

O Jesus, what is that to me,
I just let go and follow thee,
with this I do pass ev'ry test,
to find with you eternal rest.

**O Jesus, let the Fire of Joy,
consume the devil's subtle ploy,
transfigured is our planet earth,
the golden age is given birth.**

9. The very essence of life, the very essence of the spiritual path for me, is the transcendence of consciousness. The very essence of what the fallen beings are resisting is the transcendence of consciousness. I will not live my life based on the mindset of the fallen beings. I want to live my life based on the mindset of the ascended masters: constant self-transcendence.

O Jesus, fiery master mine,
my heart now melting into thine,
I love with heart and mind and soul,
the God who is my highest goal.

**O Jesus, let the Fire of Joy,
consume the devil's subtle ploy,
transfigured is our planet earth,
the golden age is given birth.**

Part 8

1. I am making this shift consciously. I am freeing myself from these judgments based at the level of things. I want to be able to look at my life and be free of all judgments of what should or should not have happened.

> Maitreya, I am truly meek,
> your counsel wise I humbly seek,
> your vision I so want to see,
> with you in Eden I will be.
>
> **Maitreya, kindness is the cure,**
> **in fires of kindness I am pure.**
> **Maitreya, now release the fire,**
> **that raises me forever higher.**

2. However difficult my life has been, I chose those situations for a reason. It is part of my Divine plan. There is nothing that happened that should not have happened. Everything was an opportunity to see something in myself and to demonstrate to others that I can grow up in a difficult situation but rise above it.

> Maitreya, help me to return,
> to learn from you, I truly yearn,
> as oneness is all I desire
> I feel initiation's fire.

**Maitreya, kindness is the cure,
in fires of kindness I am pure.
Maitreya, now release the fire,
that raises me forever higher.**

3. There is a different way to look at my life than to see it at the level of the event itself and to judge it based on the should and should not consciousness. A situation also has different components. I am stepping step back and seeing a more nuanced, more sophisticated view of the situation.

Maitreya, I hereby decide,
from you I will no longer hide,
expose to me the very lie
that caused edenic self to die.

**Maitreya, kindness is the cure,
in fires of kindness I am pure.
Maitreya, now release the fire,
that raises me forever higher.**

4. I will focus on changing myself, and I will forgive the other people and allow them to simply be who they are and outplay the consciousness they are outplaying. I will be free to move on to other aspects of my Divine plan.

Maitreya, blessed Guru mine,
my heart of hearts forever thine,
I vow that I will listen well,
so we can break the serpent's spell.

> **Maitreya, kindness is the cure,**
> **in fires of kindness I am pure.**
> **Maitreya, now release the fire,**
> **that raises me forever higher.**

5. I will stop judging my interactions with other people based on the should or should not consciousness. Therefore, I am at peace with how any interaction unfolded. I see that my actions are a product of my state of consciousness, and the other people's actions were a product of their state of consciousness.

> Maitreya, help me see the lie
> whereby the serpent broke the tie,
> the serpent now has naught in me,
> in oneness I am truly free.

> **Maitreya, kindness is the cure,**
> **in fires of kindness I am pure.**
> **Maitreya, now release the fire,**
> **that raises me forever higher.**

6. It is not my job to change other people, only to give them an opportunity to see that there is a different way to act, there is a different way to react, there is a different way to look at life.

> Maitreya, truth does set me free
> from falsehoods of duality,
> the fruit of knowledge I let go,
> so your true spirit I do know.

> **Maitreya, kindness is the cure,**
> **in fires of kindness I am pure.**
> **Maitreya, now release the fire,**
> **that raises me forever higher.**

7. When I have given the opportunity, I have done my job. I am free of the situation when I do not judge others based on what they should or should not have done.

> Maitreya, I submit to you,
> intentions pure, my heart is true,
> from ego I am truly free,
> as I am now all one with thee.

> **Maitreya, kindness is the cure,**
> **in fires of kindness I am pure.**
> **Maitreya, now release the fire,**
> **that raises me forever higher.**

8. In my interactions with other people, I will look at: What is it going to take for me to come to a point in my mind where I am completely free of this person? It is not a matter of changing the other person because my freedom does not depend on the other person. It depends on *my* state of mind.

> Maitreya, kindness is the key,
> all shades of kindness teach to me,
> for I am now the open door,
> the Art of Kindness to restore.

**Maitreya, kindness is the cure,
in fires of kindness I am pure.
Maitreya, now release the fire,
that raises me forever higher.**

9. I will be free when I am free in my mind. It does not matter how the other person is or whether the other person changes. What matters is that *I* change the way I look at that person so the person no longer has any hold on me.

Maitreya, oh sweet mystery,
immersed in your reality,
the myst'ry school will now return,
for this, my heart does truly burn.

**Maitreya, kindness is the cure,
in fires of kindness I am pure.
Maitreya, now release the fire,
that raises me forever higher.**

Part 9

1. The simplest way for the fallen beings to prevent me from getting on with the positive aspects of my Divine plan is to keep me embroiled with some kind of conflict with other people that eats up my time, attention and energy.

Gautama, show my mental state
that does give rise to love and hate,
your exposé I do endure,
so my perception will be pure.

> **Gautama, Flame of Cosmic Peace,**
> **unruly thoughts do hereby cease,**
> **we radiate from you and me**
> **the peace to still Samsara's Sea.**

2. I am going beyond the level of things and I say: "I have a Divine plan and part of my Divine plan is that I transcend a certain level of consciousness, a certain level of illusion. Could it be that this person, who is annoying me so much, is annoying me precisely because he or she is taking advantage of this illusion that I have not seen in myself?"

> Gautama, in your Flame of Peace,
> the struggling self I now release,
> the Buddha Nature I now see,
> it is the core of you and me.

> **Gautama, Flame of Cosmic Peace,**
> **unruly thoughts do hereby cease,**
> **we radiate from you and me**
> **the peace to still Samsara's Sea.**

3. "Could it be that this person, who is annoying me terribly, is actually a Divine messenger? He has been sent to try to point out to me what I haven't seen so far and what I need to overcome in myself so that I can move to a higher level of consciousness and start doing the positive aspects of my Divine plan—giving my gift?"

> Gautama, I am one with thee,
> Mara's demons do now flee,
> your Presence like a soothing balm,
> my mind and senses ever calm.

**Gautama, Flame of Cosmic Peace,
unruly thoughts do hereby cease,
we radiate from you and me
the peace to still Samsara's Sea.**

4. It is part of my Divine plan that I overcome my limitations. The fun part of my Divine plan is when I have a positive gift to bring to this earth and I get on with doing it. I will not allow these petty struggles with other people to keep me from doing the fun aspect of my Divine plan.

Gautama, I now take the vow,
to live in the eternal now,
with you I do transcend all time,
to live in present so sublime.

**Gautama, Flame of Cosmic Peace,
unruly thoughts do hereby cease,
we radiate from you and me
the peace to still Samsara's Sea.**

5. In any relationship, the other person is annoying me because I have a certain image that people should not be doing this. Any should or should not that I have in my mind, will prevent me from fulfilling my Divine plan. It will also prevent me from attaining a clear vision.

Gautama, I have no desire,
to nothing earthly I aspire,
in non-attachment I now rest,
passing Mara's subtle test.

> Gautama, Flame of Cosmic Peace,
> unruly thoughts do hereby cease,
> we radiate from you and me
> the peace to still Samsara's Sea.

6. I want to attain a vision that is not dualistic, that is not based on a judgment with two polar opposites. It is a pure vision, a clear vision, where I see things for what they are. I see every situation without any judgments.

> Gautama, I melt into you,
> my mind is one, no longer two,
> immersed in your resplendent glow,
> Nirvana is all that I know.

> Gautama, Flame of Cosmic Peace,
> unruly thoughts do hereby cease,
> we radiate from you and me
> the peace to still Samsara's Sea.

7. I want to lock in to the River of Life and see that my life is an ongoing flow. I surrender the stop-and-go view of life where there is always something that stops me from going where I want to go.

> Gautama, in your timeless space,
> I am immersed in Cosmic Grace,
> I know the God beyond all form,
> to world I will no more conform.

**Gautama, Flame of Cosmic Peace,
unruly thoughts do hereby cease,
we radiate from you and me
the peace to still Samsara's Sea.**

8. Every situation I encounter is a way to move on with my life. I see that anything that happens in life is not an obstacle to my progress. It is a message that shows me how I can get around the obstacle and move on.

> Gautama, I am now awake,
> I clearly see what is at stake,
> and thus I claim my sacred right
> to be on earth the Buddhic Light.

**Gautama, Flame of Cosmic Peace,
unruly thoughts do hereby cease,
we radiate from you and me
the peace to still Samsara's Sea.**

9. The mind is like water. My mind has the ability to see that no matter what has happened in my life, my mind can flow on. When I forgive, when I let go, then my mind will flow on, my mind will be whole and I will be flowing on as if this never happened.

> Gautama, with your thunderbolt,
> we give the earth a mighty jolt,
> I know that some will understand,
> and join the Buddha's timeless band.

**Gautama, Flame of Cosmic Peace,
unruly thoughts do hereby cease,
we radiate from you and me
the peace to still Samsara's Sea.**

Part 10

1. I am open to the conscious realization that it is possible for me to liquefy my mind. It is possible, and I set this as a goal for myself.

Sanat Kumara, Ruby Fire,
I seek my place in love's own choir,
with open hearts we sing your praise,
together we the earth do raise.

**Sanat Kumara, Ruby Ray,
bring to earth a higher way,
light this planet with your fire,
clothe her in a new attire.**

2. I am willing to look at my life and see: Where is there an event that has solidified my mind around either a certain trauma, a certain pain, or a certain view that this should not have happened? Where has my mind solidified around the view that either other people should change or the universe should change or other people should not be this way or the universe should not be this way? Where has my mind solidified?

Sanat Kumara, Ruby Fire,
initiations I desire,
I am for you an electrode,
Shamballa is my true abode.

**Sanat Kumara, Ruby Ray,
bring to earth a higher way,
light this planet with your fire,
clothe her in a new attire.**

3. Every instance that has solidified my mind some time in my past is holding me back from moving on with my Divine plan. It is preventing me from flowing with the River of Life. I am willing to look at my illusions and realize that there is nothing that should or should not happen.

Sanat Kumara, Ruby Fire,
I follow path that you require,
initiate me with your love,
the open door for Holy Dove.

**Sanat Kumara, Ruby Ray,
bring to earth a higher way,
light this planet with your fire,
clothe her in a new attire.**

4. I will not be embroiled in petty squabbles that are tying up my attention. Therefore, I liquefy the mind so that I never allow it to solidify anywhere in the past. I keep my mind with me as a mass of water that is flowing with the River of Life.

15 | Invoking True Healing

Sanat Kumara, Ruby Fire,
your great example all inspire,
with non-attachment and great mirth,
we give the earth a true rebirth.

**Sanat Kumara, Ruby Ray,
bring to earth a higher way,
light this planet with your fire,
clothe her in a new attire.**

5. I am willing to attain this goal in one dramatic shift and then gradually do the cleanup work by giving the invocations to consume the energies that are tied up in past events.

Sanat Kumara, Ruby Fire,
you are this planet's purifier,
consume on earth all spirits dark,
reveal the inner Spirit Spark.

**Sanat Kumara, Ruby Ray,
bring to earth a higher way,
light this planet with your fire,
clothe her in a new attire.**

6. My mind is liquid. My mind is like water. There is an obstacle, but I find the way to get around the obstacle and get back to flowing with the River of Life, unhindered, unobstructed, unaffected by anything.

Sanat Kumara, Ruby Fire,
you are a cosmic amplifier,
the lower forces can't withstand,
vibrations from Venusian band.

> **Sanat Kumara, Ruby Ray,**
> **bring to earth a higher way,**
> **light this planet with your fire,**
> **clothe her in a new attire.**

7. I am constantly flowing and I am looking for how I can maintain the flow. I flow around any obstacle and learn a lesson from the obstacle. The lesson is integrated and I don't need to think about it anymore. I move on to the next lesson.

> Sanat Kumara, Ruby Fire,
> I am on earth your magnifier,
> the flow of love I do restore,
> my chakras are your open door.

> **Sanat Kumara, Ruby Ray,**
> **bring to earth a higher way,**
> **light this planet with your fire,**
> **clothe her in a new attire.**

8. When I have fully learned the lesson, when I have fully transcended a certain state of consciousness, then I do not need to worry about it anymore. I do not need to think back to it. I just flow on and now I look for the next lesson or the next service I can give.

> Sanat Kumara, Ruby Fire,
> Venusian song the multiplier,
> as we your love reverberate,
> the densest minds we penetrate.

**Sanat Kumara, Ruby Ray,
bring to earth a higher way,
light this planet with your fire,
clothe her in a new attire.**

9. Life is a process where I am free from the judgment of what should or should not happen. There is no should, there is no should not. There is just the joy of knowing that I am flowing with the River of Life. I am moving constantly towards that point where I can unify with my I AM Presence in the glorious ritual of the ascension.

Sanat Kumara, Ruby Fire,
you are for all the sanctifier,
the earth is now a holy place,
purified by cosmic grace.

**Sanat Kumara, Ruby Ray,
bring to earth a higher way,
light this planet with your fire,
clothe her in a new attire.**

Sealing:

In the name of the Divine Mother, I fully accept that the power of these calls is used to set free the River of Life, so it can outpicture the perfect vision of Christ for my own life, for all people and for the planet. In the name I AM THAT I AM, it is done! Amen.

16 | SEEING BEYOND THE MATTER SCREEN

I AM the Ascended Master Hilarion. It is my great joy to watch students come to this level of my retreat where they are ready for the final initiation that I offer them as part of this course of self-mastery. This, of course, is the initiation of encountering the energies of the Fifth Ray combined with the energies of freedom.

What is, then, the initiation you face? Well, it is that you need to set your mind free, set your vision free, from this very subtle basic illusion of the fallen beings. This illusion has several levels. I have already talked about it in the previous discourses, especially in my last discourse where I talked about setting your mind free from the illusion that things are things and that they are difficult to change because matter is solid and unchangeable by the mind.

Seeing beyond the matter screen

What is it you need to start doing here? Well, when you attend my retreat in your finer bodies, I, of course, train you in the process of learning to see beyond the matter screen. It has been said that evil is an **energy veil** and what the forces of darkness, the fallen beings, have done is that they have created this illusion that matter is solid and unchangeable. Now, my beloved, is it just an illusion they have created or is there more to it? Well, it *is* just an illusion they have created but there is also more to it in the sense that there is a certain correspondence between the density of matter and the capabilities of your physical senses.

It is clear that when you are living on a planet with the density of matter that earth has, then you need to be able to sense matter. You need to be able to navigate in matter and therefore your physical senses need to be capable of sensing matter at its current level of vibration. If you take your eyes, for example, you will see that there was a time when the earth had a much higher vibration than it has today. The people who were living on it at that time had eyes that were simply incapable of seeing the dense vibrations that you find on the planet today. If you had taken some of these people from back then and transplanted them into the earth today, they would have been unable to physically see what you so easily see as matter because their eyes were simply not calibrated for such a low level of vibration.

What has happened is that as matter has densified, as your bodies have densified, your eyes have extended their range so that they can now see lower vibrations than before. Now, in itself this is not actually what forms the energy veil, the barrier of vision. Your physical eyes are still capable of detecting at least some higher vibrations, some vibrations that are beyond the physical spectrum. Some of you are able to see energy fields or auras around people. All of you know that these auras exist and that there are people who have, as the saying often goes, "had their third eye opened" and can see people's auras and chakras. Or they can perhaps see the astral plane or even see higher levels, even ascended masters.

Why you do not see people's auras

You know this is possible. The question now becomes: Why are you not able to see these vibrations beyond the material realm? There are many, many people who believe that this is because your physical eyes are not capable of seeing these vibrations; you are not physically able to see this. This is what I am telling you is incorrect, and this is part of the initiation you are going through.

I show you at the etheric level why this is not correct. I can show you, simply, the range of capabilities that your physical eyes have. I can show you that your retina is perfectly capable of receiving the light rays of the vibrations that are emitted from people's auras. You are physically able to see auras.

Now, why is it that you do not consciously see this? Well, it is because in your brain, in your visual cortex, even in your emotional, mental and identity bodies, you have certain filters. Now, again, you have to recognize that there is nothing inherently wrong with having these perception filters in the sense that if you were to receive all of the information that your eyes are capable of detecting, you might get overwhelmed at the conscious level. These perception filters can have a legitimate function in terms of allowing you to focus your attention on what is most important for you. You will know already from living in this Internet and information age that if you truly go on the Internet and look at everything that is available for you, you can quickly get overwhelmed and your mind becomes so scattered that you cannot focus on anything really. You know that it is necessary to filter out information, otherwise you quickly become overwhelmed.

The fallen beings, of course, know this very well. If you look at history, you will see that there was almost a thousand years where Europe was in the so-called Dark Ages. It was because the Catholic Church had managed to suppress all information that they did not approve of. They had burned books, they had banned books, they had physically removed books and therefore there was only a limited amount of information available to the people. This is one way that the fallen beings try to limit your freedom. If you have too little information, there are choices you cannot make.

Now, as the modern age approached and more and more technology became available for distributing information, the fallen beings realized that they could no longer withhold information. At least, there was much information they could not withhold. Therefore, they shifted their tactic to trying to overwhelm you with so much information and trying to give you so much outrageous information that people started doubting everything they heard that was beyond the normal.

Legitimate perception filters

This is their Alpha and Omega, their push-and-pull strategy, of either too little or too much. It is necessary for anyone who lives on a planet like earth to have certain filters to filter out what is not constructive. Now, what do I mean with "constructive?" Well, I, of course, mean that you need to filter out anything that would distract you from fulfilling your Divine plan. You can see that when you know that you have a Divine plan, when you have some sense of what your Divine plan involves, then you can also realize that you need a certain perception filter to filter out the information that would simply be a distraction that prevents you from focusing on the essential aspects of your Divine plan.

What I am saying here is this: You have certain filters that filter out information from your senses. There is a filter that filters out the visual impressions of people's auras or energy fields. The reason for this is that for many people it would be overwhelming to see this. There are people who have had their third eyes opened and have suddenly been able to see entities or demons in the astral plane and it has been greatly disturbing to them. It is something you need to be trained for over time so you gradually adjust to being able to see this.

However, you also need to be aware that just because it is possible to get to a point where you can see people's auras, this does not mean that it is in the Divine plan of all spiritual people to do this. In fact, I can tell you that for the vast majority of spiritual people, it is not in your Divine plan to come to see auras because it just is not necessary for the fulfillment of your Divine plan that you can do this.

Where I am getting at with this long discourse is that you need to recognize that there is a certain *legitimacy* to having perception filters. There is also an *illegitimacy* in the sense that you have been brought up to accept certain perception filters that are not conducive to the fulfillment of your Divine plan. One of the primary filters that is hindering your Divine plan is the perception filter that makes you think that matter is matter, that matter is solid, that matter is unchangeable.

Illegitimate perception filters

The reason this filter is so devastating is that it makes you look at situations on earth, and it makes you think that as soon as something has happened that has a physical, material consequence, then that consequence cannot be undone except perhaps at the physical level. What I have been telling you in previous discourses is that the reality of life on earth, of conditions on earth, is that everything is energy. Energy is always vibrating. Energy is always fluid and regardless of the appearance to your senses and your outer mind, energy can always be changed.

What has happened is that the fallen beings have managed to create (and to fool the majority of humankind into collectively creating) this perception filter that makes them think that matter is not energy, that matter is a separate substance. It is a solid, difficult to change substance and certainly it is a substance that is beyond the powers of the mind to change.

You have been brought up with a perception filter that creates an artificial dividing line. You know and you perceive that there is energy around you because you see sunlight and you can feel heat. You know that these are energy waves, that these are vibrations. Yet, your perception filter tells you that these are different from the things you see that are made up of matter. This is why you have been programmed to think that once a situation has a physical consequence, then you cannot change that consequence at the energetic level, only at the level of matter.

As an example take a disease. Medical scientists have actually recognized that over 90% of all diseases are psychosomatic, meaning that they have a psychological component. In reality, 100% of diseases are psychosomatic in that they all have a certain psychological component. Just think about the fact that medical scientists have recognized this and yet this has not led to a revolution where scientists are researching consciousness and its influence upon matter. As I said, quantum physicists have for almost a century realized that there is a deep connection between the mind and elementary particles.

Seeing that matter is energy

Still, Western scientists have not focused all of their energy and attention on exploring consciousness and its connection to matter. They still uphold the illusion, created by the fallen beings, that there is a fundamental divide between mind and matter. This is the illusion that you need to shatter here. I, of course, can do this very easily at the etheric level by simply showing you how energy is gradually lowered in vibration from the spiritual level of vibration into the identity level, into the mental, into the emotional and into the physical.

I can show you directly, by certain instruments I have, where I can display on the screen how a certain quantity of energy is lowered in vibration. I can show you directly how a certain mental matrix is superimposed upon this quantity of energy and how this gradually, as the energy is lowered in vibration, takes on form.

I used the example of a rock, and I can show you how this rock is created out of energy. Therefore, even when it gets to the physical level, it is still energy. I can then show you how it is possible to direct a beam, a stream, of high-frequency energy at a rock and transform it. Or rather, free the energy that has been captured into the rock matrix so that it begins to vibrate at higher levels and therefore gradually, simply dissolves this rock matrix that keeps the energy trapped in the matrix. The energy is set free, becomes liquid. It liquefies and can now flow either into another substance or back up into the emotional, mental, identity realms and eventually to the spiritual realm.

You can see this directly, and what I am asking you to ponder here at the physical level, the conscious level, is that you can also come to sense this at the conscious level. You may not physically see it with your eyes, but you can begin to train your mind to look at matter in a different way. You do not need to strive towards physically seeing the energy vibrations behind matter. You do need to make an effort, a concentrated effort over time, to retrain your mind to begin to see everything as energy. You need to mentally know that behind this solid form, that you see as a rock, there is vibrating energy. Within it is vibrating energy; it is vibrating, it is possible to change, it is liquid, it can be liquefied and flow into another form.

A new way to look at the body

You see, my beloved, the trick imposed by the fallen beings has many ramifications but to illustrate it let us look at the physical body. You may know that a lot of diseases have a psychosomatic component because they start in the mind. You may understand this as a spiritual person. Nevertheless, the moment you go to the doctor and the doctor diagnoses you with a physical symptom, it is so easy for your mind to slip into accepting the judgment of the doctor, namely that this is a physical disease with a physical symptom that can only be dealt with at the physical level. Now, again, I am not saying you should not go to the doctor, I am not saying that you should not follow the advice of the doctor. What I am saying is that it is possible to do this while still maintaining, in your mind, that your body is not a physical substance, not a thing.

It is vibrating energy and therefore it can be changed. Along with doing the physical things for healing, you can still invoke higher energy into the situation.

Now, you understand that at this level of the path towards the 144th level of consciousness, I am not asking you (and I am not expecting you) to be able to change things by the power of the mind alone. That is why I am saying that I am not asking you to come to a point where you say: "Okay, Hilarion has told me that matter is just energy and that therefore it can potentially be changed by the mind. So now I'm facing this physical situation but I am not going to do anything about it physically, I am just going to sit here and focus my mind and therefore change it with the powers of the mind." I am not asking you to do this.

The primary reason I am not asking you to do this is that, over time, we have seen so many students go into this state of mind and then they have failed to manifest the physical changes that they desire to see manifest. Then, they have become discouraged and they have sunk even lower than they were before they started.

There are books and courses out there that claim that they can teach people how to manifest things, whether it be gold or money or whatever they desire to manifest. They say that you can manifest something, so to speak, out of the blue, out of thin air. This is not what we are teaching you in this course because we do not want to discourage you. I am not saying that it is not possible to do this. I am saying, we are not expecting that you can do this at this level of consciousness. Therefore, we do not want you to set this as a goal. We do not want you to set yourself up for disappointment. What I am saying here is that at this stage of the path, you need to take a sensible two-prong approach.

How to change physical situations

Whatever situation you are dealing with in your life, you do take physical measures to change the situation. At the same time, you go through the process in your own mind, of first of all recognizing here that the prince of this world will come to you in any situation and he will tempt you. The tempter will come to you and tempt you to accept that this situation is now physical; it has a physical consequence that can only be dealt with at the level of matter. You take the practical physical measurements that you can take, but you do not accept that the situation is set in stone, that it cannot be changed except at the physical level. You keep your mind, as firmly as you can, locked on the image that this situation is an interaction of energy fields, of energy waves.

Regardless of the physical appearance, regardless of how solid it may seem, this is still an interaction of energy fields. What I am asking you to do is engage in an effort (and this effort will last throughout the rest of this course and even beyond the 96th level of consciousness) of training and retraining your mind to always look beyond physical appearances, to always look beyond the matter screen, as it says in my new decree, and look for the energetic component.

Then, I am asking you to do a second thing at the conscious level. It is to decide that at this point you are not seeking to create a physical change exclusively or directly through the powers of the mind. As I said, you take whatever practical, physical measures need to be taken in the situation, whether it be healing or interaction with other people. What you also do is that you fix your mind firmly on the reality that this is an energetic interaction and that your primary goal is to raise the energies of the situation as much as possible. It is not your primary goal to produce a particular physical outcome. The goal of your mind is to become an open door for a stream of spiritual energy to flow into the situation and change the situation in whatever way the energy will do so.

In other words, I am asking you to, so to speak, play a psychological trick on yourself where you deliberately disconnect your mind from the desire to produce a physical change. You neutralize this desire to produce a specific physical change. You focus your mind on the energetic component, the energetic aspect of the situation, and then you fix your mind on the goal to raise the energies. Then, you sort of set the light you invoke free to do whatever it wants to do in the situation, without you fixating your mind on a specific outcome.

What you can and cannot change

I said in my last discourse that you need to liquefy the mind and realize that in any situation your goal is to grow, to transcend, to move on with the River of life. How do you do this? What does it mean to flow with the River of life? It is not a matter of matter. You are not flowing with the River of Life by constantly dealing with *material* conditions. You flow with the River of Life by constantly dealing with *energetic* conditions.

There will always be, as long as you are in embodiment on a dense planet like earth, some physical conditions that are beyond your power to change. I have said this before: There is free will involved by other people. Even Jesus could not change certain things that were decided by the collective consciousness; he did not have the right to do this. There will always be material conditions that you cannot change. What you *can* change is the energetic components of the situation and when you do this, two things can happen. First of all, the outer situation might actually become liquefied to the point where physical changes can happen. It may not be everything that you would like to see changed but there can be changes. It can also happen that other people will be set free from their energy veils, from their energetic burdens, and they will start making different decisions that change the situation.

This is what can happen outside of yourself by focusing on raising the energy. By focusing on being an open door for raising the energy and by giving invocations, visualizations and allowing the energy to flow into the situation, you can to some degree liquefy the outer situation. This might lead to certain outer changes but the other component is that by doing this you will liquefy your own mind. You will liquefy your internal energetic situation. As you do this, you will be able to see things you cannot see today. You will be able to see that there might be a different way to react to this situation. All of a sudden, you gain a different perspective, all of a sudden the situation that seemed so serious, that seemed so devastating, that seemed so difficult to change, suddenly seems not quite as serious, not quite as devastating, not quite as locked into a certain matrix.

Suddenly, you begin to see that even if you cannot change the situation, you can certainly move on with your life so that, all of a sudden, this rock that was in the stream is now behind you and you are flowing with the River of life. There still may be a physical situation that has not changed, but *you* have moved on. You are flowing with the River of life. This, I need you to be consciously aware of as your new goal.

I need you to make a conscious decision that you will make this your new goal. I know that there are many of you who are facing certain specific situations, whether it be a disease in the body, a situation that involves other people, your financial situation, your work situation; whatever it may be. I know that these situations can seem very difficult to change. It is perfectly natural that as you have engaged in this course, you have built up certain hopes that one day there will be some shift and you will now be able to change these situations.

No particular physical outcome

Now, on the one hand it is possible that you *will* come to a point where you can change these situations. Some of you have already changed situations as you have participated in the course. What I am saying is that at this point, I need you to make the conscious shift where you say: "OK, I will set my desire for specific physical changes aside and I will engage in this experiment, as Hilarion explains, where I will focus on raising the energies of the situation. That is all I am focused on. I am focused on being the open door for higher energies to flow into the situation and I am setting the situation free, I am setting the energies free."

Here is the important point, my beloved: "I am setting myself free from this fixation on a particular physical outcome. I am allowing God to come into the situation and do whatever Spirit wants to do according to the vision of Christ, the vision that may be higher than what I can grasp right now. Therefore, I will be at peace with whatever outcome there is. I will know that even if there is no physical change, I have raised the energies and I will be willing to look at my own mind and see how this has affected my view of the situation, my ability to deal with the situation in a different way than I could see before."

If you will, my beloved, do this and if you will be open in your mind, then you will receive a different perspective on the situation. Do you see, my beloved: You have the people who study precipitation, manifestation, alchemy. Many of them have these, we might call them slightly *immature*, desires to be able to manifest things out of thin air so that they can impress other people or so that they can feel that they themselves have a certain mastery over matter. This is not our aim for this course. Our aim is to help you come to a point where you can master your outer situation in life, your living situation, your interactions with other people.

In other words, it is not our goal to get you to a point where you can manifest a simple thing, such as a lump of gold. What good would this do you if you had not really changed your consciousness? Our aim is to take you to a point where you can see what needs to change in a situation and what may not need to change because other people's free will is involved or certain other conditions are valid. You can see what *can* be changed, you can see what *cannot* be changed, and you can accept what cannot be changed and make the best of it.

Of course, you can change what can be changed, but we would much rather have you come to a point where you are able to change your outer situation rather than manifest a simple thing. I can assure you that even if you got to the point where I could manifest a simple thing, this did not necessarily mean that you could change your outer situation.

Immature dreams

We want you to be alchemists in terms of how to live life on earth, not in terms of performing what are essentially party tricks. You see, my beloved, there are many dreams that students have when they start a course like this. Many people, many spiritual students, many ascended master students, have been fascinated by alchemy and the stories of how Saint Germain was able to change the flaws of diamonds and how he was able to suddenly appear out of thin air and do other things. You see, my beloved, Saint Germain was an ascended master who had gotten a dispensation to take on the appearance of a physical body (I did not say: take on a physical body) and therefore perform these feats in a specific situation, in order to possibly change the minds of some people who had very closed minds.

This does not mean that in today's age we want our students to be able to do this so they can go out and impress people. There are students who think that if they could perform certain tricks, then surely that would attract millions of students to the teachings of the ascended masters and it would convince people that these teachings are real and that they are the next religion for the coming age. This is not our goal at all. Our goal is to make you practical alchemists who can show people, and can demonstrate this in your lives, how to live successful, peaceful, productive, constructive lives in this very complicated, very messy, situation that you have on earth.

Transforming conflict

I have said that your minds have been fixated on thinking that matter is solid and difficult to change. Now, take this to a different level. Step back a little bit and do not look at matter, as for example the stone that I have used in my example. Look at the fact that you have a planet that is made from matter. You have seven billion people who are wearing physical bodies made from matter and who have created advanced societies and civilizations.

Then, look at the fact that they have created interactions between themselves where, for example, they hold on to the image that this other group of people committed violence against our people in the past. Even though times have moved on and the physical consequences of what happened many years ago are no longer really visible, then these people are holding in their minds this matrix. They are carrying it with them and they are constantly allowing this resentment of the past to influence how they act in the present, how they act towards other people. They have a desire to punish the others. They have a desire for revenge and they have not let go of it sometimes after hundreds or even thousands of years.

Look at the fact that there are people who are carrying collectively a certain resentment and have done so for centuries. My beloved, how is this affecting their physical behavior? Can you not see that behind the vast majority of conflicts on this earth is this mechanism where people are holding a mental image created in the distant past but allowing it to influence the physical actions they take in the present?

Just imagine that you could change the energetic aspect of the situation so that the energies were raised to the point where people could overcome this emotional-mental attachment to these old images. Imagine that instead of thinking, for example, that the Arabs always have to be negative towards the Jews and vice versa, suddenly the energies could change where people could start asking themselves: "Why are we repeating these old patterns? Do we actually like the outcome? Do we like this continued conflict? We have been brought up to think that there is nothing we can do to change the situation because the other people were the ones who did the wrong thing and therefore they are the ones who have to change. And by the way, they have to be punished first before they are even allowed to change. What if we realized that *we* could do something to change, that we don't need to change the other people, we just need to change ourselves so that we can move on?"

"We actually don't care about these other people and whether they change or not, we care about ourselves and we want to move on. We want to move out of this conflict because we realize that we are as affected by it as the other people. We are constantly burdened by this and why should we export to our children what was put upon us by our parents? Why should we not question this entire process and begin to change our behavior even though the other people have not changed theirs?"

The only way to change situations

Can you see how this is the only way to actually change the situation? Look at the situation in the Middle East, my beloved. Look at what has been going on in Syria over these last years. Do you actually think that there is anything that anyone could do to create a physical change in this situation that would lead to peace? Do you think that if the international community (under the auspices of the United Nations or whatever) decided to get together and say: "Now, we are going to collect an army big enough to go in there and create peace in Syria." Do you think that this would have an effect? Do you think that this would create peace?

As you can see, it is more likely to add to the conflict. Can you see that if you look at the situation in Syria, you saw that years ago there were several rebel groups that were in the beginning stages of rebelling against the government? Certain Western nations wanted to remove the government because they thought that President Assad was a dictator. They decided to support some of what they considered "moderate" rebel groups in Syria. They gave them training, arms and money and now these moderate groups started a violent campaign against the President. Well, my beloved, ask yourself this: "How is someone who is willing to kill other human beings a moderate person?" I know you could say that those who belong to ISIS or IS are more fanatical Muslims than what was considered "moderate" rebels, but how is a person willing to use violence a moderate?

Can you see here that there is a mindset (not only in the Middle East, but also in the Western nations) that is locked and can therefore only create more and more conflict? Can you see that the Western nations might have gone in without having this specific vision that the President needs to be removed but had gone in with the vision that: "We want to raise the consciousness of the Syrian people so that they themselves can improve the situation." Just imagine that this had been done instead. Now, grant you, this may have had a limited effect in the beginning, but in the long run I can assure you that it would have had a far more positive effect than the mess you currently see.

How is it a victory for freedom and democracy that you have a country where the majority of the buildings have been destroyed by bombs and artillery? How is this a victory in any way? How is this progress?

Can you see that even if you go beyond the governments and imagine that a sufficient number of spiritual people around the world had decided to focus their attention on raising the energetic aspect of the situation in Syria, can you see what effect this might have had? I can assure you that it would have had a far more positive effect than what you see right now. Can you see that even behind this was this mindset I have been talking about, the satanic mindset, the fallen mindset? "There is a situation in Syria; it has certain physical components that we judge as not being right. Therefore, we feel that as free democratic nations we have to do something to change the situation. What can we do? We can only take physical measures to change the physical consequences and therefore we must arm the rebel groups so they can physically and violently get rid of the dictator." As we have said many times, my beloved, the leader of a country is an expression of the collective consciousness of the people of that country. What does the current situation in Syria show you? The collective consciousness simply was not high enough to get rid of Assad. Until that changes, the situation at the physical level will not change. Therefore, imagine that people had focused on raising the collective consciousness of the Syrian people and allowing it to take the time it took until they were ready for a different kind of government than what they have had so far. I can assure you that if this process had been allowed to go on, then there would have been a change by now without the country being bombed back into the Stone Age.

Freedom from material conditions

Now, I know that this has very little to do – seemingly – with a course in self-mastery, but I am using this as an example to show you that if you will change your consciousness and focus on changing the energy in a situation, rather than changing the physical aspects of the situation, then your life and your spiritual path will take on an entirely new meaning. This is the seventh level of my retreat. You are facing the energies of the Seventh Ray of Freedom. What is it I am offering you here? I am offering you an opportunity to set your mind free from the fixation on material, physical conditions.

Do you not realize that the trick of the fallen beings has been to make you forget that you are a spiritual being? How have they made you forget this? By getting you to focus your mind primarily on physical, material conditions. Can you see, my beloved, that if you engage in the spiritual path, if you engage in the course of self-mastery, but you still have this desire that the goal must be that you can change physical conditions (that you have mastery over matter conditions), then you are actually trying to walk the spiritual path with a mindset imposed upon you by the fallen beings? The spiritual path that we of the ascended masters offer, is offered from the ascended master consciousness—*not* from the fallen consciousness.

If you are dragging with you elements of the fallen consciousness, how successful do you think you will be in walking the path that leads you towards the ascended consciousness and is based on the ascended consciousness? How successful will you be? How successful will you be in overcoming a problem with the same state of consciousness that created the problem? As I have attempted to explain in my previous discourses, the fallen beings want you to think that matter is all-important, even that matter is all there is.

The ascended masters want you to recognize that matter is not all there is and matter is not all that important. It is far more important what happens in the totality of the four levels of the material universe, not just at the physical level. My beloved, there are many, many people throughout the history of this planet, even after it became as dense as it is today, who have been successful at walking the spiritual path and qualifying for their ascension but they still had certain physical diseases, handicaps or a very limited physical situation.

Look at the example of Jesus once again, as I have explained. You could look at it from a materialistic standpoint and say that Jesus was a failure because he was killed. He could not even prevent himself from being killed. Jesus qualified for his ascension by going through that, and the reason for this was that regardless of what happened at the physical level, Jesus used every situation at the physical level to change his own mind. Jesus changed his emotional body, his mental body, his identity body. Once you change the components in the three higher bodies, you can come to a point where you are ready to ascend regardless of what physical situations you are facing at the level of your physical body. It does not matter.

It does not matter what happens in matter because the ascension is a spiritual process. You qualify for your ascension in the emotional, mental and identity levels, not at the physical level. Of course, you cannot run around killing people and qualify for your ascension. You need to make certain changes at the physical level, but there are no ideal conditions that you must fulfill at the physical level in order to qualify for your ascension.

This is demonstrated very clearly by Jesus for those who have eyes to see and ears to hear, which I know that you have at this level of the course. I certainly know that you have it in your finer bodies when you attend my retreat. Therefore, I know you are capable of having it at the conscious level also when you are willing to make that switch in the mind that I am asking you to make.

Overcoming lower desires

Put aside all these desires to make some grandiose changes in your personal life or to make some grandiose demonstration to other people. Put aside all these desires for a certain physical outcome. Focus on raising the energies of every situation you encounter. Focus on raising the energies of your physical body, which, of course, requires you to raise the energies of your three higher bodies as well. Simply focus on this.

I am not saying that you will not at some point be able to create physical changes. I am actually saying that by focusing on the energies, you will shorten the time to where you can create physical changes. What I am saying is that even Jesus himself did not have the intent of creating physical changes. There are many students who have not quite understood this point so let me go into it a little bit.

Take the situation where Jesus meets a man with a withered hand. Now, as I explained in my last discourse, Jesus did not have the mindset where he instantly judged that this is wrong, this should not have happened. Neither did he have the mindset that he looked at the withered hand and said: "Oh, this is a physical consequence that cannot be changed except at the physical level and since we know no way of changing this physically, it cannot be changed."

He did not accept the condition as permanent, but neither did he judge that this was wrong and that the man's arm should be healed at all cost. Therefore, he did not go in with the intent to physically heal the withered arm. Jesus went in with the intent to raise the energies of the situation, to raise the consciousness of the person so that the person would have a shift in consciousness. It was not Jesus' goal to physically heal the arm but to set the man free from the state of consciousness he was in when Jesus met him. Jesus did not have a preconceived vision of how the man's consciousness would change because he knew that this was up to free will. He went into the situation in order to infuse the situation with higher energies so that the man might have an opportunity to change his consciousness that he did not have before.

Now, in this case the man was willing to change his consciousness and he sensed the higher energies coming from Jesus. He was willing to make such a shift that his arm was actually healed at the physical level. This was in large part due to the man's willingness to be open. It was beyond the control of Jesus: It was up to the free will of this man. Therefore, Jesus could only be the open door for higher energy to stream into the situation, he had no specific intent here. He was not trying to prove anything; he was not trying to create a miracle that would make him famous. He was simply being the open door, nothing less, nothing more. When the man's arm was healed, Jesus was actually surprised, not surprised that it was possible to heal the arm but surprised that the man was able and willing to make the shift in consciousness that made the physical healing possible.

Now, there were many people that Jesus approached the same way who did not experience a physical healing because they were not able or willing to shift their consciousness even though they all sensed the higher energy streaming through Jesus. There are people even today who have gone to faith healers and who experienced a physical healing but after some time the disease reappears. The reason for this is that while they are in the presence of a higher energy field and sensing the higher energy fields, these people are able to switch their consciousness and accept that healing is possible. When they go back to their normal life, they gradually sink back into their normal level of consciousness. They have not permanently shifted their consciousness and so the disease reappears, or rather it is recreated by the mind because they have not changed the images in the three higher levels that are being projected onto the physical energy.

Being an open door for higher energies

You are spiritual students. You are all capable of sensing higher spiritual energies. You have sensed this in our dictations. You have sensed it when you give decrees and invocations and you feel the energy flowing through you. You know when you are being an open door for the energy that is more. This is what I am asking you to do: To make this shift in every situation you encounter in life. Focus within; focus on being the open door for letting spiritual energy flow into the situation.

What does it mean to be the open door, my beloved? *Open* door. How is a door *open?* When there is no screen in front of it, the screen in your mind that has some expectation of what should or should not happen, that judges the situation based on what should or should not be.

The more you can remove the screen, the more you will be the open door and the more effective the spiritual energies will be in changing situations. This is your highest potential right now. I am not saying it is the highest potential for the rest of your time in embodiment. Right now, this is your highest potential. Focus on this and forget about physical changes, be non-attached to the physical changes. Seek to change the energies. Give people an opportunity to sense a higher energy and therefore make a different choice. Give yourself the opportunity to sense a higher energy and make a different choice to be independent of physical conditions, to be at peace, to be focused on flowing with the River of Life, regardless of physical conditions.

You see, my beloved, there are many, many spiritual people, over the centuries and millennia, who have been aware of the possibility that they can channel spiritual energy into a situation. Many times they have thought that if only a certain physical change could happen, then they could be the open door. You see, what Jesus demonstrated was that regardless of the physical conditions, you can always be the open door if you are willing to take your mind away from the attachment to physical circumstances. Only non-attachment can help you be the open door, can bring you to the point where you are the open door. Therefore, you need to look at what attachments you have in any situation, what attachments you have to a particular outcome. Perhaps the outcome you are envisioning may not be what Spirit envisions in that situation? You are saying to yourself: "But the person is ill, how could Spirit not want that person to be healed?" Well, as I explained in my last discourse, sometimes a disease can be part of a person's Divine plan. Otherwise, it can be karmic conditions so it is not in Spirit's vision that the disease is healed right now. Or it may not be in Spirit's vision that it sees this healed until the person has shifted his or her consciousness.

You see, there are many, many situations in life, in fact *all* situations in life, where the background of the situation, the conditions that have precipitated the situation, are so complex because they involve the minds of so many people. You take one person and you realize that this person is a very complex being who had many lifetimes, reaching back into the past. The person has created certain patterns in its four lower bodies that reach far back into the past, and the person is only going to progress by changing some of those patterns.

As I said earlier, everything is exactly as it should be because the conditions in that person's life are an outpicturing of the person's state of consciousness. It is because the person has not been willing to listen to inner direction and therefore needs to see an outer demonstration of its state of consciousness so it has an opportunity to start questioning that state of consciousness and changing it. Now, if you come in as a spiritual student and you have compassion for the person and you want to just heal that person and remove the physical conditions, then how is that going to help the growth of that person? The person will simply say: "Oh, now I am free of the limitations, I can live happily ever after and I don't ever need to look at my state of consciousness."

Many people have done this when they have been healed. Even Jesus sometimes healed a person who had this reaction. What you need to recognize here is that every situation you encounter in life has these almost infinite layers of complexity, far more layers than you are able to fathom with the conscious mind. That is why I said to you that there are certain of these perception filters that are actually beneficial because they prevent you from being so overwhelmed with information. Say you were to look at a situation and evaluate: Should this person be healed or not be healed? If you were to know consciously everything that is involved with this situation, you would be overwhelmed and it would take you so long to fathom this that it would tie up your time and energy for a long time. Why do you need to know this consciously? You do not need to know this consciously.

Can you also see that if you cannot know consciously what is involved in a situation, why should you have a conscious judgment of what should or should not happen in the situation? Is it not far more constructive to allow yourself to be the open door, to allow the energies of Spirit to flow into the situation and do whatever they want to do, without you having any conscious opinion about what they should or should not do. Set Spirit free to act according to its vision, and set yourself free from any attachment to the situation or to the outcome.

Non-attachment to physical outcome is the hallmark of a spiritual student who has reached the final level on the Fifth Ray. It is also the key to Buddhahood, which I assume is a goal that you are striving towards and see as a real potential for yourself. Perhaps not tomorrow, but certainly one day.

My beloved, it has been my great privilege and my great joy to tutor you at my retreat and to see you grow through these seven levels. It is with great joy that I say to you: "Well done!" It is with great joy that I send you on to my beloved Nada so that she may tutor you through another seven levels on the Ray of Peace. Certainly, if there is anything the world needs, it is peace. So peace be still and know that you are God, a God in the making.

Hilarion I AM, and with great joy, I send you on your way.

17 | INVOKING VISION BEYOND MATTER

In the name I AM THAT I AM, Jesus Christ, I call to my I AM Presence to flow through the I Will Be Presence that I AM and give this invocation with full power. I call to beloved Elohim Cyclopea and Virginia and Arcturus and Victoria, Archangel Raphael and Mother Mary and Zadkiel and Amethyst, Hilarion and Saint Germain to help me see the energetic aspects of every situation and to stop judging with the outer mind. Help me see and surrender all patterns that block my oneness with Hilarion and with my I AM Presence, including …

[Make personal calls]

Part 1

1. I am willing to set my vision free from the very subtle basic illusion of the fallen beings, namely that things are things and that they are difficult to change because matter is solid and unchangeable by the mind.

> Cyclopea so dear, the truth you reveal,
> the truth that duality's ailments will heal,
> your Emerald Light is like a great balm,
> our emotional bodies are perfectly calm.
>
> **Cyclopea so dear, in Emerald Sphere,**
> **in raising perception we shall persevere,**
> **as deep in our hearts your truth we revere,**
> **to immaculate vision the earth does adhere.**

2. Evil is an energy veil because the forces of darkness have created the illusion that matter is solid and unchangeable, and this makes it difficult to see beyond the matter screen.

> Cyclopea so dear, with you we unwind,
> all negative spirals clouding the mind,
> we know pure awareness is truly our core,
> the key to becoming the wide-open door.
>
> **Cyclopea so dear, in Emerald Sphere,**
> **in raising perception we shall persevere,**
> **as deep in our hearts your truth we revere,**
> **to immaculate vision the earth does adhere.**

17 | Invoking Vision beyond Matter

3. There is a certain correspondence between the density of matter and the capabilities of my physical senses. My physical senses need to be capable of sensing matter at its current level of vibration. They are calibrated based on the density of matter.

> Cyclopea so dear, clear our inner sight,
> empowered, we pierce the soul's fearful night,
> we now see our life through your single eye,
> beyond all disease we're ready to fly.
>
> **Cyclopea so dear, in Emerald Sphere,**
> **in raising perception we shall persevere,**
> **as deep in our hearts your truth we revere,**
> **to immaculate vision the earth does adhere.**

4. My physical eyes are still capable of detecting vibrations that are beyond the physical spectrum, I am physically able to see these vibrations. I do not see them because my brain and my higher bodies filter them out as unnecessary information.

> Cyclopea so dear, life can only reflect,
> the images that the mind does project,
> the key to our healing is clearing the mind,
> from the images the ego is hiding behind.
>
> **Cyclopea so dear, in Emerald Sphere,**
> **in raising perception we shall persevere,**
> **as deep in our hearts your truth we revere,**
> **to immaculate vision the earth does adhere.**

5. My perception filters can have a legitimate function in terms of allowing me to focus my attention on what is most important for me. It is necessary to filter out information, otherwise I quickly become overwhelmed.

> Cyclopea so dear, we want to aim high,
> to your healing flame we ever draw nigh,
> through veils of duality we now take flight,
> bathed in your penetrating Emerald Light.
>
> **Cyclopea so dear, in Emerald Sphere,**
> **in raising perception we shall persevere,**
> **as deep in our hearts your truth we revere,**
> **to immaculate vision the earth does adhere.**

6. The fallen beings are deliberately trying to overwhelm us with so much information and trying to give us so much outrageous information that people have started doubting everything they hear that is beyond the normal.

> Cyclopea so dear, your Emerald Flame,
> exposes every subtle, dualistic power game,
> including the game of wanting to say,
> that truth is defined in only one way.
>
> **Cyclopea so dear, in Emerald Sphere,**
> **in raising perception we shall persevere,**
> **as deep in our hearts your truth we revere,**
> **to immaculate vision the earth does adhere.**

7. It is necessary for me to have certain filters to filter out anything that would distract me from fulfilling my Divine plan.

17 | Invoking Vision beyond Matter

> Cyclopea so dear, we're feeling the flow,
> as your Living Truth upon us you bestow,
> from all dual vision we are now set free,
> planet earth in immaculate matrix will be.
>
> **Cyclopea so dear, in Emerald Sphere,**
> **in raising perception we shall persevere,**
> **as deep in our hearts your truth we revere,**
> **to immaculate vision the earth does adhere.**

8. There is a certain legitimacy to having perception filters. There is also an illegitimacy in the sense that I have been brought up to accept certain perception filters that are not conducive to the fulfillment of my Divine plan.

> Cyclopea so dear, the truth is now clear,
> we see higher purpose for which we are here
> we know truth transcends all systems below,
> immersed in your light, we continue to grow.
>
> **Cyclopea so dear, in Emerald Sphere,**
> **in raising perception we shall persevere,**
> **as deep in our hearts your truth we revere,**
> **to immaculate vision the earth does adhere.**

9. One of the primary filters that is hindering my Divine plan is the perception filter that makes me think that matter is matter, that matter is solid, that matter is unchangeable.

> Cyclopea so dear, we're feeling your joy,
> as creative vision we now do employ,
> in lifting earth out of serpentine cage,
> to manifest Saint Germain's Golden Age.

> Cyclopea so dear, in Emerald Sphere,
> in raising perception we shall persevere,
> as deep in our hearts your truth we revere,
> to immaculate vision the earth does adhere.

Part 2

1. This filter is devastating because it makes me look at situations on earth, and it makes me think that as soon as something has happened that has a physical, material consequence, then that consequence cannot be undone except perhaps at the physical level.

> Beloved Arcturus, release now the flow,
> of Violet Flame to help all life grow,
> in ever-expanding circles of light,
> it pulses within every atom so bright.

> Beloved Arcturus, your Violet Flame pure,
> is for every ailment the ultimate cure,
> against it no darkness could ever endure,
> earth's freedom it will forever ensure.

2. The reality of conditions on earth is that everything is energy. Energy is always vibrating. Energy is always fluid and regardless of the appearance to my senses and my outer mind, energy can always be changed.

> Beloved Arcturus, thou Elohim Free,
> we open our hearts to your reality,
> we have no attachments to life here on earth,
> we claim a new life in your Flame of Rebirth.

> **Beloved Arcturus, your Violet Flame pure,**
> **is for every ailment the ultimate cure,**
> **against it no darkness could ever endure,**
> **earth's freedom it will forever ensure.**

3. The fallen beings have managed to create this perception filter that makes us think that matter is not energy, that matter is a separate substance. It is a solid, difficult to change substance and certainly it is a substance that is beyond the powers of the mind to change.

> Beloved Arcturus, be with us alway,
> reborn, we are ready to face a new day,
> expanding our hearts into Infinity,
> your flame is the key to our God-victory.

> **Beloved Arcturus, your Violet Flame pure,**
> **is for every ailment the ultimate cure,**
> **against it no darkness could ever endure,**
> **earth's freedom it will forever ensure.**

4. I have been brought up with a perception filter that creates an artificial dividing line. My perception filter tells me that energy is different from the things made up of matter.

Beloved Arcturus, your bright violet fire,
now fills every atom, raising them higher,
the space in each atom all filled with your light,
as matter itself is shining so bright.

**Beloved Arcturus, your Violet Flame pure,
is for every ailment the ultimate cure,
against it no darkness could ever endure,
earth's freedom it will forever ensure.**

5. I have been programmed to think that once a situation has a physical consequence, then I cannot change that consequence at the energetic level, only at the level of matter.

Beloved Arcturus, your transforming Grace,
empowers us now every challenge to face,
with your Freedom's Song filling the ear,
we know that to God we're ever so dear.

**Beloved Arcturus, your Violet Flame pure,
is for every ailment the ultimate cure,
against it no darkness could ever endure,
earth's freedom it will forever ensure.**

6. I am willing to shatter the illusion, created by the fallen beings, that there is a fundamental divide between mind and matter. I want to see how energy is gradually lowered in vibration from the spiritual level of vibration into the identity level, into the mental, into the emotional and into the physical.

17 | Invoking Vision beyond Matter

> Beloved Arcturus, we surrender all fear,
> we're feeling your Presence so tangibly near,
> as your violet light floods our inner space,
> towards the ascension we willingly race.
>
> **Beloved Arcturus, your Violet Flame pure,**
> **is for every ailment the ultimate cure,**
> **against it no darkness could ever endure,**
> **earth's freedom it will forever ensure.**

7. I want to see how a certain quantity of energy is lowered in vibration. I want to see how a certain mental matrix is superimposed upon this quantity of energy and how this gradually, as the energy is lowered in vibration, takes on form.

> Beloved Arcturus, bring in a new age,
> help earth and humanity turn a new page,
> your transforming light gives us certainty,
> Saint Germain's Golden Age is a reality.
>
> **Beloved Arcturus, your Violet Flame pure,**
> **is for every ailment the ultimate cure,**
> **against it no darkness could ever endure,**
> **earth's freedom it will forever ensure.**

8. I want to see how it is possible to direct a beam of high-frequency energy at a rock and transform it. Or rather, free the energy that has been captured into the rock matrix so that it begins to vibrate at higher levels and therefore gradually dissolves this rock matrix that keeps the energy trapped.

Beloved Arcturus, illusions you pierce,
no serpent can stand against angels so fierce,
no forces of darkness can stop Violet Flame,
all discord on earth it will instantly tame.

**Beloved Arcturus, your Violet Flame pure,
is for every ailment the ultimate cure,
against it no darkness could ever endure,
earth's freedom it will forever ensure.**

9. I want to see how the energy is set free, becomes liquid, liquefies and can now flow either into another substance or back up into the emotional, mental, identity realms and eventually to the spiritual realm.

Beloved Arcturus, we love Saint Germain,
and therefore we call forth again and again,
your Violet Flame to flood all the earth,
so Saint Germain's eyes are filling with mirth.

**Beloved Arcturus, your Violet Flame pure,
is for every ailment the ultimate cure,
against it no darkness could ever endure,
earth's freedom it will forever ensure.**

Part 3

1. I want to sense this at the physical level, the conscious level. I want to train my mind to look at matter in a different way. I want to retrain my mind to begin to see everything as energy.

17 | Invoking Vision beyond Matter

> Raphael Archangel, your light so intense,
> raise us beyond all human pretense.
> Mother Mary and you have a vision so bold,
> to see that our highest potential unfold.

> **Raphael Archangel, for vision we pray,**
> **Raphael Archangel, show us the way,**
> **Raphael Archangel, your emerald ray,**
> **Raphael Archangel, our lives a new day.**

2. I want to mentally know that behind this solid form, that I see as a rock, there is vibrating energy. Within it is vibrating energy; it is vibrating, it is possible to change, it is liquid, it can be liquefied and flow into another form.

> Raphael Archangel, in emerald sphere,
> to immaculate vision we always adhere.
> Mother Mary enfolds us in her Sacred Heart,
> from Mother's true love, we're never apart.

> **Raphael Archangel, for vision we pray,**
> **Raphael Archangel, show us the way,**
> **Raphael Archangel, your emerald ray,**
> **Raphael Archangel, our lives a new day.**

3. I want to be free of the illusion that a physical disease with a physical symptom can only be dealt with at the physical level. I want to know in my mind that my body is not a physical substance, not a thing. It is vibrating energy and therefore it can be changed.

Raphael Archangel, all ailments you heal,
each cell in our bodies in light now you seal.
Mother Mary's immaculate concept we see,
perfection of health our new reality.

Raphael Archangel, for vision we pray,
Raphael Archangel, show us the way,
Raphael Archangel, your emerald ray,
Raphael Archangel, our lives a new day.

4. I understand that at this level of the path I am not able to change things by the power of the mind alone. I will not become discouraged. I am willing to take a sensible two-prong approach of both taking physical measures and using spiritual tools to change a situation.

Raphael Archangel, your light is so real,
the vision of Christ in us you reveal.
Mother Mary now helps us to truly transcend,
in emerald light with you we ascend.

Raphael Archangel, for vision we pray,
Raphael Archangel, show us the way,
Raphael Archangel, your emerald ray,
Raphael Archangel, our lives a new day.

5. I recognize that the prince of this world will come to me in any situation and he will tempt me. The tempter will tempt me to accept that this situation is now physical; it has a physical consequence that can only be dealt with at the level of matter.

17 | Invoking Vision beyond Matter

> Raphael Archangel, diseases are done,
> as you help us see that all life is One,
> we no longer do your true love reject,
> immaculate vision on all we project.
>
> **Raphael Archangel, for vision we pray,**
> **Raphael Archangel, show us the way,**
> **Raphael Archangel, your emerald ray,**
> **Raphael Archangel, our lives a new day.**

6. I will take the practical, physical measurements that I *can* take, but I will not accept that the situation is set in stone, that it cannot be changed except at the physical level. I keep my mind firmly locked on the image that this situation is an interaction of energy fields, of energy waves.

> Raphael Archangel, we're healing the earth,
> in immaculate vision we give her rebirth,
> a new era has on this day begun,
> your emerald light now shines like a sun.
>
> **Raphael Archangel, for vision we pray,**
> **Raphael Archangel, show us the way,**
> **Raphael Archangel, your emerald ray,**
> **Raphael Archangel, our lives a new day.**

7. Regardless of the physical appearance, regardless of how solid it may seem, this is still an interaction of energy fields. I am training and retraining my mind to always look beyond physical appearances, to always look beyond the matter screen and to look for the energetic component.

Raphael Archangel, the fall is behind,
as all of earth's people the Christ path do find,
we call now to you all people to heal,
as four lower bodies in love you do seal.

Raphael Archangel, for vision we pray,
Raphael Archangel, show us the way,
Raphael Archangel, your emerald ray,
Raphael Archangel, our lives a new day.

8. I am deciding that at this point I am not seeking to create a physical change exclusively or directly through the powers of the mind. I will take whatever practical, physical measures need to be taken in the situation.

Raphael Archangel, as you bring the light,
the forces of darkness swiftly take flight,
their day is now done as we claim the earth,
spreading to all an innocent mirth.

Raphael Archangel, for vision we pray,
Raphael Archangel, show us the way,
Raphael Archangel, your emerald ray,
Raphael Archangel, our lives a new day.

9. I also fix my mind firmly on the reality that this is an energetic interaction and that my primary goal is to raise the energies of the situation as much as possible.

Raphael Archangel, our vision set free,
as we can now see God's reality,
as Saint Germain's vision is manifest here,
the earth is now sealed in immaculate sphere.

17 | Invoking Vision beyond Matter

Raphael Archangel, for vision we pray,
Raphael Archangel, show us the way,
Raphael Archangel, your emerald ray,
Raphael Archangel, our lives a new day.

Part 4

1. It is not my primary goal to produce a particular physical outcome. The goal of my mind is to become an open door for a stream of spiritual energy to flow into the situation and change the situation in whatever way the energy will do so.

Zadkiel Archangel, your flow is so swift,
in your violet light, we instantly shift,
into a vibration in which we are free,
from all limitations of the lesser me.

**Zadkiel Archangel, encircle the earth,
Zadkiel Archangel, with your violet girth,
Zadkiel Archangel, unstoppable mirth,
Zadkiel Archangel, our planet's rebirth.**

2. I deliberately disconnect my mind from the desire to produce a physical change. I neutralize this desire to produce a specific physical change. I focus my mind on the energetic component, the energetic aspect of the situation.

Zadkiel Archangel, we truly aspire,
to being the master of your violet fire,
wielding the power, of your alchemy,
we use Sacred Word, to set all life free.

**Zadkiel Archangel, encircle the earth,
Zadkiel Archangel, with your violet girth,
Zadkiel Archangel, unstoppable mirth,
Zadkiel Archangel, our planet's rebirth.**

3. I fix my mind on the goal to raise the energies. I set the light I invoke free to do whatever it wants to do in the situation, without me fixating my mind on a specific outcome.

Zadkiel Archangel, your violet light,
transforming the earth, with unstoppable might,
so swiftly our planet, beginning to spin,
with legions of angels, our victory we win.

**Zadkiel Archangel, encircle the earth,
Zadkiel Archangel, with your violet girth,
Zadkiel Archangel, unstoppable mirth,
Zadkiel Archangel, our planet's rebirth.**

4. I am liquefying the mind and deciding that in any situation my goal is to grow, to transcend, to move on with the River of life.

Zadkiel Archangel, the earth is now free,
from burdens put on her by humanity,
all people are free from their inner strife,
embracing the freedom to start a new life.

**Zadkiel Archangel, encircle the earth,
Zadkiel Archangel, with your violet girth,
Zadkiel Archangel, unstoppable mirth,
Zadkiel Archangel, our planet's rebirth.**

5. Flowing with the River of life is not a matter of matter. I am not flowing with the River of Life by constantly dealing with *material* conditions. I flow with the River of Life by constantly dealing with *energetic* conditions.

> Zadkiel Archangel, the earth will now spin,
> much faster as we Christ victory win,
> for in Christ the captives are truly set free,
> bathed in Christ Light the earth now will be.
>
> **Zadkiel Archangel, encircle the earth,**
> **Zadkiel Archangel, with your violet girth,**
> **Zadkiel Archangel, unstoppable mirth,**
> **Zadkiel Archangel, our planet's rebirth.**

6. There will always be some physical conditions that are beyond my power to change because there is free will involved by other people. What I can change is the energetic components of the situation and when I do this, two things can happen.

> Zadkiel Archangel, the forces of night,
> are bound by your penetrating Freedom Light,
> the earth is now cleared by forces so dark,
> as your Violet Light provides a new spark.
>
> **Zadkiel Archangel, encircle the earth,**
> **Zadkiel Archangel, with your violet girth,**
> **Zadkiel Archangel, unstoppable mirth,**
> **Zadkiel Archangel, our planet's rebirth.**

7. The outer situation might become liquefied to the point where physical changes can happen. Other people might be set free from their energy veils and they will start making different decisions that change the situation.

> Zadkiel Archangel, we truly love you,
> and to Saint Germain we will always be true,
> help us now see our plans so Divine,
> so we on this planet our full light can shine.
>
> **Zadkiel Archangel, encircle the earth,**
> **Zadkiel Archangel, with your violet girth,**
> **Zadkiel Archangel, unstoppable mirth,**
> **Zadkiel Archangel, our planet's rebirth.**

8. My mind will become liquefied and I will liquefy my internal energetic situation. I will be able to see things I cannot see today. I will be able to see that there might be a different way to react to this situation.

> Zadkiel Archangel, there is no more night,
> a new day is born from your great Violet Light,
> transforming all manifestations of fear,
> we know that the Golden Age is now here.
>
> **Zadkiel Archangel, encircle the earth,**
> **Zadkiel Archangel, with your violet girth,**
> **Zadkiel Archangel, unstoppable mirth,**
> **Zadkiel Archangel, our planet's rebirth.**

17 | Invoking Vision beyond Matter

9. I want to gain a different perspective on all situations that seem difficult to change. I want to see that they are not quite as serious, not quite as devastating, not quite as locked into a certain matrix.

> Zadkiel Archangel, your violet flame,
> the earth and humanity, never the same,
> Saint Germain's Golden Age, is a reality,
> what glorious wonder, we joyously see.
>
> **Zadkiel Archangel, encircle the earth,**
> **Zadkiel Archangel, with your violet girth,**
> **Zadkiel Archangel, unstoppable mirth,**
> **Zadkiel Archangel, our planet's rebirth.**

Part 5

1. I see that even if I cannot change the situation, I can certainly move on with my life so that this rock that was in the stream is now behind me and I am flowing with the River of life.

> Hilarion, on emerald shore,
> we're free from all that's gone before.
> Hilarion, we let all go,
> that keeps us out of sacred flow.
>
> **Hilarion, with light so green,**
> **we see behind the matter screen,**
> **immaculate our inner sight,**
> **we see the earth is taking flight.**

2. There still may be a physical situation that has not changed, but I have moved on. Flowing with the River of life is my new goal. I am making the conscious decision that I will make this my new goal.

> Hilarion, the secret key,
> is wisdom's own reality.
> Hilarion, all life is healed,
> the ego's face no more concealed.
>
> **Hilarion, with light so green,**
> **we see behind the matter screen,**
> **immaculate our inner sight,**
> **we see the earth is taking flight.**

3. I am making the conscious shift that I will set my desire for specific physical changes aside and I will focus on raising the energies of the situation. I am focused on being the open door for higher energies to flow into the situation and I am setting the situation free, I am setting the energies free.

> Hilarion, your love for life,
> helps us surrender inner strife.
> Hilarion, your loving words,
> thrill our hearts like song of birds.
>
> **Hilarion, with light so green,**
> **we see behind the matter screen,**
> **immaculate our inner sight,**
> **we see the earth is taking flight.**

4. I am setting myself free from this fixation on a particular physical outcome. I am allowing God to come into the situation and do whatever Spirit wants to do according to the vision of Christ, the vision that may be higher than what I can grasp right now.

> Hilarion, invoke the light,
> your sacred formulas recite.
> Hilarion, your secret tone,
> philosopher's most sacred stone.
>
> **Hilarion, with light so green,**
> **we see behind the matter screen,**
> **immaculate our inner sight,**
> **we see the earth is taking flight.**

5. I will be at peace with whatever outcome there is. I will know that even if there is no physical change, I have raised the energies and I will be willing to look at my own mind and see how this has affected my view of the situation, my ability to deal with the situation in a different way than I could see before.

> Hilarion, with love you greet,
> us in your temple over Crete.
> Hilarion, your emerald light,
> the third eye sees with Christic sight.
>
> **Hilarion, with light so green,**
> **we see behind the matter screen,**
> **immaculate our inner sight,**
> **we see the earth is taking flight.**

6. I am open to receiving a different perspective on the situation and how I can master my outer situation in life, my living situation, my interactions with other people.

> Hilarion, you give us fruit,
> of truth that is so absolute.
> Hilarion, all stress decrease,
> as our ambitions we release.
>
> **Hilarion, with light so green,**
> **we see behind the matter screen,**
> **immaculate our inner sight,**
> **we see the earth is taking flight.**

7. I want to see what needs to change in a situation and what may not need to change because other people's free will is involved or certain other conditions are valid. I want to see what can be changed and what cannot be changed. I will accept what cannot be changed and make the best of it.

> Hilarion, our chakras clear,
> as we let go of subtlest fear.
> Hilarion, we are sincere,
> as freedom's truth we do revere.
>
> **Hilarion, with light so green,**
> **we see behind the matter screen,**
> **immaculate our inner sight,**
> **we see the earth is taking flight.**

8. I desire to be a practical alchemist who can demonstrate how to live a successful, peaceful, productive, constructive life in this very complicated, very messy, situation that we have on earth.

> Hilarion, you balance all,
> the seven rays upon our call.
> Hilarion, you keep us true,
> as we remain all one with you.
>
> **Hilarion, with light so green,**
> **we see behind the matter screen,**
> **immaculate our inner sight,**
> **we see the earth is taking flight.**

9. I see that behind the vast majority of conflicts on this earth is a mechanism where people are holding a mental image created in the distant past but allowing it to influence the physical actions they take in the present.

> Hilarion, your Presence here,
> filling up the inner sphere.
> Life is now a sacred flow,
> God Vision we on all bestow.
>
> **Hilarion, with light so green,**
> **we see behind the matter screen,**
> **immaculate our inner sight,**
> **we see the earth is taking flight.**

Part 6

1. I am willing to help change the energetic aspect of the situation so that the energies are raised to the point where people can overcome this emotional-mental attachment to these old images.

> Saint Germain, your alchemy,
> with violet fire now sets us free.
> Saint Germain, we ever grow,
> in freedom's overpowering flow.
>
> **O Saint Germain, your Golden Age,
> sets people free from psychic cage,
> the earth is raised to starry height,
> as we project with Freedom's Sight.**

2. I am the open door for changing the energies so people can start asking themselves: "Why are we repeating these old patterns? Do we actually like the outcome? Do we like this continued conflict?"

> Saint Germain, your mastery,
> of violet flame geometry.
> Saint Germain, in you we see,
> the formulas that set us free.
>
> **O Saint Germain, your Golden Age,
> sets people free from psychic cage,
> the earth is raised to starry height,
> as we project with Freedom's Sight.**

17 | Invoking Vision beyond Matter

3. I am the open door for helping raise the energies so people can begin to change themselves instead of seeking to change other people.

> Saint Germain, in Liberty,
> you give the love that sets all free.
> Saint Germain, we do adore,
> the violet flame that makes all more.

> **O Saint Germain, your Golden Age,**
> **sets people free from psychic cage,**
> **the earth is raised to starry height,**
> **as we project with Freedom's Sight.**

4. I am the open door for a new awareness that instead of seeking to physically change situations, we can focus on raising the collective consciousness of the people so they become ready for a different situation.

> Saint Germain, in unity,
> we will transcend duality.
> Saint Germain, the self so pure,
> your violet chemistry so sure.

> **O Saint Germain, your Golden Age,**
> **sets people free from psychic cage,**
> **the earth is raised to starry height,**
> **as we project with Freedom's Sight.**

5. The trick of the fallen beings has been to make me forget that I am a spiritual being. They got me to focus my mind primarily on physical, material conditions.

Saint Germain, reality,
in violet light we are carefree.
Saint Germain, our auras seal,
your violet flame our chakras heal.

**O Saint Germain, your Golden Age,
sets people free from psychic cage,
the earth is raised to starry height,
as we project with Freedom's Sight.**

6. If I still have this goal to change physical conditions, then I am actually trying to walk the spiritual path with a mindset imposed upon me by the fallen beings.

Saint Germain, your chemistry,
with violet fire set atoms free.
Saint Germain, from lead to gold,
transforming vision we behold.

**O Saint Germain, your Golden Age,
sets people free from psychic cage,
the earth is raised to starry height,
as we project with Freedom's Sight.**

7. The spiritual path that the ascended masters offer, is offered from the ascended master consciousness—not from the fallen consciousness.

Saint Germain, transcendency,
as we are always one with thee.
Saint Germain, from soul we're free,
we so delight in knowing thee.

**O Saint Germain, your Golden Age,
sets people free from psychic cage,
the earth is raised to starry height,
as we project with Freedom's Sight.**

8. If I am dragging with me elements of the fallen consciousness, how successful will I be in walking the path that leads me towards the ascended consciousness? How successful will I be in overcoming a problem with the same state of consciousness that created the problem?

> Saint Germain, nobility,
> the key to sacred alchemy.
> Saint Germain, you balance all,
> the seven rays upon our call.

**O Saint Germain, your Golden Age,
sets people free from psychic cage,
the earth is raised to starry height,
as we project with Freedom's Sight.**

9. The fallen beings want me to think that matter is all-important, even that matter is all there is. The ascended masters want me to recognize that matter is not all there is and matter is not all that important. It is far more important what happens in the totality of the four levels of the material universe, not just at the physical level.

> Saint Germain, your Presence here,
> filling up the inner sphere.
> Life is now a sacred flow,
> God Freedom we on all bestow.

O Saint Germain, your Golden Age,
sets people free from psychic cage,
the earth is raised to starry height,
as we project with Freedom's Sight.

Part 7

1. Many people have been successful at walking the spiritual path and qualifying for their ascension but they still had certain physical diseases, handicaps or a very limited physical situation.

> Divine Director, I now see,
> the world is unreality,
> in my heart I now truly feel,
> the Spirit is all that is real.
>
> **Divine Director, send the light,**
> **from blindness clear my inner sight,**
> **my vision free, my vision clear,**
> **your guidance is forever here.**

2. Jesus qualified for his ascension by going through a limited physical situation. Regardless of what happened at the physical level, Jesus used every situation to change his own mind. Jesus changed his emotional body, his mental body, his identity body.

> Divine Director, vision give,
> in clarity I want to live,
> I now behold my plan Divine,
> the plan that is uniquely mine.

> Divine Director, send the light,
> from blindness clear my inner sight,
> my vision free, my vision clear,
> your guidance is forever here.

3. Once I change the components in the three higher bodies, I can be ready to ascend regardless of what situations I am facing at the level of my physical body. It does not matter what happens in matter because the ascension is a spiritual process.

> Divine Director, show in me,
> the ego games, and set me free,
> help me escape the ego's cage,
> to help bring in the golden age.

> Divine Director, send the light,
> from blindness clear my inner sight,
> my vision free, my vision clear,
> your guidance is forever here.

4. I qualify for my ascension in the emotional, mental and identity levels, not at the physical level. There are no ideal conditions that I must fulfill at the physical level in order to qualify for my ascension.

> Divine Director, I'm with you,
> my vision one, no longer two,
> as karma's veil you do disperse,
> I see a whole new universe.

> **Divine Director, send the light,**
> **from blindness clear my inner sight,**
> **my vision free, my vision clear,**
> **your guidance is forever here.**

5. I am willing to make a switch in the mind and give up all desires to make grandiose changes in my personal life or to make some grandiose demonstration to other people. I give up all desires for a certain physical outcome.

> Divine Director, I go up,
> electric light now fills my cup,
> consume in me all shadows old,
> bestow on me a vision bold.

> **Divine Director, send the light,**
> **from blindness clear my inner sight,**
> **my vision free, my vision clear,**
> **your guidance is forever here.**

6. I focus on raising the energies of every situation I encounter. I focus on raising the energies of my physical body, which requires me to raise the energies of my three higher bodies as well.

> Divine Director, heart of gold,
> my sacred labor I unfold,
> o blessed Guru, I now see,
> where my own plan is taking me.

**Divine Director, send the light,
from blindness clear my inner sight,
my vision free, my vision clear,
your guidance is forever here.**

7. Focusing on the energies will shorten the time to where I can create physical changes. Jesus did not have the intent of creating physical changes.

Divine Director, by your grace,
in grander scheme I find my place,
my individual flame I see,
uniqueness God has given me.

**Divine Director, send the light,
from blindness clear my inner sight,
my vision free, my vision clear,
your guidance is forever here.**

8. Jesus did not accept any condition as permanent, but neither did he judge that this was wrong and that a situation should be changed at all cost. He did not go in with the intent to create physical change.

Divine Director, vision one,
I see that I AM God's own Sun,
with your direction so Divine,
I am now letting my light shine.

**Divine Director, send the light,
from blindness clear my inner sight,
my vision free, my vision clear,
your guidance is forever here.**

9. Jesus went in with the intent to raise the energies of the situation, to raise the consciousness of the person so that the person would have a shift in consciousness.

> Divine Director, what a gift,
> to be a part of Spirit's lift,
> to raise mankind out of the night,
> to bask in Spirit's loving sight.
>
> **Divine Director, send the light,**
> **from blindness clear my inner sight,**
> **my vision free, my vision clear,**
> **your guidance is forever here.**

Part 8

1. It was not Jesus' goal to physically heal people but to set them free from the state of consciousness they were in. He went into any situation in order to infuse the situation with higher energies so that people might have an opportunity to change their consciousness.

> Surya, cosmic being bright,
> your balance is my pure delight,
> I am in orbit round God Star,
> in perfect unity we are.
>
> **Surya, banish all extremes,**
> **Surya, shatter Serpent's schemes,**
> **Surya, balance to me bring,**
> **Surya, making my heart sing.**

17 | Invoking Vision beyond Matter

2. I am a spiritual student. I am capable of sensing higher spiritual energies. I know when I am being an open door for the energy that is more.

> Surya, there is more to life,
> than human conflict, war and strife,
> your balance gives me inner peace,
> all outer conflicts do now cease.

> **Surya, banish all extremes,**
> **Surya, shatter Serpent's schemes,**
> **Surya, balance to me bring,**
> **Surya, making my heart sing.**

3. I am making the conscious shift that in every situation I encounter in life, I will focus within. I will focus on being the open door for letting spiritual energy flow into the situation.

> Surya, what a wondrous sight,
> from Sirius you send the light,
> of one mind, I now call to thee,
> for your apprentice I would be.

> **Surya, banish all extremes,**
> **Surya, shatter Serpent's schemes,**
> **Surya, balance to me bring,**
> **Surya, making my heart sing.**

4. Being the open door means that there is no screen in my mind that has some expectation of what should or should not happen, that judges the situation based on what should or should not be.

Surya, radiate your light,
with balance you set all things right,
consuming energetic dross,
my letting go is not a loss.

**Surya, banish all extremes,
Surya, shatter Serpent's schemes,
Surya, balance to me bring,
Surya, making my heart sing.**

5. The more I can remove the screen, the more I will be the open door and the more effective the spiritual energies will be in changing situations. This is my highest potential right now.

Surya, your light is alive,
for inner balance I do strive,
the alchemy is now begun,
my heart transformed into a sun.

**Surya, banish all extremes,
Surya, shatter Serpent's schemes,
Surya, balance to me bring,
Surya, making my heart sing.**

6. I am focused on giving people an opportunity to sense a higher energy and therefore make a different choice.

Surya, come enlighten me,
duality you help me see,
extremes they cannot pull me in,
on Middle Way I always win.

**Surya, banish all extremes,
Surya, shatter Serpent's schemes,
Surya, balance to me bring,
Surya, making my heart sing.**

7. I am focused on giving myself the opportunity to sense a higher energy and make a different choice to be independent of physical conditions, to be at peace, to be focused on flowing with the River of Life regardless of physical conditions.

Surya, in your cosmic sphere,
with Cuzco I your light revere,
from your perspective o so grand,
life finally I understand.

**Surya, banish all extremes,
Surya, shatter Serpent's schemes,
Surya, balance to me bring,
Surya, making my heart sing.**

8. Regardless of the physical conditions, I can always be the open door if I am willing to take my mind away from the attachment to the physical circumstances. Only non-attachment can help me be the open door, can bring me to the point where I am the open door.

Surya, show me God's design,
I see that God is all benign,
you calm my feeling body's storm,
I know the God beyond all form.

> **Surya, banish all extremes,**
> **Surya, shatter Serpent's schemes,**
> **Surya, balance to me bring,**
> **Surya, making my heart sing.**

9. I am willing to look at what attachments I have in any situation, what attachments I have to a particular outcome. I realize that the outcome I am envisioning may not be what Spirit envisions in that situation.

> Surya, I come from afar,
> and as you show me my home star,
> I see now my internal light,
> a star I am in my own right.

> **Surya, banish all extremes,**
> **Surya, shatter Serpent's schemes,**
> **Surya, balance to me bring,**
> **Surya, making my heart sing.**

Part 9

1. I realize that in all situations in life, the conditions that have precipitated the situation are very complex because they involve the minds of many people.

> O Portia, in your own retreat,
> with Mother's Love you do me greet.
> As all my tests I now complete,
> old patterns I no more repeat.

**O Portia, opportunity,
I am beyond duality.
I focus now internally,
with you I grow eternally.**

2. I realize that I cannot consciously know whether a person should or should not be healed. Every situation I encounter in life has almost infinite layers of complexity, far more layers than I am able to fathom with the conscious mind.

O Portia, Justice is your name,
upholding Cosmic Honor Flame,
No longer will I play the game,
of seeking to remain the same.

**O Portia, opportunity,
I am beyond duality.
I focus now internally,
with you I grow eternally.**

3. If I were to know consciously everything that is involved with a situation, I would be overwhelmed. I do not need to know everything consciously.

O Portia, in the cosmic flow,
one with you, I ever grow.
I am the chalice here below,
of cosmic justice you bestow.

**O Portia, opportunity,
I am beyond duality.
I focus now internally,
with you I grow eternally.**

4. If I cannot know consciously what is involved in a situation, why should I have a conscious judgment of what should or should not happen in the situation?

> O Portia, cosmic balance bring,
> eternal hope, my heart does sing.
> Protected by your Mother's wing,
> I feel at one with everything.

> **O Portia, opportunity,**
> **I am beyond duality.**
> **I focus now internally,**
> **with you I grow eternally.**

5. It is far more constructive to allow myself to be the open door, to allow the energies of Spirit to flow into the situation and do whatever they want to do, without me having any conscious opinion about what they should or should not do.

> O Portia, bring the Mother Light,
> to set all free from darkest night.
> Your Love Flame shines forever bright,
> with Saint Germain now hold me tight.

> **O Portia, opportunity,**
> **I am beyond duality.**
> **I focus now internally,**
> **with you I grow eternally.**

6. I set Spirit free to act according to its vision, and I set myself free from any attachment to the situation or to the outcome.

17 | *Invoking Vision beyond Matter*

O Portia, in your mastery,
I feel transforming chemistry.
In your light of reality,
I find the golden alchemy.

**O Portia, opportunity,
I am beyond duality.
I focus now internally,
with you I grow eternally.**

7. Non-attachment to physical outcome is the hallmark of a spiritual student at my level.

O Portia, in the cosmic stream,
I am awake from human dream.
Removing now the ego's beam,
I earn my place on cosmic team.

**O Portia, opportunity,
I am beyond duality.
I focus now internally,
with you I grow eternally.**

8. Non-attachment to physical outcome is the key to Buddhahood, which is a goal that I am striving towards and see as a real potential for myself.

O Portia, you come from afar,
you are a cosmic avatar.
So infinite your repertoire,
you are for earth a guiding star.

> O Portia, opportunity,
> I am beyond duality.
> I focus now internally,
> with you I grow eternally.

9. I am forever striving to free my vision from the subtleties of the fallen mindset and the illusion that makes matter seem unchangeable and makes it seem separated from Spirit. Matter is in Spirit and Spirit has the power to change matter. I am in Spirit and Spirit has the power to change matter through me.

> O Portia, I am confident,
> I am a cosmic instrument.
> I came to earth from heaven sent,
> to help bring forward her ascent.

> O Portia, opportunity,
> I am beyond duality.
> I focus now internally,
> with you I grow eternally.

Sealing:

In the name of the Divine Mother, I fully accept that the power of these calls is used to set free the River of Life, so it can outpicture the perfect vision of Christ for my own life, for all people and for the planet. In the name I AM THAT I AM, it is done! Amen.

www.ingramcontent.com/pod-product-compliance
Lightning Source LLC
Chambersburg PA
CBHW030516230426
43665CB00010B/630